WORLDS BEYOND DEATH

The Sacred Key

by
Dr. Grant H. Pealer, D.D.

OZARK MOUNTAIN PUBLISHING

PO Box 754
Huntsville, AR 72740

www.ozarkmt.com
800-935-0045 or 479-738-2348

For permission, or serialization, condensation, adaptions, or for catalog of other publications, write to: Ozark Mountain Publishing, Inc., PO Box 754, Huntsville, AR 72740, Attn: Permissions Department.

Library of Congress Cataloging-in-Publication Data
Pealer, Grant H.- 1944 -
"Worlds Beyond Death" by Dr. Grant H. Pealer
Pre-life memories of the spiritual world; where we go after death.
1. Life After Death   2. Metaphysics
I. Pealer, Grant H., 1944 -   II. Title

Library of Congress Catalog Number: 2006940824
ISBN: 978-1-886940-97-0

Cover Art and Layout by www.enki3d.com
Book Design: Julia Degan
Book Set in: Times New Roman, University Roman LET

Published by

OZARK
MOUNTAIN
PUBLISHING

PO Box 754
Huntsville, AR 72740

www.ozarkmt.com
Printed in the United States of America

Table of Contents

DEDICATION

I dedicate this work to my "Soul-Family Tribe".

My Loved Ones.

Those who have blessed me with their presence in this great life journey.

AUTHOR'S NOTE

Many individuals have questioned where the following information has been gained. While much is based on pre-birth memory, commonly called Universal Consciousness, one should understand that at each level you ascend, a massive amount of knowledge pertaining to that particular plane or dimension will be absorbed. However, since I have often mentioned the institutes called Mystery Schools, a few have wondered if some of this knowledge has been obtained from their teachings. Nothing could be further from the truth. While their so-called mysteries pertain only to the physical universe and the lower levels of the astral, what is offered here will take you on a journey into the core of Creation, more than a dozen dimensions away.

There are two types of knowledge; head knowledge and heart knowledge. Head knowledge is what you have learned through reading or being taught by someone. Heart knowledge is that which you know to be true because you have experienced it for yourself. What I am offering is a little bit of both. While we start out with head knowledge, the intent is to lead you into heart knowledge, helping you remember for yourself the wonderful worlds you have already experienced, but forgotten.

INTRODUCTION

Why is this book different and what is so special about it?

What you are about to experience may very well be unlike anything you have previously read. There are a multitude of reasons for this, but the most important is that this book, which is based on personal experience, not only examines the astral, but also explores those worlds that very few become aware of while in the physical body. It can serve as a personal instrument, enabling you to become a true Cosmic Coworker.

As you work into the Coworker state, the fear of death dissolves, pre-birth memories return. There is an awareness of Higher Worlds, and you discover you have new physical and spiritual abilities.

In this study, we are not only exploring what happens and where we go when we leave this world, but we will also discuss some of the many ways to open our subconscious (and pre-birth memories), to better understand the higher vibrating spiritual worlds long before our transition (physical death) takes place.

The exercises that help trigger our memories are based on "Inner Movement". This is nothing like astral projection. While astral projection is limited, this form of movement opens worlds that the projectionist is simply never aware of. In this experience, it's not even necessary to leave the body to gain knowledge. Many become aware of things at a great distance while they continue to maintain whatever they are doing in the physical.

Another surprising thing I discovered is that all religious teachings reach only as high as the fourth plane. Through this form of mind expansion, we can gain knowledge from planes reaching far beyond that state.

Unfortunately, the very few that have dared to attempt to describe those worlds existing beyond the fourth, have failed to awaken the student's awareness, because they made them sound like something existing outside of the seeker's being. These worlds are not distant, nor are they someplace we have never been. The truth is we have just temporarily forgotten about these wonderful worlds. This presentation is intended to awaken the consciousness so we may once again remember.

Through the assistance of spirit (since we are Coworkers with spirit), we will be shown how to pass not only the tests of this world, but the tests of the higher worlds as well, long before we face them! God bless, and happy journey.

SECTION ONE:

EXPLORING

THE WORLDS OF TRANSITION

(DEATH)

CHAPTER ONE:

THE DEATH EXPERIENCE

THE KEY

Everything vibrates. There is nothing in this world that is not humming at a certain rate of vibration. Our body vibrates; everything we can touch or see vibrates. Even that which we are not aware of, will be found to be vibrating at a certain pitch.

In becoming a Coworker with God, we must understand there is no such thing as perpetual energy in the physical world. Everything here had to be manifested from an outside source. Moreover, it needs to continue to be maintained by this outside source, or it will cease to exist. Thus, here is our proof of life beyond the physical!

Next, we need to understand there are many levels of life and each of these levels are referred to as planes.

Every plane (just as with the physical) has its own special rate of vibration, and we come to understand that each of these planes has its own particular set of laws. What we may not be able to accomplish on one plane, can be accomplished on a higher one.

In the physical, we might call this magic. To perform a certain thing, all we need do is adjust our vibration to match the rate of the plane offering that particular ability.

The true Coworker will discover they are soon able to assist, not only their families and loved ones, but even complete strangers.

THE ULTIMATE EXPERIENCE

You are about to embark on the greatest adventure of a lifetime. In this account, you will be taking a journey only a handful of modern day explorers are even slightly aware of.

3

Regardless of the religion one may have been reared in, they soon see how inadequately and ineffectively mankind has been served with this very limited vision, once they are able to gain a glance into the true God Worlds.

While most religions are interested in only this world or the next, we find that God is far greater in scope than most have been able to understand. That which we call God not only made all of the universes and planes of existence, but "Is" what these universes and planes are made of. That includes the most precious Gem of all – the Human Soul!

Also, we will be quick to discover that God is much more than an Entity. God is a Force far beyond our comprehension.

In this book we explore the mystery of God, and you can be assured your life will never be the same again. How could it be, once you understand concepts the average individual has hardly ever dreamed of?

Perhaps one of the most important things to understand is that it is far more than some religious teaching. It is a real and living account. The following is based on true events. Every word and every description given is totally factual. and every point made is within your power to activate!

We will be studying from two different aspects. There are many individuals who can recall what happened before being born into this world. This is not as unusual as one might think. Most of us have some subconscious memories of the higher vibrating worlds, and usually it only needs a nudge to awaken the conscious mind. In my case, it was undoubtedly due to a cosmic fluke we will be discussing later. From that memory, we will actually take the journey I took when my past incarnation ended.

Second, we will relive a similar inner movement experience I have particularly strong memories of. From these vantage points, we will be able to examine the differences in these two experiences, enabling us to probably have a better understanding of the higher planes than those who are presently there!

As you will see, when we attempt to gain spiritual knowledge while still in the physical body, we have a better opportunity to understand what really happens when someone leaves the physical world.

A CHANGE OF CONSCIOUSNESS

There is an old saying that you can't see the world as it is - but the world IS as you see it. We are a multi-dimensional being, and actually have the ability to travel back and forth through the various ranges of vibration, to control to some extent what might come to us. A good example of this would be the law of karma, which states what goes around comes around. This coupled with our attitude about our circumstances pretty much sets the stage to gauge how happy or unhappy we may be.

We are actually what you might call a multi-lane consciousness. While we think we have only a physical consciousness, there are many layers of consciousness above that. All we need do to move our consciousness to a different level is focus on what we desire for ourselves. There is an old teaching that where the mind goes – the body must follow. Simply put, we are going to live at whatever level we accept for our consciousness. If we think we are happy, we will be happy. If we live in fear and dread, then that will be our state. While some would be very content to live the lonely life of a lighthouse keeper, finding solace and peace in the surrounding as well as in himself, to another it might seem to be an unbearable horror. You might say we are a mold that can create our surroundings. In that case, if we hunt for the meaning of life, we will only end up with what others have perceived it to be. Instead, we create our own perception, our own happiness, and our own state of spirituality. This is done purely by vibration change; by raising the vibration of our consciousness.

When we depart from this world, we leave only the physical body behind. We still carry these other levels with us. They are part of our makeup. They are what we have become since we entered the physical world. It is also here in the lower levels of astral vibration where we find our subconscious.

The subconscious plays a very important part in our physical and spiritual development. It is through the sub that various spiritual energies and intelligences are able to guide us, and make sure we learn the particular lessons that are determined essential.

While we think we are doing something mysterious and awesome by studying life after death, we are actually only opening our understanding to what we are and where we came from. By having a better understanding of our true nature, we are able to make leaps and bounds in our development and ultimate graduation from the physical level. We will find, by some strange process, we have also developed a host of strange physical and spiritual powers.

Not the least of these abilities is the opening of the door to becoming aware of the many wonderful forces and spiritual teachers that can assist us – once we give them permission to do so.

We call the physical consciousness "reality", but if we were to move our awareness to another viewpoint, *that* particular consciousness would become our reality. We think we are the primary state of awareness because this is all we remember. Most people consider anything outside the physical universe as strange, unusual and possibly very fanciful.

When someone hears about an existence beyond the physical, they might roll their eyes, make funny expressions or laugh out loud, saying the speaker wasn't being realistic.

But what is reality? We are pretty much like the ancients who believed the Sun and all of the planets and stars revolved around our small planet. Although we know better today, we are still very primitive with our understanding of Spirit. We are not the center of reality. All of the worlds of Spirituality do not revolve around us – even though we would like to believe so.

Always remember that whatever consciousness we reside in will be our reality. While we might become frightened to come upon a snake, that snake is often just as terrified to encounter us. There is as great a difference between an elevated awareness and what we presently perceive real. To that higher entity we may seem very childish and backward, but these entities realize we have been sent here to learn certain lessons to help us better fit into the esoteric worlds.

Since we came from a higher dimension (with it not being the other way around, being created in the physical world and trying to climb higher), then that previous exalted awareness would be our reality. We are a spiritual being presently living in an illusion that we are something less.

Anyone experiencing moving from one consciousness to another has always said it was like stepping out of the darkness into a bright new world. And it is like this each time one moves from one consciousness to the next higher one.

Since we presently reside in the physical, we can laugh at or doubt the existence of higher worlds, but that doesn't change what has happened to us in the past. We came from worlds far beyond the comprehension of the average person, passing through multiple degrees of awareness to reach this low vibrating world. That means we are located at the lowest and darkest consciousness possible.

WELCOME TO OUTPOST HELL

Even when I was a child, I had the humorous idea that maybe we weren't really alive at all. I mentioned to many of my playmates maybe we were dead and had gone to hell. While most didn't know or care what I was saying, it seemed to make their parents very upset. I remember a couple of occasions where they grabbed up their child and rapidly retreated.

Once when I asked my mother, wouldn't it be funny if two angels in heaven were talking and one asked the other where I was, and he said "Oh, haven't you heard? He's dead and gone to hell", she became very upset. With everyone's different reactions, I soon learned to keep my thoughts to myself. It seemed if we *were* in hell, most people didn't want to hear about it.

Even in this day and age I find it quite amazing how many people still believe there's a devil and demons inside the earth. And it's even more amazing they don't want to know any better. It's like they want to cover their ears and run away when anyone attempts to explain what hell really is.

At the lowest level of the harmonic scale, the lowest vibration, the students of spiritual development are free to practice and learn about the responsibility of becoming Godlike. That's why they came here. The physical plane is nothing more than a school; a learning ground where the Little Gods can learn about being responsible for their actions.

When we hear about the horrors of hell, the gnashing of teeth, or the endless torment, we only need to look about to see this is due to man's mistreatment of man. Only our own individual actions will determine how hellish or heavenly we can make it.

DEATH, WHERE IS THY STING?

(Previous transformation - 1923)

The day had been long and hard, but tired as I was, I agreed to make a delivery on my way home from my shop.

After struggling with a fairly heavy box for some time, I finally reached my destination. As I crossed the street, I heard someone yell out to me. Turning, I slipped on what seemed to be a pebble. It was just enough to throw me off balance, throwing me backward, where I hit the side of my head solidly on the edge of the curb.

More embarrassed than anything else, I tried to get up. I remember reassuring a woman who had rushed to my side, that

I was all right. But when I was only half way up, I let out a moan and collapsed again.

There was no pain – except for that first sharp blow, but I was unable to move. I immediately felt a strange but soothing vibration come over me. I just wanted to slide off into a deep and relaxing state.

While it was relaxing to me, it only increased the anxiety of those who had gathered around. My physical body would be in a coma for three days, but for me it was like a nice peaceful sleep that seemed to hardly last more than a few hours.

Coming out of that peaceful state, I recognized an old friend I hadn't seen for many years. I gave him the same cheery greeting that I usually gave.

"Hey, I haven't seen you in a long time!" I said with a big smile.

As he smiled, nodded, and stretched out his hand, my smile quickly disappeared.

Slowly, my astral memory was beginning to kick in. Of course, I hadn't seen him in a long time. I hadn't seen him since he came to my side – my bloody side – on a battlefield. The last time I saw him, he had come to take me back to the astral after I had been slaughtered.

"I'm not dead!" I seemed to scream. "How could I be dead? I just bumped by head!"

"No, you're not dead," he answered with that wonderful smile of his, while he continued to reach out to take my hand into his. "You're very much alive!"

Relaxing again, I touched his hand. While his soothing vibration ran through my entire system, I remember him asking me to close my eyes (the eyes of my astral body). I quickly complied, as I remembered doing many times before.

I knew I was changing from one dimension into another and to my fragile religious understanding, I imagined he was taking me past the gates of a fiery hell. And I knew I definitely wouldn't want to see that.

9

The truth was, of course, there was no fiery hell, no demons, no dragons, no distorted monsters, or anything else of that kind. These pictures of death had been painted by poor misled artists, who served as tools for the fear merchants who sought control over the masses through superstitious nonsense.

I later discovered this was a usual request of the newly departed by their escort (to close my eyes) only so the frightened and delicate soul would not be too shocked seeing himself withdrawn from the physical body. On the other hand, if the individual had gone through a long and painful illness, he would be more than ready to depart from his old coat of clay.

Even though he had reassured me I was still very much alive, I was still apprehensive about taking this journey that had always symbolized a full and complete departure from a previous life.

I suggested that perhaps I should return to the physical body. I was more worried about my wife and children than anything else. I knew they would be greatly upset and crying to see my comatose body.

Gently, he reminded me that there was no such thing as death and that I was truly very much alive, but that body I had used while being known as Peter Lynch, was no longer a suitable vehicle.

A tremendous anguish swept through me. I tried to explain I had to return to that body. Even though soothing vibrations seemed to blanket me, I resisted them, continuing to insist we return.

The understanding he gave, that the physical body can only be allowed a very limited time disconnected from its spiritual nourishment (life giving vibration) before the body becomes completely useless, only heightened my insistence that we should return immediately.

Finally, the understanding came through that I had nothing to worry about. All of my matters were in the hands of spirit. If my being upset was due to my desire to return to the physical, then I would be permitted to do so.

With that understanding, I then insisted the return should be soon. As my guide had explained, time was an essential element to the physical body. Again, the understanding came through that I should no longer have any apprehension about time. We were now operating in a different set of vibratory rules. Time in the physical was completely independent from the measurement of time by astral standards. What could be only moments in the Astral, could be an extensive time in the physical. Or even the opposite could be true. In a moment of physical time, a great deal of astral time could have passed.

Another understanding I had was that everyone's observation of the transition experience (leaving the physical world) would not necessarily be the same as mine. Although a spiritual guide will always be present when one leaves the physical body, that does not mean the individual will always see him (or her). Many will be aware of only the loved ones who may have come with the guide. Some will take little notice of anyone around himself until he enters into and becomes bathed in a soothing, peaceful white light. Others may seem to just awaken in a beautiful garden, and a few will even think they are still in bed in a hospital room. Just as people will have many different attitudes (and fears) about leaving the physical body behind, there are just as many different ways one will experience the transition state, that is mistakenly called death.

I was asked if I had any questions I would like answered. While it is true you can receive as much knowledge about esoteric matters as you desire, nothing will be given to you that you are not ready for – or that you presently show no interest in.

Because I had a deep curiosity about life on other planets, I probably would have been shown some of that life had I asked, but instead, I asked to see what Earth's moon was like. Quickly becoming bored with the Moon, just as my guide knew I would be, we left the physical plane.

While the physical consciousness might be fascinated exploring man's greatest mystery, the Moon, the next level of awareness demands something more than merely rolling over barren waste.

As we "transform" (not die) from one state to the next, we move into a deliriously grand state of understanding. Even without exploring every crater, mountain range or valley, this higher consciousness was instantly able to show me the Moon was nothing as glamorous as Earth. There was only an endless sea of dust and rock. It was actually rather depressing.

There was an awareness that life forms had walked the surface (in ancient times), but again, while this would be mind-blowing from a physical point of view, the astral consciousness offered the understanding that if I desired to learn about other life forms, I would need to move on. (These life forms had undoubtedly been space travelers who visited Earth, and perhaps established a base on the Moon).

Another thing that needs to be clarified about this next level of awareness is that while all of us seem to be independent and separate from one another, we should understand we are "an extension" of divine or cosmic consciousness. We are all interlinked.

There is only one consciousness. All individual personalities come from this. This is how we can understand things not previously known. The closer we get to the ultimate consciousness, the more we become able to absorb what it knows.

Through this astral awareness, I finally realized there were endless other and greater things to explore.

Although I was in a dream-like state, I was still aware of many wondrous sights passing below us. Even though I had a great desire to explore these fantastic visions, we sped on. I was assured I would be able to examine them fully before my return to the physical.

When we first return to the astral, we are very much like small children. We are led around having little real awareness about where we are or what might be going on.

My guide took me into what seemed to be a tremendous hall. In the midst of unexplainable beauty, we finally approached a great, shining and reverent being. I thought this must be God.

Quickly though, my new astral awareness began to expand further, and I was able to see that this temple-like place was not the throne of God, nor was this being (even as great as he was) God. I could sense there were many others such as himself here and they served in a capacity similar to that of a Counselor.

This was the place that many religions spoke of as a "reviewing" place. The Christians called it "the Judgement". They mistakenly believed it would be at this stage that every deed and every thought we ever had, would be reviewed by God. Of course, I quickly saw through that, realizing this was only another attempt by some misguided individuals to control and frighten their followers.

As my attention centered on the communication between my guide and him (and not on anything that I may had ever said or done), I realized the Counselor was attempting to offer me a great reward. It was determined it would not be necessary for me to return to the hard and harsh physical world.

Instantly, my emotion again escalated, fighting back the calm vibration encircling me, I insisted I had to return. Seeing my anguish, the Counselor seemed to cast wave after wave of tranquility over me, but with each casting, my blazing emotion seemed to burn through. It was very much like a blanket being thrown over a raging fire. It would seem to kill the blaze for the moment, but then a flame would lick at a small hole until it would burst through again. Finally, I was so highly sedated there was no more emotion, and most of my memory of the physical had been removed. At that point I became aware only of what was transpiring between the two. While it was true that I did not have to return to the physical, it was seen how my return could be of a great benefit not only to myself, but perhaps to others as well.

Finally, it being settled that I would return, my guide offered our love and we withdrew.

At that point, I seemed to fall into a deep sleep. This was undoubtedly due to the enormous amount of soothing vibration I had received. When I awoke, I found myself in a very familiar surrounding. There were beautiful gardens, majestic waterfalls and ecstatic observations in all directions. I remembered being here before. In fact, I remembered being here many times before.

I was immediately surrounded by loved ones that I had not seen in a very long time, and it was not at all difficult for me to make an adjustment to this world.

This was the relaxing stage one experiences while still being a student in the lower vibrating worlds (above the physical, but still below what is called the higher worlds).

It was almost impossible for me to know how much time I spent frolicking and dreaming in these gardens, but I was periodically removed to be taught something about the astral or one of the higher planes.

The first astral visit I made was to a place I remembered seeing before. It was called the Mountain of Light. This fantastic mountain was undoubtedly a hundred times larger than any mountain existing on Earth, and the powers it had was phenomenal. It actually received Cosmic energy from a higher plane and then redistributed it throughout the astral and physical worlds. I instantly understood this was the power transmitter that gave life to all things below the third plane (the Causal plane). And I realized the energy that was being released was so great that if it were not properly regulated, it had the power to wipe out the physical plane completely. Not being able to understand God, I was told this was hardly more than one puff from the breath of God and that it would take some time (and many more revelations) before I would be able to gain even some grasp of what God might be.

Just as I had said many times before – I was determined that when I returned to Earth, I would let the whole world know of this place and the true spiritual wisdom here. Unfortunately, no matter how many times I became determined to reveal the truth, it seemed each time I was reborn, the memory was washed away while in the physical body.

Shortly after my visit to the Mountain of Light, I was taken to a great temple. In this awesome place I received spiritual teachings from a mighty Being that I again confused with God. Quickly, my guide explained that while many will accept this Being as God until they can gain a greater spiritual understanding, He was actually similar to a Governor. He was the Governor for this particular astral location.

With gentle and loving eyes, he offered me a lesson. The context that I absorbed was basically as follows. (Note: although the following is presented as dialogue, the reader should understand much of what I received was through "impressive thought forms" and not hard, physical words. But the context will be found to closely convey the same thought – as much as humanly possible.) "Most people in the physical don't realize they carry five bodies around with them," he said, as his musical vibrations flowed through me. "Just as you need a physical body to operate in the physical world – and you needed to have an astral body to come to me – you will need a particular vibrating body that corresponds to each of the planes below the true God Worlds, if you wish to visit them. That is not a difficult thing to accomplish though, since these bodies have always been with you ever since you entered into these lower vibrating worlds to receive spiritual instruction. Everyone has these bodies available to them, even while they are still in the physical world. They only need to learn how to use them.

"But now I will give you some further insight about these layers that is not taught in even one of the Earth's religions. Not only do you have these bodies surrounding you, but each of the planets are also surrounded by them.

"Your instruction in these worlds is not by hit or miss. It is very definitely planned, and while in these worlds, most will stay in a particular schooling system until they finally graduate to the higher worlds.

"When anyone thinks about the astral world or any of the other worlds, even Heaven, they think of there being only one level of its existence. But that is not true. Every planet, even though there are endless billions, each has its own astral, Heaven sections, and so forth. For you see, even though most accept that Heaven is the final goal, it is only the last stop before the seeker graduates on into the true God Worlds.

"It is because of this that when someone dies in your Earth world, they return only to Earth if they are to reincarnate – and not to some distant galaxy that would seem strange to them. And the same is true for those souls in those distant places. They, too, will return only to that which is familiar to them, and not to your world."

At first, this lesson seemed complicated to my understanding, but then I was able to see that there was far more law and order in this schooling system than most had been able to understand. It also helped me to comprehend a much grander plan than any religion had ever been able to relate.

After each lesson or adventure I shared with my guide, I was always returned to my wonderful home among the gardens.

Also, now that I had been able to overcome my very primitive and carnal limitations of physical emotion, I was shown a great deal of time had passed on Earth since I had left it behind. I could also see that my wife and children had been able to adapt, and there was no longer any feeling of pain or anguish on their part. With their believing that I was residing in some eternal Heaven, their hearts had come to peace. And it was that peace that finally released me from my own emotional pain.

With this problem removed from my aura, I was finally able to be taken for visits into the higher vibrating worlds. There I learned that even though it would be a long time before I could even begin to understand what God was – that I, and all other living beings, were very much a part of God!

As I prepared to enter into the God worlds, having fully graduated from "the school of hard knocks", an old decision that had been passed down from the Counselor returned, as you might say, to bite me in the butt.

Instead of going to the Fourth and then the Fifth plane, I was to return (reincarnate) back into the first, my Earth world, where I had previously so desperately desired to return. While it may have seemed to be a cruel joke to me at the time, that was not the case. When the Counselor had agreed to let me return, it was not to satisfy my childish temper tantrum, but because He and Spirit saw I could serve in a useful position in the enlightening "Spiritual Revelation Period" about to dawn on this physical Earth world.

Again, showing that I was not the spiritual being I may have thought I was, I became greatly upset.

As I was escorted from my personal surroundings, I was led to another even grander and greater garden. Here, I was introduced to two females who would be my sisters in the next incarnation. I was also shown some of the highlights that would "probably" take place during that time period, including the date I would leave the Earth world for good (which has been changed at least three times since I returned – which also shows nothing is written in stone). I was also comforted with knowing that my parents would not be strangers to me. I would have the same mother and father that I had in my two past incarnations. That did seem strange to me – that these two people had been able to find each other and marry one another in another life. But it did show that spirit controls our lives on a much higher elevation than we may have ever perceived.

After the time of the preparatory period had passed, I instantly found myself surrounded by what seemed to be a long tunnel. Instantly, I remembered this stage from my past encounters with it. Here, my astral memory would be erased. The thought horrified me. The whole purpose of my agreeing to return was to let the world know there was no such thing as death, and to tell them the things I had seen here. There had been so many other times where I was determined to write about this and the other worlds while I was in the physical body, but each time my memory had been wiped clean.

I was determined this time would be different. This time I would remember.

I concentrated with all the strength I could muster to remember at least some of the things I had seen.

As the hall seemed to go flying by, in something similar to a hypnotic wheel, I could feel gaps of memory slowly being released.

I became angry and admonished myself, saying that I would forget, that I always forgot, that I was just too much of a weakling to remember.

That snapped me back slightly, but hardly enough. There was just too much to try to remember and every time I was able to bring it back up, I would then feel it start to wash away again.

In desperation, I remembered some insignificant thing I had been told before I left the garden. My guide had said if I could base my life on the number four, I would be more successful. Four would be my lucky number.

Soon, being able to remember only this, I burned it into my memory. Over and over again I repeated, "I hate the number four! I hate four! I hate four!"

The soothing flow of the tunnel tried to bring peace to me, but I refused to let it in. I managed to hold on to the thought of four being an evil number to such an extent that it actually served to help me remember most of the incidents I had experienced.

Finally, the flow began to slow – and I had managed to hold onto some memories.

Then, I dropped and swooped and felt the most excruciating pain one could imagine. I was being born, and a tool the doctor was holding grabbed my ear and tore some of the tender flesh away.

My predominate thought was, I had been delivered unto the barbarians. I floated above my new body, and became terrified by the frightening scene of masked beings who stood around me.

This fear then left, as I lapsed back into an infantile state of mind.

As I grew older, bits and pieces of my astral memory would return and my parents were often quite perplexed by some of the things I said or asked. Even though I was a normal child, my mother became quite worried when I insisted I had two sisters and wanted to know where they were. (By the way, one sister was born when I was eleven and the other when I was thirteen.)

Once when I asked my mother why four was a bad number, I was totally shocked to hear her say she didn't know four was a bad number. I asked how she couldn't know that. Everybody (so I thought) knew four was evil.

Parents really should pay more attention to the strange things their children might say. While we may often pass off their silly talk as imagination, there is probably a far greater thing here than may be apparent.

When I was four years old, I was walking beside my mother as we went up some stone steps that led into a butcher shop. About half way up I tripped over her foot and smashed my head against the edge of one of the steps. It caused a gash that took a lot of stitches (and a mark that would last the rest of my life). Shortly there-after I started babbling nonsense that only served to frighten my parents further. But even stranger was my insistence that I wasn't born until after I tripped over my mother's foot.

Even though she could definitely prove that I lived before I took the fall, I still had to say that I didn't know why I said it, but that was when I was born.

It would take some time to finally grasp some understanding about what had taken place. When I was born, I was outside and above the scary scene watching my birth take place. Then, just as I was pulled downward, I felt that most horrible pain. Even though I had forgotten about it, the memory was still in the subconscious. This, paired with the new event, re-opened the terror. Again, I was able to view these most horrifying beings all

19

dressed in white and wearing masks as I bobbed above my tiny body after receiving a dose of ether. The two events merged into one, leading this poor confused four year old to say he was born at that time.

I was still quite young (about twelve) when my memory began to fully open, and I was better able to explain to my parents (and to others who were interested) what really happens when you die.

As I entered into my twenties and was able to make a full recall – with the help of various spiritual exercises, I received validation for the things I had been teaching.

Here, then, is the presentation that not only my guide and Counselor had intended for me to share with you, the true Spiritual Seeker, but which will hopefully assist spirit in its work in the "New Enlightened Age", now dawning around us.

CHAPTER TWO:

THE SPIRITUAL DOOR

WHAT IS INNER MOVEMENT?

Inner Movement is "the ability to reach a state of awareness normally beyond the borders of our carnal limitations". But in addition to this, it is also conceivably the oldest form of religion known to mankind.

Pythagoras, a great spiritual teacher and mathematician, and Zoroaster, a Persian mystic, both taught this esoteric science hundreds of years before the birth of Jesus.

In the ancient mystery schools of Greece, the great minds taught that this was the original form of communication between God and Mankind. And that it had been the previous major teaching of the elder civilizations (presumably Atlantis and Lemuria).

Also, every major religion was formed out of this ability, whether it be by reaching a state of Nirvana through meditation or physically leaving the body, traveling to a distant plane of existence, observing what is there and returning to teach about the remarkable visions and revelations that one had seen.

This should not be confused with astral projection. While astral projection is a crude, highly limited, and very difficult feat to accomplish, we find that Journeying is not only highly refined, but results come almost automatically.

Those who believe they don't have the ability to leave the physical body should understand they leave their physical body every night.

One who has experienced jumping or jerking awake may be very surprised to find the reason for that jerk was they returned to the body a little too fast.

Leaving the body is what the process of sleep is all about. As the body relaxes to recharge itself, the individual, the soul, rises anywhere from several inches to a few feet from the physical body and comes to rest in what is called the dream bubble.

It is here that the individual can get in touch with the subconscious, which fully controls the bubble. From this state of awareness, the subconscious can either relax the hold and permit the mind to learn things coming from sources outside the bubble (i.e. learning about something while "sleeping on it") or it can restrict the hold, unifying the bond of communication between the sub and the conscious mind.

It is during this restricted state we find we are not able to run or move very fast in a dream. This is due to the very nature of the bubble walls.

As for the difference between astral projecting and journeying, an important point is that astral projecting is the separating of the astral covering (breaking or tearing it away from the other bodies that are held within our etheric proximity, which is what makes the process of projecting so difficult to do). Meanwhile, journeying is a unifying move, leaving the bodies intact. Also, astral projecting can often leave the practitioner with a slight headache (due to such separating of the sheaths), while he who has experienced the inner movement (leaving the sheaths intact), will arise feeling perhaps better than he has felt in a long time.

These sheaths (or bodies) are a part of the many bodies that surrounds each of us. Although we are only aware of the physical body, we should understand that each plane of existence has its own vibratory rate and for anyone to function within the boundaries of any particular plane (particular vibration), he must have a corresponding vibrating body.

If one were to function at the astral level, he would need the astral body. If the information he desired was located on the etheric plane, then he would need to use that particular body, and so forth.

While we are aware of only the physical body, we actually have five bodies at our immediate disposal. The other four are: the Astral, the Causal (often called Casual), the Etheric and the Soul Body.

So, we see that by separating the astral sheath from the others, we limit ourselves, operating solely on the astral level. In comparison, by moving away from the physical as a solid unit, we discover we have the ability to go wherever we desire, unimpeded by the different rates of vibration. Regardless of the plane we desire to contact, we find we have the proper body to function at that level.

In addition to knowledge, the practitioner can also become aware of what exists at each of these levels. With this awareness comes the related spiritual enlightenment relative to each particular plane.

Instead of being limited within the boundaries of our known three dimensions, we find we have access to twelve planes of wisdom that can be fed to the subconscious, even if we are unable to fully digest such wisdom at this time.

We also discover that we can have unlimited access to the time track. This is accomplished by engaging the use of the soul body (our fifth and most refined body). Having such access, one is also better able to understand the laws of personal responsibility to himself, his fellow souls, his Eternal Source, and even to the realms that he is yet unable to comprehend.

Of all the creations of God, the soul is the most prized. All other things were created for the benefit of soul and so the exploration of these other planes is nothing to shy away from. Since these planes were created for our benefit, then it only stands to reason that by reaching out to them can only lead to a higher degree of enlightenment.

When we view the time track, we easily see why Jesus and other religious teachers taught, "Do unto others as you would have them do unto you." Because, from this spectacular position, we are able to understand the fantastic reactions of cause and effect.

By observing the actions carried out at any point of the track, we see it automatically causing a reaction at another point.

The law states: "For every action, there has to be an opposite and equal reaction." This goes not only for individuals, but any group, institute, religion, and yes, even every country or planet.

So, by traveling along the track, we see that everything comes back to us, whether it be good or bad. By this same token though, we can be assured that our attempt at learning to journey must be matched with equal results from the cosmic!

THE TECHNIQUES OF JOURNEYING

(DISCLAIMER: Although there is mention of ancient mystery schools in this work, that is not to insinuate I am speaking for any institutions who claim to lay hold of ancient mysteries. I do not speak for or represent any organization, and it is not my intent to suggest they represent or assist me. Also, although there is mention of guides, spiritual workers, and some individuals by name, that is not to suggest I have any connections anyone else in the world might not have – for you do! Finally, all of the work presented here, spiritual exercises included, are not the private property of any group, institute or individual. These exercises have been adapted into the mainstream of modern-day meditation and are openly available to all.)

While experiencing inner movement, it will become a personal matter to you (meaning that once you have grasped the fundamentals, you develop the method most comfortable to you), you will be operating within the scope of one of four major methods of journeying.

These four methods that activate the ability within you are: sleep, imagination, visualization and sound. Even though there could be dozens of different variations you discover that work effectively, they will all come from one of, or a combination of, these four techniques.

First, we should have a firm understanding of what is happening when we experience inner movement, and why we should make every attempt to open ourselves to this flow. To do that, we need to understand who we are and why we are here.

What we consider to be of utmost importance in this world is actually of relative little use in the realm of spiritual development.

While we concentrate our entire energies in the direction of gaining money, there are very few that are able to see beyond this world's illusions. Understanding anything more than being a game piece, moving around a game board, where the objective is to get all that we can, in order to be the big winner.

A more accurate view of life would be that we are students and that this world is only a school.

If we are to firmly believe that we have always existed and that we will continue to always exist, then it must follow that this period in time that we occupy is meant to serve some purpose. That purpose would then be to receive training, and to elevate ourselves to a greater level so that we may be of more spiritual benefit to that which we call God.

With this broader concept, we are more apt to understand that, just as in our schooling system, we are expected to progress on a daily basis. So, it would be more accurate to say that what we experience during the dream state, would be our lessons, guiding us with implanted knowledge to the subconscious.

In this dream state, the inner movement consists of two functions, volunteer and automatic.

Volunteer is where we instruct the subconscious, informing it to respond to our commands. Automatic is where we are fed symbolic information from a higher spiritual source.

JOURNEYING IN THE DREAM

Automatic: One of the most mysterious of all things to the average individual is his process of sleeping. He can have precognition dreams, where he can see little bits and pieces of things that will occur in the near future. He, too, can experience such a dramatic change of consciousness that once he awakens, he will wonder, "What the heck was that all about?"

He will remember things that made sense at the time of the dream, but are totally absurd later. In the dream, he can be riding a bicycle that turns into a pig and then a pig that changes into an airplane and then, a few minutes later, he can find himself in a classroom or a shopping mall totally nude.

This is due to the great amount of activity that the brain is engaged in while the majority of the body activities are shut down. Not only is the conscious mind in direct communication with the subconscious, but from the dream bubble, it can receive impressions from the time track, be intercepting communication from the various bodies, and receive information from the Higher Self. And at the same time, be receiving broken up pieces of coded information fed to the subconscious (from the lessons we are meant to learn).

All of this activity can be very confusing to the dream function of the brain and whenever the soul separation takes place (when such coded information has been received by the sub to do so), this will seem to make the dream even more complex, leaving the sleeper totally unaware that he has been away from the body at a great distance.

Another strange occurrence of the dream state is when we find that we have fallen asleep for a short period of time, but have exposed ourselves to a totally different life than we know.

In this type of dream, not only do we live someplace we have never lived, but we could be married to someone we don't know, have different children, work at a strange job and even be discussing something that took place last year, or maybe several years ago, but which never really happened to us.

Then when you wake up, you will notice you have been asleep for only a few minutes. Within those few minutes though, a complete life has been formed and lived. A file filled with a lifetime of memories will have been created all in less than a few seconds!

Of every capability of the human brain, this is undoubtedly the most amazing. It is also a good example of automatic journeying. As the individual separates from the dream bubble, he can absorb massive amounts of information not only from the time track, but also from soul mates or from people of similar nature and even from cosmic intervention (lessons being received from a spiritual guide).

Automatic journeying is the form that most experience until they are ready and willing to engage in their own particular form of spiritual exercise.

Volunteer dream travel: Volunteer dreaming is comprised of giving affirmations to the subconscious. These affirmations are commands that are directed from you (the Commander-In-Chief), to your internal security staff.

To better understand what is happening, let's compare your body to a kingdom. You are the king or the queen and the ultimate figure in authority, while the subconscious is like the royal palace guard.

Just as with real palace guards, the subconscious does not need to receive constant orders from the king in order for it to function. The palace guard has its own commander, whose duty is to protect and assist the king even in many ways that the king may not be aware. It is not necessary for the ruler to constantly pass down orders to the commander, but that in no way limits him from doing so, if he so desires. Also, when any such orders from the king do arrive, those orders must be obeyed.

The whole key of passing these orders from the conscious to the subconscious (or from the king to the commander) is to send them through the proper channels in the proper way.

An affirmation is clear, concise and leaves no doubt about what is wanted and when it is wanted.

A good example would be, "On this evening I desire to travel to the astral plane, to the highest level that I am attuned. I desire to see what is there and then to return with complete memory of the journey."

This is a good affirmation because it leaves no doubt about what is wanted. However, if you should say, "Sometime, I desire to travel someplace," that order would be ignored. Not only because it is vague, but because there may be doubt that such an order came from the governing body. Since the lower command is very effective and efficient, it will always take it for granted that the higher authority is too.

With the proper command, we must also know how to send the command. It should be given at a time when you are fully relaxed. Bedtime would be ideal.

The room should be quiet; no radio or television playing. There should be either darkness or subdued light and it would be ideal to be alone, but that is not totally necessary, as long as your bed partner is not disturbing you.

Once your affirmation is prepared, take several deep breaths, hold each for a couple of seconds and then release them.

After waiting a minute or two (until your breathing has returned to normal), repeat your command three times.

Even in the metaphysical schools, the students were taught to issue affirmations in series of threes.

The first time is to get the attention of the subconscious. The second time is to give the information, and the third is to verify the command.

It is very much like dealing with another entity entirely. Just getting their attention is not sufficient. The subconscious has literally thousands of pieces of information passing through its files on a daily basis and if it were to attempt to give complete attention to each scrap, it would never be able to carry out its proper duties.

So, on the first send, it may be put aside for some sort of follow up. If such follow up is not forthcoming within the next few minutes, it could be discarded, making room for the next batch of incoming.

When it receives a second command, the information is removed from the side file and is given more attention. Also, due to the fact that the body and brain are in a calm and quiet state, the sub is not distracted by any other matters for the moment.

Now, while the sub has its full attention on the command, in comes the third affirmation, giving verification that this order is indeed from the ruling body. The sub can easily understand what is desired, so all of the forces of the royal guard are brought into play, carrying out the royal command.

Journeying Through Visualization: Visualization can be used during bedtime to aid dream traveling, or it can be used as a meditative exercise during the day.

To meditate, one should sit comfortably in a chair with hands either folded or resting against the arm rests. The feet should be flat on the floor and the back should be fairly straight.

Take three or four deep breaths to draw in the surrounding prana (spiritual energy that always completely surrounds us) into your lungs. Then concentrate on the area between the eyebrows, just above the bridge of the nose. This is the area of the Third Eye.

You only need to develop some very pleasant thoughts of a particular place and then visualize it completely.

When you have done this, you have activated the spiritual law that states, "Where the mind goes, the spirit must follow." This is an infallible law.

All things are magnetized. There are two major things you need to understand. First, no matter what it is, everything vibrates and holds some degree of magnetic attractiveness. And Second, our magnetic fields will attract or repel the magnetized conditions that surround us.

Just inside the aura, we have billions upon billions of units of energy spinning around. Some of these units are positive and some are negative. Those that are positive have been found to spin clockwise, while the negative spin counterclockwise. This spin is what spiritual magic is all about.

This spin of the energy units was taught even in the ancient mystery schools before the birth of Christ, but it has been only in the last few years that our scientists have been able to verify it.

Another thing that was taught by the ancient masters was that this rotation is controlled by our thoughts. The more positive our actions and thoughts, the more units will spin clockwise, opening many new things to us that also spin in a like rotation. However, the more negative our actions, the more negative the energy field becomes, and the more easily these units attract situations and conditions that we may not desire. These conditions are not really bad, but are lessons to help us correct our incorrect thinking! We must never forget that all of this life is really only a school. Never forget that everything that comes to us is either a'"reward" or a "lesson". But since this is a school, we should understand that we are not expected to be perfect. There is never any reason for us to feel bad for having our very imperfect nature. It is because the student needs to learn, that he is in school. When the student no longer needs to learn, he is given a diploma and he moves on.

Those religions that teach we are evil sinners simply because we may have some faults, are the ones who are really acting wrongly. They will act in this manner usually to hold onto and keep control of their followers. What they don't realize, is that just as in the case of individuals, these religions also polarize and attract "corrective measures" to themselves. For they too must learn through lessons.

Some will try to tell you that you cannot know God or cannot receive any miracles simply because you are not good enough; that you have faults and therefore you are imperfect and miracles cannot come to the imperfect.

However, there is an ancient arcane teaching that says, "For those who believe they are not good enough to receive miracles, should understand that one does not have to be perfect to receive spiritual gifts, they only need to follow the middle way."

The Buddhist religion says that the middle way means one should not be too bad, but on the other hand, does not need to be too good. You have to be something in between. Basically, what that means is if you are too bad, you will be removed from society by the law. If you are too good, then you will be unable to stay on Earth, because even great entities who come to this world must take on some disability. They are not perfect, for nothing perfect can exist in an imperfect world.

Armed with this knowledge, we find we can develop an inner peace that literally permits miracles to come to us!

Activating the Imagination: When we speak of the imagination, we are not making reference to anything that is not real. In our society, we associate anything coming from the imagination as something not tangible, and therefore has no life in our world.

The truth is that the imagination is the seed from which all things spring. There can be no progress without it first being formed in someone's imagination. That would include anything from the advertising on Madison Avenue to falling in love and having a family. The imagination provides the form and then all creation in the world comes from that.

So, it would be better to say that we are Image-ing. That is precisely what we are doing when we use the imagination to perform an inner movement.

To begin the procedure, it will be the same as visualizing. Position yourself so that you are comfortable but with your back fairly straight. Keep feet flat on the floor. Or from the bed, take a position stretched out comfortably, head slightly raised with a pillow.

Then imagine that you are above the body, looking down on it.

This will take time and practice. The mind is like a monkey. It is very difficult to make it behave, and you will find that you have no sooner brought one section under control then it is jumping around someplace else. When you try to make the mind a blank, it will seem that all kinds of garbage will be flying in at you from every angle. This is a protective measure from "specially coded instructions" that were fed into your system even before you were born. The purpose of this implant is to keep you from consciously leaving the physical to enter into the spiritual realms.

The law that explains this is the one of "reversed effort". We are all aware that the harder we try to do something, all the more difficult it becomes.

This law is implanted for much the same reason that very few of us have pre birth memories.

While most people are afraid of the process we call death, the truth is they would not want to stay here if they could fully remember the joys of the other worlds.

We are like the unfortunate student that has been sent off to boarding school, having to leave the comfort and happiness of the very privileged family that we came from. Meanwhile, spirit realizes that many students would try to runaway back home if given an easy opportunity.

This is also the reason that the first out of the body experience is the most difficult to achieve. However, once it is seen that the practitioner is not going to offer any trouble about returning to the physical body, it becomes easier and easier to pay short visits to his true home.

It is not that we are not wanted in the spiritual realm, for that is our home, but this block has been staged as an act of "mercy" for us. The guiding intelligence is very aware of our difficult times, and it knows that by limiting our memory we will be far more agreeable in our schoolwork, with a lot less pain to our heart.

So, one might wonder how we will manage to get the opportunity to prove ourselves for the first time.

Actually, the answer is really quite simple. We will use the law of reversed effort in our favor. If we seem to seal ourselves into our body by trying to get out, then it would only seem appropriate to release ourselves by trying to prevent a release.

But how do we do that? It might be compared to a child that is being taught to overcome his fear of water. All that he knows is that the harder he tries to stay on top, the more he will sink. It is only when he is taught to stay under the water that he finds it is impossible to do. The more he fights to stay under, the more he comes bobbing to the top.

So, to begin, we will not try to quiet the hyper monkey mind. Instead of trying to maintain a blank screen at the third eye, we will imagine that we are laying on the bottom of a pool. We see ourselves being completely covered with water and our major concern is to try to keep the body there, not permitting it to rise back to the top.

This exercise should be performed preferably at night, preparing to go to sleep. Then when we do drop off to sleep and automatically rise anyway, we will have managed to escape the dream bubble itself.

One thing to always remember is that you are never alone. Although you may not be aware of this, you are always protected.

The students of the arcane mystery schools referred to this as "the presence of the Inner Master". It is often only at the time that we journey, or go through physical transition (commonly called death), that we are able to understand just how precious we are to the Supreme Consciousness. It will be then, that we are able to see how protected we have been all of our lives, and what is meant by, "God is always as close as your heartbeat."

The Blank Screen Method: Once you have overcome the rampant mind, you will discover that the blank screen method is even faster and sometimes more effective to do your journeying.

In this method either position is correct. Simply take a few deep breaths before you begin and rest comfortably. Remove all thoughts from the conscious mind and concentrate solely on the area at the center of the eyebrows.

Picture a great spiritual light before you and imagine that all of its energy is being focused into a fine point of light, like a magnifying glass can do to the sun's rays. Then, in the same way that this glass can concentrate the energy onto a piece of paper, feel this beam focusing directly on the third cye section.

After a few seconds, you will be able to feel the vibration that is being set up. In turn, this will cause a chain reaction that reaches to depths behind the third eye, and establishes a link between your inner self and the spiritual light.

As you keep your attention on the energy vibration, you might see a blue light or a blue star (this is verification of a Divine Presence). You may see a yellow ball of light (which signifies the presence of a loved one or a teacher). Or you could see the picture of a place forming on the blank screen.

The blank screen is a complacent exercise, meaning that instead of requesting a certain result, you are opening yourself to receive what has been deemed important for you to experience.

The Sound Technique: The sound technique is best performed while being in a sitting position. If one is able to sit in a yoga or meditative position, that would be ideal, but if not, then one of the other positions will do.

The important thing to know in this exercise is that you will be choosing which level (or plane) you will visit by attuning yourself to that sound.

As already explained, everything vibrates and that is especially true for sounds and colors.

Not only the physical worlds, but all spiritual realms were created through sound. This sound can often be heard during a meditative exercise and sometimes may seem quite loud.

It is this sound that maintains these many, many worlds. We know of it as part of The Holy Trinity. This great wave of musical sound that creates the music of the spheres is that which is called The Holy Ghost – or some religious scriptures refer to it as The Voice of God.

When we practice with the sound technique, our main goal is to use the finer bodies that surround us, with the intent to travel beyond the astral plane.

The physical world vibrates at the lowest rate, where the atoms are close and the vibration heavy. The astral is next, with a little higher rate of vibration and a little less density, and so on, up through the many planes, where the vibration will increase on one hand, while the distance between the atoms spread on the other.

With our knowing that a certain sound has an unmistakable rate of vibration, all we need do is chant that particular sound to raise our vibration to that level.

The most common chant is OM (drawn out). This raises our consciousness to the vibration of the fourth plane, and usually opens the third eye of the seeker to the point that the inspiration, love and knowledge of that plane will enter into the consciousness.

Sitting in a meditative position, take several deep breaths, concentrate the energy flow to the third eye and then begin to chant.

Those who practice the religion of Light and Sound prefer to use the chant HU. This sound is also drawn out for as long as possible and is presented as if it were being sung.

The vibration of HU is the same vibration as the twelfth plane, so the student will find this the most desired of all vibrations.

The sound technique can be used to produce a variety of different results. You can experiment and possibly open doors especially adaptive to you, by using other sounds that have special meaning to you.

When choosing a particular sound, the only requirement is, if it can't be drawn out, then it be limited to just two syllables.

An example would be the name Jesus, using half the breath for the first syllable and half for the second.

At this point, we have pretty much established the fact that sound and vibration are one and the same thing. Since all of our atoms vibrate, we can now understand that everything is not only given life, but literally held together by this most holy of all things , this Voice of God.

Just as in ancient times, students today are taught to listen for the holy sounds that surround us in all things. Actually, it is impossible to ever separate ourselves from this sound. This sound not only gives life – but is life.

So, here we have briefly covered the several ways to journey, from the simplest to the most elevated. We have seen how we can have an inner movement without even trying, at one end of the scale, and how we can attune ourselves to God, by using sound, at the other.

We can now also comprehend much of the great mystery that has always existed in the relationship between mankind and that from which it came.

UNDERSTANDING THE HIGHER SELF

As we look into outer space, we may wonder about the mystery of life. It is easy for us to realize how little we know about our plane of existence, as we gaze up and stare out into that vast blackness.

Another interesting thing that may come to mind is how we, ourselves, may appear to microscopic life.

As much as our world is confusing to us, there is even a greater mystery about who and what we truly are.

Scripture tells us, "Man is made in the image of God", but unfortunately that has only led us to believe God is only human. That which we call God is not an old man with a long flowing beard, sitting on some golden throne. God is a very complex force, multidimensional and exists on – and is a part of – all dimensions.

Although we may not be aware of it, we too, are multidimensional. We are not the body we see in a mirror. We are actually a Spark residing in the pineal body, which we call the third eye. And from there, we control not only this physical body, but to a certain degree, we can exhibit influence on the higher planes.

This is also the reason for practicing spiritual meditation. When all of our attention is focused on the things of the physical, getting all of the money we can, or seeking power, we are lowering our vibration to the lowest possible rate of the physical world. When one seals himself at this level, he will develop the character of a "low" life.

This is a most appropriate term, for that is precisely what it means, "to be very low on the harmonic scale".

Have you ever noticed how money grabbers or power seekers have very low morals? How they care about nothing except themselves?

It is simply because our world has lost the true knowledge, has learned all of the wrong values, and moved itself to the lowest vibration of the physical. It has become populated with those who pray only to the dollar, are corrupt in action and bankrupt in character.

The more we seek our refuge and security in money, the further we grow away from spirit; the further we separate ourselves from our true security.

When we practice a spiritual meditation, it is not just because we desire to leave our physical body. It is to attune ourselves to the higher worlds so we can experience more of what we should be gaining.

In the earliest religious teachings, this was the knowledge imparted to the masses, but with the passage of time, many of the original teachings were lost. The lesson's intent was to explain that one should maintain a high vibration rate, so spirit can flow through us at a higher level. It also attempted to show that the more mundane a thing was, the lower a rate of vibration it would have. Because it is a fact that money is the servant to the gross needs of the physical, it vibrates at the low pole. Then, for a person to worship this money would also anchor him to this bottom scale.

It was not the intent to show that money is evil, only that it should be used and not loved. When we leave this world, not one penny will go with us. All that we will take with us is what we are and what we know.

Money is only loaned to us while we are here. Because of its nature, we can never truly own it; it can only own us.

There are so many that have more money than they could ever possibly use in this lifetime, and still they hunger for more. This only shows they are just as sick as any alcoholic or gambler. By the way, the alcoholic, the gambler, the pervert, the cheat, the liar and all the rest are the way they are due to being a prisoner at the lowest vibration of the physical.

This is also why so many things were classified as a sin. It wasn't really a matter of such things being evil, or because they were scorned by God, but was due to the very nature of their vibration.

So, the sex addict can be just as much a prisoner as the alcoholic. In either case, they are both being ruled instead of being the ruler. And, again, it was not the objects themselves that were being warned against, but the attraction to them to such an extent that it affected their aura, lowering and tying them to very base desires.

A good example of lowering your vibration through attunement would be an actor playing a certain part. Everyone knows to be a good actor, one must become that which he is portraying. To add to this difficulty, if an actor should be type-cast and that particular type of character is not desirable quality, the actor's constant attempt at becoming one with it will cause him to become that character.

This takes us back to the teaching of positive and negative spin. Since we control the spin through our thoughts and actions, enough of the energy units will be changed through pretending, that the negative becomes a reality.

It is a very sad thing to relate, but it is for this reason that actors and actresses often have such messed up lives. This is all due to the conflict caused within the mind as the character and soul clash in a vicious battle for control.

If one finds himself trapped at the lowest vibration and desires to escape, all that he needs to do is practice the highest form of inner movement, by using the sound technique. That is not to say that the gambler will automatically be cured, or that the alcoholic won't desire to drink anymore. That is something that will take effort on their part, but the mere fact that they have the sincere desire and are willing to seek vibration assistance, it is a great start.

Unlike what some religions teach, it is not necessary to give away all of our money to get to Heaven. That is really absurd! We only need to know how to handle our responsibilities without becoming trapped in this quagmire.

Meanwhile, if we desire to get ahead of our class, we will start to take an interest in the other four bodies that surround us.

With these bodies we can explore the worlds up to and including the fifth plane, called the soul plane. Once we are able to elevate to this level, we are better able to understand much of what has been taught in religion.

The physical worlds are like being in grade school. The astral is like going up to junior high (or middle school). The causal plane is compared to high school, and the etheric is our college training.

Then, when we have shown sufficient desire, by applying ourselves, we will all finally graduate into what is called the higher worlds or the God worlds. It will be at this point we complete our lower world training, and acquire powers and abilities still beyond the average person's ability to understand now.

The fifth plane is also the location of what mystics call "the Higher Self". This is something far greater than we may have previously believed.

When we entered into the lower worlds for schooling, we did not come alone. You see, we are not a complete soul – we are only half of a soul! If we were complete, we would be both male and female. But, if we were complete, that would hinder the learning process. If we did not have that animalistic desire to mate, the school would cease to exist.

So, as the soul left that essence called the "higher self" on the fifth plane, and proceeded to journey to the lower worlds, it was split in half. Half would be male and half would be female. Each would be complete in all ways. Both would be able to function without the aid of the other. But because they were split apart, each would seek to unite with the opposite sex. This is the basis for the teaching about Soul Mates.

That did not mean that they would *have* to find each other, for that is rarely the case. It only meant that the progress of the higher self would be sped up, having two working toward the completion of the assignment, instead of only one.

It has also increased the assistance of each soul, for each could draw on the benefits of the other through this higher self, even though neither was aware of the other.

The purpose of the sheath called the" higher self" is it acts much like a cosmic bank. All of the good that each does is accumulated and kept in this essence. It makes no difference if the acts (or thoughts) are only slightly good or are of monumental humanitarian benefit. All is sent to the essence and kept there and that which is considered undesirable is passed off.

What a fantastic conception!

Only the good is kept, all of the good – and none of the bad! Also, remember every time you do a spiritual exercise, it is like sending a check to be deposited.

Even though one of the partners might not be aware of the fantastic progress of the other, it makes no difference. They will find many miracles coming into their lives, and they will begin to have greater and greater experiences during the dream state until they are able to learn about the ancient science and the spiritual exercises that it engages. Then, when both partners are doing these exercises, the troubles of the physical become almost nonexistent.

Above the Ancient Temples was the inscription "Know Thyself". This was not just some idle reference as might be expected in today's society. It wasn't making a reference to their physical body, their emotional makeup, or even their knowledge. Instead, it was a constant reminder that we are spirit.

Those students who knew spirit and soul were both composed of the same thing were placed within the Circle of Spirit.

As long as the student thought of himself as a person, he was doomed to remain outside of the circle, but when he could see that he was truly spirit, he found that he could perform miracles.

The soul that functions at this point has the power to give assistance not only to their own counterpart (soul mate), but also to others that they and their soul mate may have loved while in the physical.

Can you even begin to comprehend the magnitude of that statement?

Because of others that may have loved us, they can elevate us, which in turn will elevate our soul mate. Also, any that have loved our soul mate and elevated them, will in addition elevate us. It doesn't have to be just a soul mate helping us.

According to the school of Pythagoras, "On this higher level of spirit and soul, we do not find the greed or the jealousy that is a part of the physical world. There is only love and compassion for one soul to another. Here soul once again becomes whole – and in this transformation can see clearly, knowing truly that all of us are of one grand family, and each and everyone is most eager to share this blessing of spirit with all."

Unfortunately, almost everything you may have been taught in this world has been geared to lowering you. The fear merchants would rather discredit God than to permit you to know the truth about yourself.

To them it was far better to discredit God, making It a Him, and making Him an "angry and vengeful God," than to permit souls to escape their control by finding out the truth about themselves.

OPENING THE DOOR

Regardless of our race, religion or culture, there is one thing we all share and that is that one day each and every one of us will leave this world.

For this reason these writings have always been of interest to the populace. Also, as we are God-manifested human beings, it is our right and privilege to know fully where we came from, why we are here, and where we will be going when we pass through that misty portal in ignorance we call "death".

Remember, even though on various occasions the word death may be used, we must understand that there is really no such of a thing as death. There is only change.

Nothing can be destroyed.

A drop of water can be consumed, passed off, vaporized, condensed – all to only once again return to its normal state of being a droplet of water. A mighty tree can be burned, turning it to ash, which in turn returns its nutrients into the soil, making it rich with vitality – thus encouraging the new seed.

No, there is no such of a thing as death, only change, which we call transition.

To better understand our biggest transition (the one that occurs at the culmination of our physical experience on this planet), we first must turn to those who have had the experience of being able to move back and forth between our world and those places of the higher worlds (meaning higher vibration).

There is an old saying that none of us can ever know what lies beyond death until we travel that road ourselves – because no one has ever returned to tell us, but that's not exactly the truth. Most religions are based on what their Seers have seen and translated into our world.

There is one major difficulty with what these Seers, Astral Projectionists, and Journeyers have related. While they can give a very broad account of what they have found, they have not been able to fully explain the true beauty, the vibrant harmony and the feeling of these worlds.

This is because there are certain senses that the human body does not have. Even though we will develop them after our graduation from this world, they still remain hidden away in our heart region. They are emotions that the herded masses will never understand while in the physical world.

To better explain this, we will use our interpretation of sex as an example. The pleasant vibration that passes through the brain, causing the entire body to heave and convulse is actually an extremely low vibration.

This vibration does not really belong to the physical plane, but is an astral vibration. However, this astral vibration is close enough "in sync" with our physical bodies that it can be sensed by all creatures and, in turn, guarantees the procreation of all animals (including the human animal).

Many lecturers have remarked about the wonderful vibrations they enjoyed while performing astral projection. They were quick to realize the feeling of love and compassion that accompanies sex was really a vibration the physical brain was able to sense and translate into physical response.

This, then, is our first step in understanding there is something beyond our physical realm. Without our receiving vibrations from a higher state, there would be no such thing as sex!

Procreation would not be a pleasant sensation; there would be no feeling of emotion; there would be no physical attraction; and more than likely, the act of sex itself would be bothersome, unappealing and even irritating. Physical creations would most certainly become extinct.

To speak of sex without experiencing the love vibrations would not give us a clear understanding of it. Writers could write about it and teachers could explain the mechanics of it, but both of these would only be a dull and dry biological explanation. Not until we could sense and feel that vibration, could we come to fully appreciate and use it.

Thus, when writers attempt to introduce you to the many worlds they have seen (and the worlds you will one day experience), they will be speaking of worlds accompanied by, and composed of, vibrations the human body cannot grasp or comprehend. With their being armed with only words, most students are not able to absorb the true nature of their euphoric state.

Even the senses you have in the physical are greatly expanded after the process of elevation has taken place. Some teach that your senses are expanded a hundred or even a thousand fold. Sights are far more beautiful, sounds more musical, smells more radiant, and the feeling of love is far more vibrant and pure.

An atheist believes in only one plane of existence, the physical. The religionist believes in two planes, the physical and some distant heaven. And the fanatic believes in three planes, the physical, a heaven – and a burning hell. But through teachings revealed in the ancient schools, we find there are at least twelve planes of existence (and not one of them a fire and brimstone hell).

Now that we have established the fact that there is Life after death, let's clarify what hell is actually supposed to be.

The original teaching suggested all souls had to be put to the test of trial and error, and this was to be done by being exposed to a trying and sometimes difficult school of lessons.

To receive these lessons, the soul had to be removed from its content and complaisant state and sent into the lower worlds. But remember, here we are speaking from the higher worlds. The physical is a part of the lower worlds. We are the lowest because we have the lowest vibration.

To suggest there is some lower world inside of the earth is not only foolish, but remains in contrast to our present day spiritual evolution. This was a control factor used by the fear merchants to maintain a hold over ignorant peasants.

Also, to believe in such a thing as eternal punishment and damnation controlled by hideous, evil beings, is to give little credence to the concept of a "loving and gentle God". If you couldn't toss any of your children into an oven and roast them, regardless of how bad they may have been, then it's foolish to believe the Spirit of Love could do so. This concept was instated to insure that the populace would support the teachings out of pure fear. So, while we state emphatically there is no hell, we most assuredly must agree that there is a school – and that school can be as hellish or as peaceful as we see fit to make it.

We are in the physical world only because we vibrate at the physical level. If we are able to raise our vibrations slightly, we may become a little euphoric or drunk-like. If we can raise it even slightly more, we may be able to find ourselves outside of the body, looking down on it.

Spirit is forever passing through us. This is important because spirit is our direct link with the higher planes. At the moment of death (transition) of the physical body, our innermost core (with the assistance of this spirit) will begin to vibrate to the highest level we have opened ourselves to in this life.

But another surprising thing is that you don't have to wait until you are ready to leave this world to share in the pleasure of experiencing the higher vibrations. We can begin on this very day. We will also be opening our God Doors, where perhaps for the first time in our lives, we can discover who we really are – and bring miracles into our lives.

As already stated, the closest vibration to us is the one associated with sex. The next highest vibration is the Heart Region. There is a very good reason love is associated with the heart. The heart is actually only an organ, and is not really capable of feeling any emotion at all. However, the region of the heart will become warm and even start to feel ecstatic when true love is felt.

While most adults have drifted away from this vibration, it is most easily touched by children. Take a moment and try to remember what it was like when you were in the third grade or so. Can you remember your first crush on the opposite sex? Can you remember what that wonderful feeling in your chest felt like? It was a wonderful feeling that would come to you time and time again, making childhood the wonderful thing that it is. It was a glorious feeling that kept you in touch with the astral from which you came. And it was this great force that was always with you – and it would always stay with you – until the days of puberty set in.

With puberty came physical and psychological changes that would make you forget your "Dear Friend" at the heart region. Suddenly, you've taken a step into adulthood and another step away from the sanctity of the worlds of higher vibration. The new emotions came on strong with strange sensations in the brain and loins, and the heart region was quickly forgotten.

Now, though, we will begin to reopen old channels, reconnecting with the higher vibration and we will use it as we never dreamed possible as a child.

ACTIVATING THE HEART REGION

While the heart region can be used to send love, it is most widely accepted as being a receiving station. This means that the best way to activate the region is to open yourself to receive love vibrations being sent to you. That does not necessarily mean there has to be someone crazy in love with you and thinking of you twenty four hours a day. While that may be quite unlikely, there are divine love vibrations forever pouring out from the various planes.

The heart region is most closely attuned to the astral plane, so this would most likely be the first vibration to enter our heart receiver.

To activate, simply relax, concentrate lightly on the general region of the heart. There is never any forcing or trying. You simply gaze across it with your inner vision.

Gently feel the energy come. It may have been many years since you have been in awareness contact with this love, so it will not come on in great strength, but will move ever so gently into your field of action.

Feel the Love come to you. Try to remember that feeling you had as a child when the mystery of the opposite sex was absolutely Awe-inspiring.

See yourself as that eight or nine year old again. Feel the thrill you felt when someone of the opposite sex looked at you in a loving manner.

Feel it. Enjoy it. It may even make you smile a little. It has nothing at all to do with sex. It deals purely with the majestic beauty of soul – and the mystery of life.

Almost immediately, once you relax, you will start to feel a glimmer of that warm glow in the area of the heart.

If after several minutes you still have any doubts about making contact, all you need do is look into a mirror. You will notice how soft, gentle and loving your eyes have become. The eyes never lie. The brain may be cynical, but the eyes serve as the doorway to the soul.

The longer you choose to stay in this meditative state, the more it will grow.

The actual response will vary greatly from individual to individual. Some might see a beautiful landscape flowing below them, or they might hear beautiful music. You might even get the impression someone who greatly loves you is near.

Again, it will not be a knock down, take over experience. It will not be something you will see with physical eyes or hear with physical ears. It will be gentle, compassionate, and flowing smoothly as an impression on the blank screen of the inner mind.

At first, you may more feel the experience than relatively see it, but with the feeling, there will soon be a picture coming to the mind.

This will be the first step in being reintroduced to your true home.

Putting yourself in a passive state is more than just a healthy thing to do for your body. In addition to lowering your blood pressure and removing stress from the nervous system, it will attune the mind and body to the higher vibrations that surround us. Even though our physical vibration is relatively low, we should understand the higher vibes are still around us.

When one speaks of a higher plane, he is not making a reference to a far off or distant place. Most religions think of Heaven as someplace Up. They are not sure where up may be, but they are sure that it's someplace far away.

How often we have seen the drawings of winged angels playing harps, floating among the clouds while a great Pearly Gate rests upon a nearby cloud bank. But just as lower worlds do not mean inside of the Earth, higher does not mean up or in space.

When we relax and learn to take advantage of the wonderful vibration that flows through the heart region, we also open ourselves to other spiritual wonders. We may be able to experience Illumination or what is called "Cosmic Consciousness".

The phrase "As Above/ So Below," acknowledges that all we have to do to reach a higher state is to become like that vibration.

This is where Imagination becomes such an important aspect of spiritual liberation. Even if we only imagine we have begun the flow of spirit through the heart region – it will instantly come to us.

Just as spirit is the divine tool of God to perform miracles, our imagination is our Divine tool to manifest miracles.

This is perhaps one of the greatest secrets about the working of spirit. It will always follow the will of our imagination, just as long as our thinking is clear, pure and does not harm another in any way.

With spiritual liberation comes a freedom basically unknown to most of our fellow humans. Whether we attract the divine flow, bringing miracles to our surrounding or whether we flow to higher states, opening our senses to what life is like beyond transition, the end results are the same. We have succeeded in raising our vibration to a higher degree than the majority will reach.

The feeling in the heart region will be a mystical, magical and ecstatic love that may make your heart race, just as when you were a child. Astral love is always like having your first love affair – where magic pounds in your chest and blood rushes to the brain.

From this vibration, we will be able to reach just a hair higher, opening the door to those vibes that the physical body did not previously touch.

While in a meditative state, there are certain slight impressions that will come to you. They will often be so slight you may not be aware of them until they have passed, and you are better able to analyze what you saw or heard. We will be dealing with delicate impressions that the bulky brain is not used to receiving. Some sounds you might hear are: a buzzing, a rolling of thunder, a waterfall, birds singing, or even musical sounds similar to a flute or bagpipe.

Each of the planes has its own distinct identification sound. This offers us another unique opportunity. We can check to find out exactly how spiritually advanced we are, simply by listening for which sound we might hear.

When one can detect what seems to sound like distant bagpipes, they will know they are very close to the fifth plane.

As for inner visions, the astral always appears similar to the physical. There are trees, gardens, waterfalls and scenic temples. This is the place most vibrate to when they translate from the physical plane. Everyone pretty much returns to a familiar surrounding, someplace they had previously been, before they entered into their Earth journey.

Memories are instantaneous, and one will find that all they had forgotten during their journey through the physical, has at once returned.

When one picks up the vibes of the third (causal) plane, they will find glorious landscapes that even dwarf the beauty of the astral. The feeling is complete love, peace and contentment, the likes of which have never been previously experienced in physical life.

When the vibes of the fourth plane become a part of your physical makeup, it is likely you will be able to improve not only your life, but the lives of those around you - without your even trying.

The ability to touch the fourth plane during a spiritual exercise is the closest thing to Divine that the soul can experience while still in the lower world (physical universe).

Those worlds above the fifth plane are called higher worlds. Those who reside in these worlds have graduated back to their true home.

CHAPTER THREE:

EXPLORING THE OTHER WORLDS

THE VEIL OF GOD

As we explore the higher worlds, we must remember we are attempting to describe conditions far superior to the trials and tribulations of our Earthly school. There are also many obstacles that face us in regards to attempting to share the knowledge with others.

We are confronted with the difficulty of trying to relate higher states of consciousness using only an inferior tool (the physical mind). We are saddled with the burden of explaining high vibrations to a world of very low vibration. We are engaging in cosmic laws completely foreign to our understanding of physics. We are speaking about important emotions the Earth bound cannot feel, and we must never forget we are dealing with explanations that often make their home in realms existing beyond Time and Space.

Now, if all of this sounds complicated, we must never lose sight of the fact that all of this information of the other worlds is being presented at a physical level, as if we were only taking a journey across the country. We need to remember that although you will maintain the physical consciousness while on this journey, there is a change of consciousness at each and every level.

When you make this journey for yourself, instead of reading about it, you will quickly note there is a tremendous amount of knowledge absorbed as you progress. This is necessary to be able to comprehend the magnitude of each plane.

Also, this absorption will help you understand the laws of the particular plane you are on, enabling you to perform certain acts that sound fantastic to those of the physical realm.

With that in mind, let's begin our journey, which is very similar to what millions have experienced.

Almost as quickly as my eyes closed, I awoke and saw the twinkling of city lights beneath me.

Even though great joy surged through my being at such an awesome sight - a sight that I would prefer to spend the night exploring – instantly I was aware that would not be the case.

A great vortex encased me, raising my consciousness to a higher level. There, I could detect the presence of a Spiritual Traveler, and instantly I remembered the words of my teacher. He said there was never any need to be afraid, because there would always be someone at my side while I was learning. This also went for all who opened themselves to spirit.

I was immediately aware that somehow I would be escalated to tremendous spiritual heights, being escorted by this great one.

The lights below me began to zoom past; then other lights and other cities quickly flashed past my vision.

Faster and faster the scene changed below me – one city after another – until I could quickly detect that all these cities were not just this world.

Before being lifted into the higher realms, this Guardian seemed to be able to read my mind about questions I have had for many years. Without even needing to ask, he showed and confirmed that life not only existed elsewhere in the physical universe, but that the universe was literally saturated with life.

The hundreds, thousands, and millions of flashing sights below us showed that life not only existed elsewhere, but my consciousness was flooded with the massive variety of such life.

I saw everything from mud hut hovels to civilizations so far advanced from anything I had known on Earth, that even with my heightened awareness, I could not begin to touch their knowledge.

I saw planets of various sizes and characteristics. Some had multiple suns; some had very strange creatures that towered over the trees; some planets were so large they could have held dozens of our Earth; and some were so small that an individual could walk completely around the circumference in a time equivalent to a couple of our hours.

I saw worlds that flourished with life – and others so barren that life as we know it, could not possibly exist. While some were rich in water and vegetation supporting carbon based life forms, there were just as many that seemed to support only soot and ash, and gave life to horrible creatures from which nightmares sprang.

There were creatures of every imaginable scope, size and capability. And even though I desired to stop and investigate what was being shown, my efforts were ignored by my Guide. Much the same as a parent would ignore the enthusiastic reactions of a child in the back seat of a car, refusing to stop at every sight, every few yards, as the car sped along.

But even in the great haste, I was able to absorb knowledge. I was quick to see that within the host of creatures I witnessed, it was apparent the Homo Sapien, although a highly spiritual creature, was not the ultimate life form. Some life forms who had at one time been sub-servant to mankind, now exhibited knowledge far exceeding my own Earthly culture.

The knowledge received was so massive that even if we were not to rise to the higher planes, it seemed that what I had absorbed in only a few moments would take the balance of my life to recreate, filling thousands upon thousands of volumes.

Even as I was thus engaged, a great vibration covered me completely. I seemed to vibrate from head to foot. (If in fact, I still resembled my Earthly form. For now, while traveling, I was aware that to some I would appear to be a Golden Ball of Light.)

With the vibration came an exalted consciousness expansion, and I could still see cities flashing below me, but now I was aware they were vastly different from the former ones.

Where the previous cities sparkled by man-made light and were reflected by illumination from a supporting sun, it was quite easy to see that these cities gained their glorious light from some mysterious force that poured down upon them from another spiritual plane.

"Witness the astral," came the thought-form from my Guide, within whose comet tail I seemed to soar along. "Even as great as the physical universe may seem to you, know that the astral worlds and universes are three times greater in size. Even in its greater size, you will find only peace and love here."

We continued to soar along, far above an ocean of gold and blue texture, until a great sight fell upon my eyes.

There, before me, was a glorious mountain of Light. I could clearly see billions of rays of energy pouring from it. Instantly I remembered when I had been shown this great mountain before.

As my astral memory returned, I remembered having spent some time in this wonderful city before I began my lessons on Earth in my present life.

I remembered standing before this wondrous Mountain of Light many years previous, and remembered how badly I wanted to return to Earth to tell the people of this place. At the same time, I was amazed that the people I left behind were so ignorant they could not conceive the existence of this mighty power transmitter.

I marveled even then, so many years previous, that they never wondered even once where the Force that gave them and their planet life, came from.

Even the great scientists that had taught there was no such thing as perpetual energy (that all energy needed to draw its life from another source) failed to have faith that the higher planes existed.

This was shocking to me. They would say, "Show me and I will believe," but, yet, was not the continuance of life itself proof enough?

How did they think the hundreds of functions of the body alone, were able to carry out their various duties? Without ever taking into regard the operation of nature, what do they think makes the heart beat, the blood to flow, the organs to function?

If they cannot believe there is a higher existence and they can dare to say, "Show me," then all I could offer them would be the words, "If you are so blind, then show me your wonderful science by creating a simple machine that can function in such a manner."

No, they cannot – and neither could our world exist without this Redistribution Station of Power located in the astral – and especially from this capital city where I now stood.

We gazed together upon the majestic sight, watching the strange forms and visions that formed within it and then shot forth with a power and a velocity that could no way be comprehended by any that could not witness the sight for themselves. Through my higher understanding that was opening, I easily realized that each and every one of the billions upon billions of rays that shot forth every second, had the capabilities of a million times a million nuclear bombs. To my fragile being, it seemed that even just one of these rays would be enough to run our Earth for hundreds of years – or even destroy it completely.

"As powerful as this Force is," my Guide continued, "it has been cut thousands upon thousands of times before it is permitted to enter into the astral plane. If this were not so, the Force would be far too much for this plane to handle. Instead of bringing life to the astral, it would bring great disaster. And that is not to mention what would happen to all physical universes. They would just simply cease to exist; all going out at the same time in one great explosion.

"The pathetic and fragile human animal believes in its mind that he or she would like to stand in the presence of God, but there is no way such a thing could occur until they have been properly prepared. If this Force, which is only 'The Breath of God', could destroy the lower planes, then I ask you, what could it do to a mere delicate atom that we call a soul?

"So it is that when the newly arrived soul has returned to the astral, after their day in school has been completed in the physical, this soul usually first desires to seek out God. Thus, he or she will first be shown this mountain. If they are truly spiritually advanced, they will realize the power of the mountain, realize that it is but one puff from God, and will realize that this is the most they will be able to comprehend of God while they remain on the astral.

"However, if they are not so greatly advanced, they will gaze upon the mountain, marvel at its stature and then turn and still seek to find God.

"Unfortunately, one lesson not very well taught in the physical school is what God really is. Most believe It is a very, very old man, with a long flowing beard, dressed in a golden robe and sitting upon a jeweled throne.

"Since they cannot understand what God actually is, they attempt to lower the concept by insinuating God is only a man. This is really a shame for more reasons than one. For in truth, if they could have understood God while still residing in the physical worlds, they could have made their prisons a paradise.

"If they could have understood they were not really physical beings, but Little Gods, they would have forced the tests and the elements of the physical world to bow before them. They could have had – and demanded – anything from the physical and it would have been granted. This, because they would have discovered they were the true Sons and Daughters of God.

"Even in your culture and your religion, the man known as Jesus tried to teach this to the people. His teaching was that mankind was the true Son of God, and that it was sacrificed into this world so it could be purified and return to its true home and position.

"There was nothing in His teachings about Him dying for your sins. Such a thing is not only outrageous, it would serve no purpose. Do you really think such a great man said, 'With my death I will absolve all crimes now and forever into the future. And because I am to die, it means that all individuals, even thousands of years into the future, can commit crimes against one another and they will never need to worry about any retribution of any kind, simply by saying that I died for them'?

"Unfortunately, that is not the Christos Teaching Jesus attempted to bring into the world. It was His intent to awaken the people to the very ancient teaching that we, too, are composed of the same thing as God. We are in the Image of God, but God is not in the image of man.

"But, still, perhaps now more than ever before, these souls leave the Earth world, return here and their first desire is to journey to the Throne of God. So, we of the astral will present to them what they expect. Since they believe that God is a man, they will be presented with several different Faces of God; with each step they climb toward spirituality, changing their understanding, so does the Face change.

"Until the soul has grown enough spiritually, he must be introduced to God very slowly and carefully. Just as a child beginning school could not understand the classes of a college student, so it is with the physical Soul, trying to understand the very advanced World of God.

"By the time the soul has met each of the different Faces of God, he will be prepared to enter into the twelfth plane, the true home of God."

With that, he pointed in the far distance at a great statue. At first I could not see where he was pointing. All I could see was something that looked like a great copper beam rising high into the Heavens at an angle.

Although I could not see the statue to which he was referring, I was greatly impressed with the tremendous size and magnitude of this copper beam. I realized the base took up many miles of space. The base was so tremendous in size that if such a thing were to exist on Earth, one would have to travel perhaps as much as forty or fifty miles to go around it just once.

"Expand your vision," he mused at me. "You are much like the man that could not find the forest because the trees were in his way.

"If you will use your Astral vision, and not look at this world as if you were looking at it through your physical eyes, you will be able to see that the great towering beam is but one leg of the statue to which I am pointing."

Then, in total amazement, I realized what he was saying was true. As great as the beam was, it, indeed, was but one leg. I could now see the slant was due to the fact it merged with another great leg that also rose up into the ethers from far away, and atop of that rested an even more incredible body that towered far into the Heavens.

I could now also comprehend that the distance between the two feet was anywhere from a hundred to two hundred miles. The sight of such a thing staggered me almost as much as the Mountain of Light had done.

Seeing that I could now encompass the full scope of the statue, he continued, "This statue is dedicated to He who is known as the Governor of the astral universe. He, of course, is not God, but for those that come here and believe they have earned the right to meet with God, and simply will not accept the truth about who and what God is, they will be led to Him."

"Who could build such a thing as this statue?" I asked.

"Even in this world," he answered, "where many residents have memories that date back thousands and thousands of years, they can only tell you that it was here even before their arrival. Actually, it was built in the misty ages of the astral, back when the physical and the astral were merged together as one, by an advanced race that can no longer be found living in any of the lower planes."

Then he motioned for me to travel gently with him and we floated above this strange and beautiful city.

At this time, he granted me the pleasure of exploring wherever I desired. I could now understand why he had no desire for me to waste too much of my time in exploring the worlds of the physical previously. He had sped me along so that even greater eternal questions lodged in my mind, could be answered.

"There," he said as he pointed in the direction of the Hall of Memories. "Whenever one leaves the physical in what is deemed death, the newly departed will be brought here so they can see the results of their classroom work. What they accomplished while still on Earth, or one of the other planets. Some religions try to teach it is a Judgment of some kind and something to be afraid of, but nothing could be further from the truth.

"It is simply a viewing for your own benefit, to see what tremendous good you may have accomplished – even if you might not have been aware of it. It is a matter of the student getting a glimpse of his report card, allowing him to know why he is being so richly rewarded – and why there are so many souls who love him so dearly.

"And there!" he exclaimed as he pointed at another fantastic structure. "That is the greatest museum known to any; either in these worlds or in the physical. Anything that has ever existed on the astral or in the physical will be found in this museum of museums. And not only that, but anything that will ever be invented in the physical is already here"

Even as great as all of the physical universes are, or as great as the astral universes are, it was easy for me to believe such a claim. The size of this incredible place was again beyond what I could understand using my untrained senses. The basic structure of the main entrance could have stretched for hundreds of miles and the number of wings spreading out from that entrance was beyond my ability to count.

As I looked upon it, he again began to speak to me in thought forms. "One might wonder how anyone could locate any particular thing in such a vastness, but when the time is ripe, whatever one of your Earth's scientists or inventors needs to see, will be shown to him. This is usually accomplished in the dream state.

"There are a great number of your inventors that have said they were shown what they needed to know while asleep. Well, this is that sleeping place. They are brought here from their dream bubble, and carefully shown just enough to help the world to continue on with its slow progress."

We paused just long enough that I might get a glimpse of some of the things that will be invented in the Earth world while I am a resident. There was really no danger that I might carry this knowledge back with me though, and thereby upset the balance of things by bringing something that the world was not yet ready to receive, because, for the most part, I had no idea what I was looking at, nor did I know how it was to be used.

Even as intriguing as the place was, I felt a deep urge beginning to stir within myself. Without using words, my Guide focused my attention on still another structure in the far distance.

As my astral vision brought it into focus, I felt a warm glow. In physical words, I could only describe what I saw as being a majestic temple or mansion, but those words could do it no justice. Its size easily equaled the Mountain of Light or the Statue; perhaps it was even larger than either of those, but that was not the reason for my excitement.

Instantly, I remembered when I had been brought here before - when I had died in a previous life and returned to this place. At that time I thought I was approaching the throne of God. Now, even as I knew better, it was still very much like returning home.

I felt great love for this Being when I thought He was God. Now shouldn't I love Him, simply because I now know He is not?

A great warmth filled me as we neared His Temple. Even though I loved this wonderful Being with every fiber of my being, it seems that I had forgotten about Him while I was on Earth. I had even heard His true name mentioned many times by various spiritual teachers, but the truth was that since I had not known His real name, it had brought no memories to me at that time.

There was another great change of consciousness that overtook me as we began to approach this most holy ground of the astral. To relate it to the physical consciousness is almost impossible. The law of physics as we know them simply do not apply here. The only thing close that the physical consciousness could compare it with, would be the state that we reach as we sleep.

When we are asleep, things are easier to understand. We will often experience things (and understand them) where the awakened consciousness is left totally confused. That is pretty much the case here, for we are dealing with Laws that are entirely different from the physical. Now, though, since my awareness had been greatly expanded, I was not the least bit surprised to find myself flying about, nor was I surprised by the great abilities I now knew I had.

I and my guide soared down to the fantastic entrance, around which I estimated a thousand angelic beings seemed to be standing guard. With no more than a loving smile offered by my guide, the beings, each and every one, parted the way and seemed to be singing praises and blessings upon us.

They showed they were as happy for me as I was happy. "The Beings here are quite different from those you have left behind on Earth," the guide offered. "In your culture there is much pretending. Most will say they are happy for someone when something good has happened to them, but, unfortunately, they, unless being a loved one, could probably care less. Here their love and happiness is genuine."

As we entered the great hall, I was aware that my guide and I had changed from the shining Golden Lights that were our soul bodies, into the astral sheath that was at our disposal. I was also quick to realize we were automatically switching to the astral bodies with no effort on our part, because that body was the right vibration for this plane. As far as how we looked, it was easy to see that the ancient teaching that taught that the astral and physical bodies are similar, was very right. The only difference I could see was that any limp or any imperfection or fault of the physical body had been corrected or improved in the astral one.

Moving along the inner hall I noticed large murals, paintings and statues that adorned the way as we progressed into what many call the Throne Room.

Again, I urgently wanted to stop and learn more about what these things represented, but my guide continued to hurry me along, for there was still much I needed to know and our time together would be limited.

Soon, we were no longer walking along the hall, but were floating over the radiant shining floors and steps. Suddenly we emerged from the hall and found ourselves in the center of the Throne Room.

Then, before me... there He was!

His glorious shining body was more than my senses could encompass! For a moment I felt as though I were falling to my knees – to pay loving homage. But, my guide quickly gave me support. "When you were last here," the guide said, "you believed this was God. And then, too, you wished to pay homage, but now this Loving Father welcomes you not as a subject but as a Coworker. It is not His desire to be worshipped, but to teach and prepare those who are ready, so that they may enter into the higher worlds.

"This is the loving Governor of the astral for which the statue had been built. For those who believe they must meet God, He will greet them as the First Face of God."

After my guide had transmitted this knowledge to me, there was a moment of silence as we gazed upon this gigantic Being. He presented Himself to us, appearing to be maybe a hundred feet tall and shined with the brilliance of a bright sun. He was so great that He could be looked upon only with astral vision. No physical eyes would be able to look directly at Him and, perhaps, this was one of the reasons He never presented Himself in the physical worlds, although He was the Lord of those worlds also.

"Welcome!" came booming at me. It was more of an inner awareness though, than a sound.

Then a tremendous flow of knowledge began to pass through me and I realized many mysteries of the cosmic were being removed from my mind, so that I might understand the great concept. (And again, as with all presented dialogue, the translation has been based on the memory of the impressive thought-forms and the impact of the understanding received.)

"The time has come for you to learn about God – and so it is that I am to give instruction to you on the Veils of God.

"Do you know what the Veils of God are? God must be hidden behind many veils and there is a very good reason for that. It is for protection. Not for the protection of God, as you may think – but for your protection.

"At least, it is for your protection until you are better able to grasp the true force of God. As your guide has already informed you, the force of God – the force that gives life to all things – could just as easily destroy all of these worlds, simply by permitting too much of the force into these worlds!

"The first Faces of God will be to impart knowledge and protection to your frail existence, but the last of the veils will be especially to protect the essence of the fountain from which all things flow. It will be at that time that you will finally be permitted to stand before God. And there will be many wonderful surprises that you simply would not be able to understand now."

As the knowledge flowed to me, I felt the ecstatic waves that rolled out from His Greatness and they were so wonderful and powerful that it was as if I were hypnotized. Wave after wave pounded against me and with each, I realized I was being pushed into an even greater state of awareness.

There was nothing physical about this encounter, since here lower laws did not apply. Sometimes I seemed to be floating up before Him and sometimes I seemed to be experiencing a split existence, where I was here with Him and at the same time aware of things taking place a tremendous distance away. And all of this was taking place with no effort on my part.

It was not like I was a restless child, because that could have been understood by the physical consciousness. It was more like I was absorbing abilities from Him. This massive display had nothing at all to do with attention, understanding or even endeavor. It was simply a Gift given to me, opening my consciousness for what was to follow, when I would be leaving this Grand Hall.

There are billions upon billions of souls in the physical universes that believe this astral presentation is God and they worship Him in such a manner. This, however, is not due by request or desire of the Governor, but due to the fact that this was the duty for which He has been prepared and assigned by the True Eternal Existence.

It is at this stage mankind learns that all of us are identical. There is no separation by race, religion, or even species. At this veil, purification of mind takes place.

Also, the developing soul can finally see that spirit and religion are not always identical.

As the knowledge and blessings were passed to me, I was aware of a pending question. "Do you believe that Law and Justice are the same?"

Then, instantly, I had the answer. It was quite evident the two were drastically different. Many laws have nothing at all to do with justice. Just because a certain law is being enforced by a court, it didn't necessarily mean that law was just.

Slavery has been a law in many cultures, but that didn't insinuate it was just. The same is true for religion. Just because a certain religion tells you what you should or shouldn't do, or how you should feel about certain subjects, or even how you should react to a thousand different situations – have nothing at all to do with spiritual development. That is another purpose of this stage; to further emphasize that which is Truth, and to wash away all errors that may have been picked up along the way.

At this Face of God, all finally learn who they really are. You are far more than you may have ever dreamed or believed possible. It is easy enough for a spiritual master to teach, "We are all Flames from the Great Fire called God," but not until one awakens to the awareness of the Inner Planes, will they ever gain a proper perspective to the full implications of that teaching.

"From here," the flow continued, "you will gradually make your way to even higher veils. Your understanding of what God is will grow with each different encounter, because at each level you will be shown that God is still more than you had learned at the preceding level.

"At each encounter, you will be tested to see if you are still unaware of the ultimate truth. So, at each level there will be an attempt to convince you that you have arrived at the end of your journey. If you had not been previously instructed about this test, you would, undoubtedly, believe that nothing could be more than this – and you would turn away, seeking God no further.

"While the school may seem complicated, the lessons are really very simple. There are only three things to know to become a Master. Know that you are a part of God; know that God is unlimited; and know that you, as God, are also unlimited. You must never forget that you are a little God!"

BEYOND THE ASTRAL

As we left the Grand Throne Room, it seemed we floated out over a massive body of water. I was so dazed by the event that I lost contact with what was happening around me and it took some time for me to realize we had left.

I felt a glow that covered me completely. It was as if I had been placed in a trance. I was unable to communicate, and all of my senses were in some kind of suspended state.

I was barely aware of my surroundings and I was totally unable to move on my own accord. If it had not been for my guide taking charge of me and moving me from the temple, I'm sure I may have spent eternity floating and bobbing there beside this astral Governor – and to my mind, I would have been very happy to maintain that condition.

Once we had traveled a far distance, my guide carefully maneuvered me into a countryside setting, placing me at the foot of a tremendously beautiful mountain that shone in a majestic hue of velvet.

I have no idea how long it took me to regain enough of my senses before I could fully realize we were no longer in the presence of that fantastic Being.

"Just take it easy," my guide suggested. "Enjoy it while you can. When you get back to the physical you're going to remember this, and you are going to hunger to feel it again."

Yes, it was true. Another piece of knowledge was mine, as the knowledge of the Spheres was absorbed into my inner being. I could see very clearly why the memory of the soul was erased as it began its journey into the physical world.

There were actually two good reasons for this curtain to be drawn around the student's awareness. The first was as an act of mercy. The cosmic is very aware of the human's frailty, and desired for these Gems of God to know as much happiness as they could while clothed in their temporary Temples of Clay. Happiness could never manifest if they were forever homesick. The second reason was to insure against suicide.

All souls should know that suicide is one of the ultimate of all crimes. Of course, the suicide is one of the most pathetic of all creatures, for they feel all is lost. However, although the teachers and masters may feel great compassion for them, it makes no difference. It is the law of the lower worlds that he who commits suicide must return immediately and be placed in a very similar situation that he had previously left, except that it must be just a little worse than before. It could be compared to a prisoner who has attempted to break out of prison. He will be captured and returned to the world he left behind – except, now more time must be added to his sentence. By trying to escape, he did not erase his debt, but only added to it. So it is with the suicide. By leaving the memory intact, it is feared many would not only abandon the purpose for which they entered the world, but may try to return home – without using the proper method.

I could now see that this world (and even the worlds beyond the astral) were not really hidden from us in the physical, but merely put on hold until we could learn more about proper perspectives, and more about what is true spiritual knowledge. It would be then, that the earthbound would know we had never really been separated from God. We would only need to adjust our vibration through the use of a spiritual exercise to go wherever we desired, whenever we desired.

I returned my attention toward my guide, and found I was slowly beginning to function more satisfactorily.

"I'm not ready to go on to the next plane yet," were the first words I heard myself say. I knew, perhaps by his smile, that he had many more surprises for me, and I knew by his previous actions that he was not one to linger any place too long. But there was still so much I wanted to see and do before the journey continued to the higher planes.

With the full return of my astral memory, I could remember where I had been here in the astral, at the conclusion of the three different lives I had lived on Earth.

At the conclusion of each life, I had always been met by the same individual, who served as a Coworker, and who had chosen this position of service, after his final departure from earth. As my guide, he returned me here among my loved ones and long time friends each time.

Now that I was floating freely in the astral, I was eager to be with my friends and those I loved, who had departed from Earth some time ago.

My eyes met his and I could sense he knew what was in my heart.

"Your mother and father are no longer here," he informed me in a loving and kind manner, for he knew how much I loved them. "At this time, your father has returned into the physical to perform a very important function. He, like many millions such as himself, have chosen to be born again into the school to carry out some very important duties. If you desire to see your mother, you will need to travel with me into the still much higher heavens. For, she will be waiting for you on one of the higher planes."

Then, he made a casual gesture in the direction of the valley to insinuate that the choice was mine. It was as if he was making an attempt at trying to make me think I was in charge of the decisions being made – but I knew better.

With the thought of seeing my mother again, I returned his smile and with no further discussion of exploring the astral any further at this time, he began to prepare me for the next higher vibration.

"As you may remember," he continued, "whenever you received a lesson about moving from one plane to another, the incident was always related in a physical way.

"Whenever you heard a story about a student exploring the higher worlds with his teacher, each plane sounded pretty much like a previous one. And not only that, but when they were leaving one plane and going into another, they would walk over a mountain, or they would follow some secret path, or go through some hidden entranceway, or even pass through a tunnel. Do you remember?"

I nodded. It always sounded like going from one heaven to another was hardly much different than going from one country to another.

"Well, that is not really the way it is done. The change was presented in writing this way for the students of your world, so they could better understand that a change was taking place. Going from one state of awareness to another is nothing like going over a bridge. In fact, going from one plane to another is easier than physically moving from one place to another.

"Again, here is the lesson on vibration. Just as we left the Earth world together and were able to come to the astral, so shall we be able to enter into the third and then the fourth and so on, using only our ability to control the rate of our vibration.

"Even when you desire to return, not only to the astral, but to the capital city that we just left, manifesting in the presence of the astral Governor, you only need to use that particular exercise to do so."

I thought for a moment and recalled that special exercise. I remembered that when one wanted to draw a blessing from Him, all they had to do was use the exercise of the sound technique.

This was accomplished by sitting in a position that was comfortable. Taking several deep breaths and holding each for a few seconds and then exhaling each completely. Next, the attention would need to be placed at the center of the third eye with the practitioner chanting the Holy Name of Niranjan, breaking it down into three syllables. It would be pronounced Ni-run-jun. It would be performed in a series of three, three times, resting for a few minutes between each series to fully feel the effect of the consciousness change.

I knew when the exercise was activated, there would always be a master or a teacher available to escort the student. It didn't matter that they were not members of any special organization or even any particular religion. Such things are not even considered in the higher realms. All that matters is that the seeker is dedicated and that he cares enough about searching for truth. That he is willing, for the time being anyway, to put aside the insatiable desire to gain wealth; or to satisfy the lust that floods the brain, to seek something that is more permanent than this world.

One of the first teachings is that the seeker always has spiritual assistance at his disposal, and this is especially true for the inexperienced traveler.

After the student can fully comprehend the lesson that we are all a part of God and that God is unlimited, then he will find himself well on his way to mastership, and will be allowed to travel freely out of the lower worlds. He will also discover that he will be permitted to travel alone.

In my journey, although I was to enter into the highest of vibrations, there was no way I would be permitted to really move around on my own.

My guide and I were fully aware of that fact, but he was always kind enough to pretend that the person who was temporarily in his charge, was in control of the decisions being made.

"The third plane is not any more difficult to reach from the physical, than it is from the astral," he continued. "If we were truly moving from one place to another, we would have to go from point A to point B and then to point C. We would have to traverse all of the land masses that are in between.

"To give an example, in the country you come from, let's say you are in Florida and wish to travel to New York. It wouldn't matter if you drove, took a bus, a train, or even an airplane, you still would need to cross all of the states in between. That is the way of the physical world.

"So now you can start to understand what it means when you hear a teacher speak of something as being Beyond Time and Space. It's not really as complicated as it sounds. In fact, it's a very useful tool. While the beginning student cannot understand how anything could be beyond time or space, the more advanced student will often wonder how he was able to survive without it.

"Being beyond time and space means you can travel from point A to point C, or D, or even to Z, without having to first go to those destinations in between. Thus, we find we can travel into even the highest of heavens without having to go through all of the other vibratory planes first.

"You are being led through them one at a time, just as if we were traveling within the rules of time and space, but that is only because you are being carefully prepared, which is the prescribed way of doing things. Once you have confronted and gained some control over each of these planes, there will no longer be a need for you to travel to each in order to carry out your work.

"Now, with this added to your information, let's continue on to the next plane."

With those words, I felt a strange sensation sweep over me. The scene around me changed and a whole new kind of joy swept through me.

The wonderful vibrations that engulfed me when I left the physical to enter the astral, were not even half as great as what I was feeling now.

Each time a plane is left and you enter into the next higher one, it will always seem as though you are stepping from darkness into light. Each plane appears to be bigger and better than the one left behind.

As an individual enters a different plane, it always seems this must be the ultimate heaven, because nothing could ever be better than this. And the individual will think this each time.

While the astral is a beautiful place and filled with love and contentment, the third plane is filled with an emotional melody more felt with the soul than heard with any ears.

Instantly, before me was a land that was able to reach out and touch my soul. The only physical sense that could begin to understand what is felt here would be that which originates in the Solar Plexus. It is very much like listening to some of the most harmonious music in the world, while watching the sunset, being encircled by a host of billowing clouds, reflecting those last rays of brilliant color, just before it disappears behind a mountain or into the sea.

71

The land was soft and one would seem to bounce as they walked along, if, indeed, they did desire to walk, for all one had to do was desire to move and they would find themselves moving swiftly in the direction of their choice.

Just as the previous two planes, this one was filled with majestic mountain ranges, spacious plains, beautiful gardens, cascading waterfalls, and conceivably any other setting one could desire to place themselves in.

"This plane is not as highly populated as the plane below nor does it have as many residents as the fourth plane," my guide told me. "That is because this plane is especially dedicated to the control of lessons and the handling of Cause and Effect.

"The individuals that live here are those who chose to serve as karma workers. You see, once your education has been completed, you are allowed to choose how you will serve God.

"Of course, you are being educated to fulfill a purpose in the grand scheme of things. You weren't sent into the physical world just for something to do, or just so you could pass time. You were sent to learn what you need to know, so that you can fulfill the purpose for which you were ultimately created. Just as the student needs to obtain an education so he can be of service to his fellow beings in the physical world, so, too, he should be of service in the cosmic worlds.

"This is the purpose for all souls, to endeavor to seek greater and greater depths of spiritual understanding. Once the soul has returned to the twelfth plane, the place from which he originated, he is then considered to be worthy of the title of Coworker with God, and can then choose what position he might desire to serve in.

"That is not to say he must serve in that capacity for all time though. He is free to pick and choose what he desires, for we must remember that at this time, the soul has been graduated to the same stature as a God!

"Another interesting aspect is, when that particular atom was formed into a soul, it was formed with certain abilities that would make it different from all other atomic souls. This gave it a special aptitude towards doing a very significant position – a special job – that perhaps he could do better than most. But that in no way was ever intended to limit him to performing just that position.

"There are Coworkers still living on your physical Earth that have been chosen to perform certain duties when the time is right. There is something very special that has been picked for them, but this is because it is so agreeable with who and what they are. It is something that spirit knows will greatly please them, but that doesn't mean they have to do that thing.

"All of the worlds and all of the planes are filled with those who have completed their education and are now serving in some position to help assist spirit.

"That means not having just completed their education in the lower worlds, but also having journeyed in the higher worlds and made their way back to where they were originally formed: the twelfth plane."

As he spoke I could hear and understand what he was saying to me, but at the same time, I was able to hear many other lessons of this third plane coming through to me. It was like I had a dual consciousness or maybe even a tri, a quad, or even a quin-consciousness. There were many things registering on my inner awareness, and I could make out at least four different pieces of information being fed to me at the same time.

There was no difficulty in my receiving these multi-lanes of information flow, nor was there even the slightest hint of any confusion. I was in complete control of the situation and felt I could even digest greater amounts of knowledge.

I felt very much like an exalted sponge. I was exalted because I could now understand why some mystics had made the strange remark, "I have been to God, and now I am God!" If being God meant being more than a human, then I certainly would have met that requirement. For one thing was definitely sure, I now was no longer like any human I had ever known. And I was a sponge, because I could easily absorb knowledge like it was nothing more than little puddles of water formed on a counter top.

As he was speaking about the Coworkers with God, I was way ahead of him on another channel, where I was being shown what some of these duties of a Coworker might encompass. I could see how millions of individuals on Earth served in this capacity every night while they slept. The largest majority of them didn't even have the slightest idea they had been away from their body nor that they were assisting spirit.

I was shown that anyone could become a Coworker simply by giving their permission to spirit to use their abilities while they sleep.

This was done by using the exercise of volunteer dream travel.   .

Some of the things that a person might experience during this time, would be finding themselves floating over a beautiful landscape. They may be giving love and sympathy to some poor downtrodden soul. They could feel a tremendous surge of benevolent energy flowing through them as they hover over some sick person or critical event. They could even find themselves giving verbal advice to someone that could gain from the knowledge that the Coworker had.

These situations are common, but so are a hundred other circumstances one may find themselves engaged in. The important thing is that the Coworker always feels wonderful and can feel the Joy of Spirit flowing through their veins. This has to be so. It would be of little use to one in need, if the Coworker that has come to assist them was feeling miserable himself.

Meanwhile, on another of the inner channels, I was aware of the rules and laws of the third plane, and how they were to be applied to those students of the physical world.

On this channel, I was being visually shown how the laws of Cause and Effect are so completely involved in every little detail of our lives. I was shown there is nothing that doesn't respond to this law. I could see how there was an effect in everything from the multimillionaire who sought to crush his competition, to the bum in the street expecting the world to give him a living. I saw how it affected the dictator that desired to rule the world, down to the common laborer working for a minimum wage. But mostly, I saw how it affected each and everyone of us in our actions, whether we passed out love or hate, or whether we chose to give or take.

Even something as simple as dropping a gum wrapper on the ground, or picking it up, will trigger some sort of response on the inner world of our being and we will be met by a like response somewhere in the near future.

Still, on another channel, I was being shown the affinity of all living things. In this lesson, I was shown that all planes are made of vibrations, and all living things were made of the very same atoms.

It was very clear that in the grander scope of things, we should offer our love and goodwill to all forms of life. It also showed me that even in times where we must kill the lower life forms, whether it be for food, or due to their invading our private space, that in essence, we haven't really killed them at all, for Life can never be destroyed. What we have done is simply move their existence elsewhere.

It is very much like some sort of fabric laid out on the floor. Where we see a lump (a life), we push down and that lump simply pops up in another spot.

When such a case arises, we should offer our love to the situation. Even the American Indians were aware of this law. When they sought to hunt and kill an animal for food, they always offered their love to the kill, and asked spirit to forgive them for their need. In today's society, though, such a thing is hardly considered, for one can easily imagine there will be scant love or compassion found in a slaughter house. The idea even crossed my mind that perhaps that was why there was such a rampage of cancer in today's society. I could also see that since we cannot give the proper blessing to the kill, the attitude of saying grace was adapted.

On the other hand, when we have to exterminate some life forms because they have invaded our lives and are making things tough or unsanitary for us, we should never engage the attack as if we were in a war.

If one desires to get rid of a pest permanently, he must first offer his love (or at least his sympathy) to the invaders. After the spraying has taken place, he should once again offer his regrets to the spirit of that life form.

While this may seem strange, I could see that all lower natures of life forms are guided by what is called a vortex. While it may be hard for us to understand, this vortex is their accumulated consciousness. One only needs to study the actions of an invading army of ants to see there is most assuredly some higher consciousness guiding them, so that even the simple actions of just one ant will be in complete compliance with the actions of the whole.

We should understand the ants didn't invade because they decided on it. It was the vortex that brought them in. Now, we must see to it that the vortex doesn't return. That is done by offering the proper respect and love to spirit – which controls the vortex.

There is a well known story about a monastery that was overrun with ants many years ago. The monks that occupied that monastery belonged to a sect that cherished all forms of life, and it was against their doctrine to take any life.

But once the ants had infiltrated all of their flour and other foodstuffs, and had invaded the beds and blankets, they knew some drastic measures would need to be taken.

In the Abbot's prayer, he asked that they remove themselves from this place. He explained this was a condition where the nature of one species had violated the natural rights of another. He concluded the prayer with an explanation that they didn't desire to destroy them, so, instead, were asking them to leave the monastery and its grounds and to bother them no further.

It is now a point recorded in their records that upon their return that evening, not even one ant could be found.

But even as I could see all of this, still, there was other knowledge pouring in on my consciousness.

On yet another channel, I was fed facts about how all of us on Earth should watch our attitude regarding all things. "Know that you do not see things as they are. Know that things are as you see them!" came the command.

Instantly, what that meant was quite clear.

Without our even being aware of it, we weren't just poor, pathetic mortals acting as helpless pawns, left to the whimsical actions of an uncaring God. Instead, we should know we are Little Gods who have complete control of our events.

It was our attitude that made our lives miserable or kept us in a joyful mood. This could be seen in all things. It made no difference if it was about where we lived, what occupation we might have, how we regarded our neighbors, or even down to the different foods we eat.

"One man's hell is another man's heaven" is a very common phrase – and a very true one.

One individual may think he is truly in heaven when he holds a position where he will be exposed to a great deal of quiet and solitude, but to another man that would be a living hell. He takes great joy in noise, activity and being surrounded by people. One may desire to live in a tropical climate all year around, but another might complain of the constant heat and desire to enjoy the full season changes. One may love a certain kind of strong food and will desire to eat it everyday, while another could become nauseous at the very smell of it.

The list goes on and on. We should understand there aren't necessarily any really bad things or situations in this world, it is only a matter of how we regard them in our attitude.

We should also be very careful how we look at ourselves. If one believes he is always sick, then he will feel the pain and agony of that sickness everyday. If we always act happy and always have a smile for everyone, then not only will we be that happy person, but through the actions of the karma energy units that surround us, good and happy things will return to us all day long.

This also presents the problem of pretending. If we are going to pretend about anything, we should be aware we are activating this assumption into our field of energy and the karma units will act upon it.

A person who always wants attention and sympathy might pretend he is sick, but as time goes by, he will soon discover he is no longer pretending. The chronic complainer will find he does have the severe ailment he sought pity for.

On the other hand, one who pretends all is right with the world, refrains from undue strenuous attitude, will be healthy and taken care of. This, of course, as long as he makes the necessary effort that goes hand in hand with that attitude. We must never forget this is a school and that we do have lessons to learn.

Then, suddenly, above all the knowledge I had been absorbing, I could again make out the voice of my guide.

"It's quite exhilarating, isn't it?"

My attention quickly snapped back to his direction.

"What you have been experiencing is an expansion into the higher dimensions of your mind. I told you that you were a Little God, and that you would soon come to understand what that meant. With your ability to master the third plane, you have been filled with the priority lessons of this plane.

"This plane is predominantly occupied with some very important things. This is the plane of Cause and Effect. In addition to that, it offers information on your affinity with all living things as well as your attitude. For both of these things will start a reaction in your personal Cause and Effect. It is also highly interested in the workings of the Coworkers with God, for they are like the star pupils of this class. The Coworkers will often discover that although they must live in the physical world until their present assignment is fulfilled, they will be able to see they are not of that world.

"This place is the Distribution Center for the energy needed to carry out the karma actions of every individual, no matter who they are or where they are. So, those Coworkers who may be interested in the position of being a Karma Worker, will find that they return to this plane every night when they sleep. With you having this knowledge, it's very easy for you to see that all Coworkers or Dream Travelers are just like pet students. Not only do they find they can have many miracles brought into their lives, but by offering their assistance to spirit and to the higher worlds, they have so greatly affected their own karma units of energy that they will discover they are no longer subdued by the physical's harsh conditions. They are free to enjoy all of the bliss of God's Worlds."

He had no sooner finished speaking than I found we were once again in flight, zooming across a flowery plane, passing some of the most incredible waterfalls one could ever imagine. Over and over again, I could distinguish that there were areas of population. Some of the areas were like a small village; some were like a city; and some were fantastic mega-metropolitan cities that had thousands upon thousands of structures that stretched into the heavens. But one thing was very clear about all of these areas. Regardless of their size, all were extremely futuristic.

Soon we came to the end of this particular land mass and I found we were soaring over a blue and golden ocean. Then, within what could have been seconds, another land mass was seen below us.

This was similar to the one we just left, but through my inner absorption I realized somehow it was vastly different.

Then there was the ocean again, then another land mass, then another ocean, then another land mass, and so on, and so on. There seemed to be no end to the repetition, but with each land mass, I could realize it was different than all of the others in some mysterious way.

"Each of these masses are approximately the size of a continent back on your Earth," my guide offered. "And each is highly skilled in one particular function, that may not be apparent in one of the others. If we were to travel to all of these continents, we would have to pass over thousands of them. And remember, that each is specialized in one way or another. So even if a Coworker may think they are not interested in being a Karma Worker, there is still a great deal here that would interest them.

"Now, let's continue on to the fourth plane."

GRADUATION OF THE COSMIC STUDENT

Once we pass beyond the laws of the physical and astral worlds, we find we are faced with the same problems as those mystics who have traversed the planes over the centuries.

Whenever they would attempt to relate what they experienced, they found words would simply not do the job.

Even among themselves, they had to develop a special hand language so they could understand what another was referring to in those planes beyond the astral.

This is even more so, when that explanation is being given to one who cannot relate to those vibrations.

In the ancient mystery schools (one of which was the school of Pythagoras), they attempted to overcome this problem by creating a new form of language where an infinite subject could be at least slightly grasped by a finite mind.

This was done by taking simple concepts and giving them a numerical value. An example of this would be the word "ecstasy". First, the school would establish in the student's mind the fact that a true state of ecstasy could not be reached while still in the physical world. It would only be when the student was able to travel into the astral that he could experience this ecstasy.

Second, to keep the concept simple, the word "ecstasy" would be given a numerical value of one hundred.

Then, they compared our earthly existence with a value of from five to forty. Five would be the rating vibration of a miserable sort of person; one who was selfish, nasty and with virtually no redeeming factors. Twenty to twenty five would be the rating of the average individual. This would be the person basically kind, who had a loving nature (most of the time), and tried to always keep a sense of humor. Forty would be the highest vibration of earthly happiness, and would usually be reached only through artificial means (such as under medication).

Now, under this concept, the teacher was able to show that even at the happiest they could have ever been while in this world, it was not even half the joy one would feel when entering the astral.

Then, they tried to show that this high degree of joy would be magnified every time one passed from one plane to another after having passed through the third plane. (In this concept the third plane was just an extension of the second.)

By this standard, the happiness that one would experience at the fourth plane would be considered Sublime Ecstasy. And it was quite easy to imagine the impression that this evaluation had on these students. If drunken bliss could rate no higher than a forty, what in the world would it be like to all of a sudden be at one, two or even three hundred?

However, this caused another perplexing problem once they began to teach of the higher worlds beyond the fourth.

To relate in words was ineffective, because words were vague. To continue to give a numerical evaluation would be inadequate, because numbers are precise.

Two things that cannot be applied to the spiritual worlds would be anything that was precise. Spirit is real, but at the same time it is elastic, having to bend to fit the different laws of each plane. Also, once the finite mind has been impressed with a piece of information, to continue along with this line of explanation is futile. We find that not only words, but now numbers mean very little.

The reason for this misconception in some of the lesser institutes was due to the fact that they were overlooking the Law of Transition.

Pythagoras was one of those who fully understood that all of this world, all of its students, and all of our lessons are based on vibration. Thus, where there is vibration, there has to be transition. That means that everything that vibrates must change. It must progress. And something does not progress just for the simple reason that it increases in size.

Ecstasy is a state of mind and being such, it must change. It must progress into another state that is yet higher.

An example would be that instead of ecstasy reaching a vibratory rate of a thousand, it would change into what is called Divine Love.

Then, as the vibration increased in this Divine Love, it would change again into what is called Omnipresence, and that, in turn, would progress and transform into Omnipotence.

Another problem in discussing any planes that go beyond the physical is that every plane has its own distinct laws.

In the physical we are limited by our very precise binding and unforgiving rules which are always far more demanding than any of the other vibrations.

For an example, say we were standing on a ledge of the fiftieth floor of a skyscraper. If we were to lean forward until our center of gravity moved beyond the safe footing of that ledge, we would undoubtedly fall to our death. It is highly unlikely that the laws of the physical are going to change as we plunge downward.

However, when we are engaging the astral body, we find that it is immune to all of the laws we have always been subjected to in this life.

The astral body, which vibrates only at the pitch of the astral plane, obeys the laws of its own vibration and not the physical, and does not have to answer to gravity.

When we leave our regular body safe behind at home and are traveling about in the astral body (or any other of our higher bodies), we find it doesn't matter if we travel to the Antarctic – or to an active volcano – we do not feel the cold nor the heat. We feel only the established comfort range as prescribed by that astral vibration.

We can travel through rain and not get wet – or even explore the depths of the deepest oceans without affecting these bodies, or without it even affecting our breathing.

The higher vibrating bodies cannot be cut, burned, drowned, or blown apart by some great explosion. There is virtually no effect at all that the physical can force upon another vibration.

Here, we see another difficulty in explaining the laws of the other vibration levels. All of a sudden, we are faced with circumstances and effects upon the soul that can only be felt and not described with words.

Often, much of the description will be withheld by the one making the journey, in his attempt to avoid making the explanation sound too fanciful, when speaking of soul's movements, abilities and encounters.

A true teacher can only suggest you listen with your heart and not with your intellect as you set out to explore these other lands; lands that answer to an entirely different set of laws.

Another point that needs to be made is that this account is not being related only so the curious can gain some insight into the higher worlds, but so the reader might be able to recall from deep within their subconscious memory bank, some place or some emotion being described. This is also the meaning of listening with the heart. For it will be only by your feeling, that the subconscious can open up and bring these memories forth to you.

At first, the memories will seem vague and you won't be sure if they are true facts or some flight of the imagination. But, as time progresses, you will find these memories are like drops of water leaking from the wall of a dam. They will come slowly at first, but as the dam (the subconscious) weakens under the continued pressure of memory vibration, the drops will come faster and faster, until, all at once, the full flow will finally register with the physical consciousness.

With this in mind, we will now continue our journey back to our true home.

Upon entering into the fourth plane, we are able to absorb knowledge about particular things without having to be taught about them. Even though the knowledge may be new to us, it is more like we remember it, drawing it from some ancient and forgotten section of our intellect.

One such piece of knowledge would be that we are now aware the fourth plane is divided into two major sections.

The lower etheric is like a settling station. By this, I mean many of our eternal questions can finally be answered, simply by using our expanded awareness.

Many have wondered if there is an animal heaven. When one is able to attune to this vibration, they will find not only is there a heaven, but that this heaven is engaged in even more intricate details and responsibilities – which can answer other more complex questions.

When mystics spoke of lions and lambs that can live together, this was the place they envisioned.

Although it is an endless array of beauty, it still is not as we of Earth may interpret it. This is not really some great zoo where all animals simply go to spend eternity. Nor is it a place where their previous Earth masters come to frolic and play with their beloved pets for all time.

While that may sound a little sad, the truth is far better.

Remember the first rule of the universe. Everything vibrates. That, of course, goes for all pets we have ever had. And when we look at the second rule of the universe – that everything must progress – we quickly see that the animal kingdom is no more limited in its progress than the human is. What is true for one, must be true for all.

Does that mean that they will one day become human? Does it mean that we used to be animals of a lower nature?

Many of the great minds of the physical world claim they remember being something other than human. Plato was one of hundreds who taught progress meant "Evolution of a Species Into A Higher Species". He claimed he could remember being a turtle in very ancient times.

But all of this does not really concern us. What is important to the human race is what it is becoming, rather than from where it might have evolved.

One most outstanding characteristic of this lower etheric plane is that soul is being prepared for something it still cannot comprehend.

By the time one has reached this level, they will have experienced the vast absorption of knowledge, but it may be here that soul realizes for the first time that there is not - nor has there ever been – any obstruction due to language barriers. In fact, it may very well seem to the explorer that they have been speaking and are comprehending in their own particular language, but it will be only when he stops to take a more careful look, that he will discover his comprehension is beyond words.

In the fourth plane, he finally comes to realize that what we call communication, has become very refined. It is like we have driven onto the superhighway of information.

Here, a thousand words can be transformed into a solitary thought form and sent to another, who receives it and understands everything completely.

Once the seeker becomes accustomed to receiving and sending thought forms, he will even find having to speak or write (upon returning to the physical), is very troublesome.

It is much easier to send an image than to use those thousand words or vocally to paint a picture on paper. Also, in the physical, when something is spoken, or even written, it still can be misunderstood. This is never the case with an instantaneous thought form. Both the sender and the receiver are always in perfect rapport.

Also, one can easily see how barbaric our learning methods in the physical are, once they can be looked at through the eyes of a resident of the fourth plane.

From the etheric level, we can see there never was anything bad happening to us in the physical. There never were any punishments dealt out from some great being who was angry with us. Instead, we have been exposed only to tests or altered corrections.

By altered corrections, what is meant is we must receive the corresponding lesson to help us better understand the test we may have failed.

When we speak of karma, we think it means rewards or punishments, but that is just not the true meaning. By incurring negative karma, the inner energy field of our aura (where the Karma Energy Units are spinning), will alter a correction, giving us a lesson, so we can better understand the test. It may very well seem like a punishment to the student who would rather not bother with the test any longer, but that isn't the case.

Punishment would never serve any purpose. The whole intent is for the soul to progress. But, regardless of what some minds may think, when anything or anyone is punished, it is only an act of sadism carried out to please the mind of the one dealing it.

Punishment should only be considered as a preventive measure (such as capital punishment – to frighten would be murderers) and never as a correcting measure.

On the same hand, if that karma is rich in positive reaction, then the individual must receive a corrective measure from the cosmic. Meaning the cosmic, itself, must be properly adjusted, so the individual can receive his passing grade.

Through the proper understanding of karma, we can see we all have Cosmic Bank Accounts. Everything we do will either make a deposit into this account, or it will cause us to make a withdrawal.

With a deposit, it looks like we are being rewarded, with us finding many great things coming to us. But when a withdrawal is made, we find we have bought a lesson.

Just as in a college, a good education can be very expensive. So, the best thing for us is to be a good, attentive student, learn our lessons quickly and get ourselves into the position we are preparing ourselves for, as quickly as possible.

Another aspect of the fourth plane is that we can now also conceive complex matters very simply.

There have been many science fiction stories about some spacecraft or other physical body that is bigger on the inside than on the outside. Of course, we simply pass these stories off as fiction, knowing such a thing is not possible according to our physical laws. But once we begin our study of the spiritual planes, we find we are confronted with this exact same condition.

On one hand we have learned as we vibrate higher, we are able to see each plane is much larger than the previous. But, on the other hand, we have been taught only the low vibrations reach outward, going deeper into the mundane. That would mean to progress to the higher vibrations, we would have to go inside. Inside where it is much larger than the outside!

So here, we are faced with the same situation as presented in these science fiction stories.

Over and over again the masters taught their students the door only opens inward.

The only way to get out is to go in.

If we concentrate on the third eye and push, we only succeed in getting a headache after a while. We could never escape the physical body with such actions. When we push, we are moving away from our higher body sheaths and forcing ourselves into a physical grounding.

Since "for every action, there must be a reaction", we find by pushing, we have only activated physical organs and tissues that react in whatever way they were designed. But as far as anything spiritual, forget it.

What we are doing when we go inward is making a connection with our inner sheaths. We must remember the entire underlying theme of this study – that everything vibrates. We can only reach the proper vibration of a higher plane by contacting our various inner bodies which are properly attuned to these planes.

We cannot reach any particular vibration unless we can adjust soul to vibrate at that same rate. And since we are not advanced enough to make our own adjustment at this time (while we are in the lower worlds), we need to use these already adjusted inner bodies. Once one of these bodies is engaged as a vehicle, we instantly find ourselves in a larger and grander plane.

When Jesus and others taught "the Kingdom of God lies within", they were conveying two important points. First, they were teaching we were more than the body seen in a reflection, and more than others could see when they looked at us. That we were (and are) a soul. Second, they were trying to show how easily we could go wherever we wanted (even to heaven) by attuning to these inner sheaths.

One other important lesson of this plane is that we must never inflict our opinions about anything on others.

That is probably the single largest violation committed in our world.

There are many who attempt to recruit or convert people to their way of thinking. Looking at this closely, we see there is no difference between this and the mind washing techniques used by less honorable cultures that seek to destroy religion.

There are many who teach that all non-Christians are doomed to hell.

That singular statement should not frighten you, but leave you appalled. Instantly you should wonder about all non-Christians in the world. What if someone just happens to be born in a religion that does not happen to be Christian? Remember, Christianity is not even the largest following in the world. Does that mean that no matter how good they may be, no matter how much good they have done, no matter how devote and dedicated they are – they must burn in some eternal hell?

And what about all people born before the formation of Christianity? Does that mean everyone born before 60A.D. when the religion was prepared in Constantinople, are all in hell?

No, such a thing is totally outrageous. This and many other things people have been forced to believe (out of fear), are not only in error, but have caused a great deal of karma alterations to those who have forced their opinion on others.

Many self-appointed saviors cannot understand what has gone wrong when they are not held in the exalted position they expect.

No, we should never force our opinions on another, regardless if that opinion is on religion or anything else. We must never think our way is the one and only true way. By the time the spiritual student can roam freely in these etheric planes, he should be able to quickly see there isn't just one true path to God. From this point in time and space, he can see that every individual is his own true path.

When the student passes from the lower etheric to the higher, if he can fully grasp this concept already, he will find he is ready for graduation into the true God worlds. If he is advanced enough to understand what has been said, he will not need to spend a great deal of time in the higher etheric - unless he so desires.

Immediately upon entering the higher etheric, what one finds will depend largely on what he expects to find.

This is the highest plane or heaven described by many of Earth's religions.

Yes, there is a Christian Heaven here. And there is also a heaven for any other religion you have heard of – and perhaps even thousands of heavens you have never heard of.

But the most interesting thing is that since each individual will be finding exactly what he expected to find, he will say, "Look, we were right. We are the true religion, for there are none here in heaven except us!"

Even though these heavens can be exceedingly large in size – and not limited by any apparent walls, such as we picture of heaven's gate – only the truly enlightened will be aware that others, not of their faith, are also on this plane.

For the student that learned his lessons well, or for those who have been informed ahead of time (such as yourself), they will be given the Second Grand Test before they are permitted to enter into the true God worlds. They should pass it with no difficulty – as long as they have faith in the ancient teachings.

The First Grand Test is what we call physical death. We have been plagued and threatened with it ever since we entered into the physical worlds, and even though we have experienced it a multitude of times, we always seem to forget about it and find we are threatened by it again.

This first test is given to us, giving us a passing grade, simply because we could spend all of eternity hung up on this test without some help. We do not need to show our faith by agreeing to die. In fact, no matter how hard we try, we can only postpone it, but can never cancel it. That would be self defeating. Our whole purpose is to progress, and further progress cannot come while we still reside in the very low and base physical vibration.

Once we can learn the basics of our education – kindness, love, compassion – we are moved quickly through the next two planes, bringing us to the etheric (and heaven) where we just need to learn some very obvious facts. While we are at this Station, we learn that 1. God is Love. 2. That we are the Sons and Daughters of God. 3. That all living beings were created from the same atoms. 4. That we must attempt to progress, even if we believe we have reached the highest heaven conceivable, and 5. That nothing will ever be hidden from us as long as we make an effort to continue to progress.

That will be the entire curriculum as we play, love and frolic in this totally indescribable world of beauty.

Sometimes the information becomes so involved it leaves us on Earth at a loss to understand it. Taking the bliss of this world and attempting to put it into simple words is very inappropriate. Simply know any happiness or beauty you may have known on Earth is magnified a thousand-fold here. After all, this is the heaven we fought and suffered for so desperately while on Earth. So, it is only appropriate it be all we ever imagined – and even more than we imagined. However, all of this beauty, all of this harmonious happiness does add to the difficulty of taking the second grand test.

The first test we passed automatically because the cosmic knew we would not enter that great unknown on our own. With this being the case, even though we might be facing great trials and tribulations in this life, how much more difficult might it be for us to agree to leave this heaven, to enter into another state of awareness.

While we are on Earth, we may desire to reach into the highest of heavens (as long as we are taken by the hand and led there). Many ancient students often wondered why everyone wasn't making a mad dash to get to the pure God worlds, but once they could conceive this heaven, they understood.

Although the spiritual student is taught he should always progress, it is still very difficult for him to give up complete and total happiness – just to enter into another unknown factor.

The first obstacle here on the fourth plane is the testing force that will make every attempt to convince you there is nothing beyond this wonderful place, and that you should be content to end your journey. This force is known as the second face of God.

The astral governor was the first face of God, and now the student has evolved sufficiently to know this is the heaven they had been promised when in the physical.

Armed with this understanding, they now (for the most part) again set out to stand before God.

He who is the governor of the etheric is known by many different names, depending on the religion one was reared in, but one thing that needs to be made very clear is that this governor most definitely is the Creator!

Taking a moment to think clearly, we can see there has to be a creative force that forms and maintains the entire schooling system, which would include this and all planes below.

Since this Governor carries out that action, He is known as The Creator. Those that believe the Creator of the physical world is God, then He would most definitely be God to them.

But, at this point, we need to step back for a moment and look carefully at the laws we understand in regards to the functioning of these lower worlds.

First of all, we know we must have a positive and a negative pole to create a spark. If something were all positive, we would lack the necessary ingredient to establish the energy needed to create.

So, we can now see that the force known as the Creator has to be both positive and negative.

That which comes from God (and I mean that in the very highest sense of the Name) is only pure spirit. There is no negative charge.

Pure spirit, operating under the laws of the higher or God worlds, does not need a counterpoint (a negative pole) to maintain those planes from the fifth up to the twelfth. This is what separates them and makes them so different from our school. This shows us that God is, therefore, composed entirely only of pure nature and in no way is found to be a dual nature.

As this spirit expanded outwards, creating the different planes as it went, the laws of spirit would change at each of these planes, each time becoming a little less perfect.

By the time spirit had created eight planes outward (or downward), the laws had changed so drastically that spirit needed to divide to carry out its work.

When this happened, another whole heavenly division was created. This would be known as the lower worlds and it would be the duty of this sector to serve as the training ground for soul's development.

In the lower planes, just as in the higher ones, there had to be a controlling factor (a higher consciousness), that would ensure the stability of those planes, protecting them from destruction.

Each of these controlling factors could be interpreted as human so we could better establish our relationship with them and we would eventually come to look upon them as governors.

The controlling factor established to create the school of the lower worlds had to have the ability to handle the new energy flow developed from this division of spirit. This governor was established on the fourth plane but would be responsible for the creation of the entire lower structure.

Under this governing factor, there would be other or lesser sub governors who, in turn, would be responsible for their particular plane. The structure is very much like a public school where the fourth plane governor could be considered the principal and the other governors similar to the teachers.

This fourth plane governor force would be different from all other governing factors though – both above and below due to the fact It had the ability to create matter, using both positive and negative energy.

An ancient portrait of God, located in one of the oldest of mystery schools, showed a Great Being, legs spread apart standing on two different planets, while a great light beamed down into the top of his head (significant of pure spiritual energy). From each of His palms, there was a radiant beam with which He was forming other worlds. The right hand depicted the energy from the positive pole, and the left was the energy from the negative.

Since that which we understand requires negative energy to create, then we would have to say all of the physical worlds, the

93

astral, causal and etheric could not have been created by the ultimate God or that which we consider the Eternal Father. But until the resident students of the fourth plane are able to conceive this fact, they will be subject to whatever illusions are cast before them.

THE WALL OF DARKNESS

Another important thing at this stage is that the student explorer has far greater senses and capabilities then could ever be understood by one who was still anchored to a physical body. On the fourth plane the range of contact is so spectacular that (to his knowledge) there is nowhere that he cannot see, visit or communicate with.

The senses here are so far advanced from our physical ones, that it would be like comparing the Sun to a match.

If these senses can be developed while we still reside on Earth, we will find we can communicate with anyone in the entire world. We can contact any planet in this almost infinite Universe. We can reach beyond the borders of death, seeing and speaking with those who have left Earth. And we can explore great worlds of wonder that neither religion nor science know anything about. All of this with the same ease as picking up a telephone to speak with someone.

When we can see something with the physical eyes, we have no doubt that thing is true, because we have complete faith in our eyes, our interpretation of what we see, and our intellect to evaluate this occurrence.

With such faith put into these faulty, lower senses, it is easy to imagine how much credence the seeker will allot to the higher ones. In the higher senses, if something is true, then he will be shown it is so. If something is false, then the seeker will also know it.

While we can see something with the physical eyes, and then find what we thought we saw was in error, the higher senses make no such mistakes. These senses are not subject to any

94

illusion or error. The knowledge that it conveys is always clear, concise and accurate. This Tool is given to the student not only as a reward, but something needed in his arsenal of incredible, growing abilities.

This could also be an obstacle if the seeker is told there are no more worlds beyond this one and this trustworthy ability demonstrates that it can neither confirm nor deny that statement. The student can only assume if these worlds did exist he would be able to see them.

When the student is ready, upon approaching the Second Face of God, the knowledge received and confirmed by the senses that this is the Creator will leave the student in total awe. Then, add to that, he is confronted with the information that this is the end of Creation, which the senses are unable to react upon – and we find the stage set for the graduation test.

Next, while the seeker is in this awesome presence, his vision is shown a great wall of darkness. It is so vast the senses can find no top to it, no bottom, no beginning to the right and no ending to the left. Add to this the fact that these all powerful senses cannot penetrate even one inch into this darkness.

The thought form that this is the end of creation can very easily be believed.

Now, an important point needs to be understood. These seekers for the most part (except for those fanatics with closed minds), are aware this is a test.

Spirit makes this knowledge available to all or else none would pass into the higher worlds.

The whole objective of this test is so you can see the strength of your own faith.

How strong is your faith in God? Can you trust completely in God, when all other things seem to say something contradictory to what you have been taught – even when this Governor seems to say something different?

Actually, the magnitude of the test is due to having an unsure mind. Those who have been prepared beforehand will eagerly approach the darkness with the ease of someone just entering into another room, which is exactly what they are doing.

The seeker is not even required to enter the darkness alone. He will be accompanied by his teacher or a master. How much easier could it be?

The real test is not so much confronting the unknown, as it is in testing the initiative of the student. Faith is important, but the student must want, must long for, must hunger to reach the Godly state.

Whenever we stand on one side of an unknown thing, we always demonstrate fear. It's the fear of change, the fear of destruction, and even the fear of not being able to return, if one should change his mind.

However, every soul upon passing over, will glance back on the experience with gleeful amusement at the true simplicity of the test. Once across, the soul may even feel it was a very childish experience. It was nothing more than telling a child to go into the next room and turn the light on.

The eternal quote is, "Death, where is thy sting?", for in place of the darkness and destruction they may have expected, they find only light, love and joy. The same is the case here.

Much of what we want to understand in the Bible can now be seen and understood, once we enter the darkness.

The first thing the seeker will see is the Light of the Master, which gives sufficient illumination to remove the darkness of the land and the mind. Even as great as one may have thought he was previously, he now finds the true meaning of divine love.

Knowledge and love pour forth from this light – this incredible beautiful, radiant and divine light. It will only take the seeker a moment to realize who and what this divine light is.

The One that comes to greet you and your escort, displaying this unbelievable Light of the Master, will be He to whom you are dedicated.

To the Christian, it will be the Jesus force. To other faiths, It will be He who has laid down their scripture. To still others, It will be a Divine Consciousness. But It will be the One you have placed all earthly love and trust in.

This place is not actually the fifth plane, but sort of a dividing line that exists between the two planes.

As the three of you make your way across this strange land, you will come upon a very dark flowing river. It will then be made clear to your consciousness that this is the River Styx written about in many religions.

It is not the river one will cross when they are condemned to hell, as preached by some individuals, but the river that gives liberation. Once you have traveled along this river for a short distance, you will find it flows out of this dim world, much like flowing from out of a tunnel, into the true God worlds.

Entering into the fifth plane brings emotions that really cannot be described. It is love and peace, but greater love and peace than one could ever understand while living in a world partly composed of negative energy.

Creation here is not maintained by a spark manifested from two conflicting energies. Instead of the abrupt and coarse energy fields we have come to associate with the maintenance of life, we find the force is more like a smooth flowing river, offering a scenic and harmonic form of ecstasy.

The fifth plane still offers us a landscape we can easily associate with. There are still gardens, mountain ranges, waterfalls, rivers and the such, but, yet, they are completely different from anything we have previously known. You become a part of the vibrant love of each and every landscape you see. To bathe in the glorious Lake brings great emotion to the heart region. Not only does the golden nectar of knowledge fill you as you enter into this water, but you enter into a sublime state the likes of which could never be known by one who is forced to live in a negative world.

The fellow beings you encounter here seem to be the most joyful of all souls previously known. They seem to represent the ultimate of what the human race could ever hope to achieve.

THE PARAMAHANSA

Although there are no longer any class distinctions, we do find that this fifth plane is composed of three main groups. The first and most numerous are those who are called the Initiates. These are the ones who had previously been referred to as a student or seeker. Once they have entered into the soul plane though, they have been promoted to a very distinguished group called Initiates.

Most of them will have spent some degree of time on the fourth plane before they entered this plane, however it is common knowledge that thousands have achieved this promotion while still residing on Earth. While it may seem unlikely we would be blessed in such a manner, it is actually the desire of spirit that this happen. It is hoped by spirit that we will achieve this prior to the date we are supposed to leave the Earth.

The second group of individuals that make their homes here are Adepts, Masters, Teachers and Cosmic Workers also known as Coworkers with God. They are here due to a decision on their part to do a particular job associated with this plane. The third group though, are the only real, permanent residents of this place. They are called the Paramahansa, which means Beautiful People.

They are the kindest, most gentle and loving individuals encountered up to this time on your spiritual journey. Being residents of a place that receives all of its light and life from pure spirit, they have absolutely nothing negative in their makeup. They represent only the highest attributes and it is taken for granted on their part, that all they encounter are the same as they.

One difficulty that does occur between the Initiates and the Paramahansa though, is that if one of the Initiates who does not make his home here (one who still lives on the Earth world), is to work in close proximity with a Paramahansa of the opposite gender, he will fall helplessly and hopelessly in love with that one.

This is another of the reasons why it is so difficult to penetrate into the true God worlds while we still reside in the lower worlds, even after one has achieved the distinction of becoming an Initiate.

It is not due to the cosmic's desire to keep the two species apart, for there are many instances where the two have chosen to become as one, but the separation is an attempt to protect the Earth bound soul.

It is feared (and rightly so) that once the soul returns to his schooling, he will abandon whatever lessons and whatever duties he was to achieve. He (or she) will simply pine away, entering into the depths of depression, possibly becoming an alcoholic, or something similar, and lose all interest in living in this world.

Although spirit is pleased to bring great joy and happiness into our lives, It must always be careful of exposing a soul to a condition beyond his capabilities to handle.

The duties of the Paramahansa are mainly to assist the governor of this plane, which includes helping souls entering into, or coming back from the physical world.

Every soul, before entering into the physical will be exposed to this great lake of ecstasy. It is called the Lake of the Paramahansa and the soul is taken there to give it the first taste of what can only be called sublime, divine ecstasy.

It will be this memory, hidden deep in the subconscious, that will supply the spark, giving soul the desire to begin and then continue Its search for divine love.

This is also why such divine love and innocence can be seen in the eyes of a child. The world seen through the eyes of a child is much different from that of an adult.

It will be many years before the full effect of the encounter with the Paramahansa will wear off. In fact, it may be only after one has become sexually active, that this pleasure will replace the previous one.

CHAPTER FOUR:

KNOWLEDGE GAINED FROM
THE SEVENTH PLANE

SOUL MATES AND THE HIGHER SELF

Once we become active on the soul plane, we next become familiar with what soul mates are – and the real meaning behind the story of Adam and Eve.

When the soul (the complete soul) is ready to leave the twelfth plane and enter into Its training to become Godlike, It is encased in divine matter with an atomic base and is sent forth to experience, learn and grow.

This unit is usually referred to as a monad by most spiritual teachers.

It will pass down through the planes, sometimes spending a little time on each one, in an attempt to acquaint the Little God with the realm he will one day have complete control over.

What concerns us at this point though, is that when it arrives at the fifth plane (from the twelfth), this monad, this higher self, will remain on this plane while the soul continues on, going deep into the very bowls of this apparently difficult and frightening school.

This will occur only after the soul has spent some time on the fifth plane though. There are still many preparations needed.

One of the first things soul will experience will be that it is divided into two very different personalities. Some ancient scriptures describe this as a splitting or a rendering apart of the divine soul, but that is not the case. It is really more like a flame giving life to another flame. The first flame becomes no way less than It was, It simply brings forth an equal.

The only real change is that where the divine soul was complete unto itself (having both positive and negative capabilities), now one personality will be masculine while the other becomes feminine. (And God took a rib from Adam and created a woman.)

As far as the divine soul was concerned, this was the beginning of creation. Up until this time, the soul existed in the greater planes, but did not have free will or desire. It would be only now the soul (souls) would come to know passion and emotions.

Great things are awakened within the core of these two new beings. As they are exposed to the sweet emotional nectar of the lake, they become more and more aware of the things that surround them and they develop a tremendous, insatiable desire to learn and experience. They even soon come to understand there is a vast difference between them – and both will agree they like that difference.

The snake is a universal symbol for the physical universe and the forbidden tree of knowledge is representative of the lessons (passions) learned there.

As the souls' desires grow, they both soon long to travel into the physical universe and experience the powerful emotions that rule everyone's life there.

When Adam and Eve (the two souls) were cast out of Eden (the soul plane) it was not to punish them, because they were supposed to desire to leave. It was to give them the education for which the school had been created.

This, also, did not mean that Adam and Eve could not return to Eden. Quite the opposite. They were cast out of Eden so they could develop and experience life. Then they could return to better understand and appreciate the surroundings they had been incapable of comprehending.

When it is felt the two souls have developed sufficiently, they journey forth enjoying each of the planes and spend a little time on each until it is time for them to slide into the physical together.

That does not mean we are necessarily supposed to find and marry our soul mate while on this Earth. In fact, it will probably be quite the opposite. They *could* meet and marry in the physical. They could come together in the astral at the conclusion of each individual life. And they could progress back to the fifth plane together but, for the most part, these two souls may never be in each other's company again until both have completed all of their training in the physical and are entering into the fifth for the final time.

This is why some of the master teachers have denied there is such a thing as soul mates. They, of course, know better, but they have denied it so the overly romantic will not waste their lives, looking for something and for someone not in their present game plan.

Whenever there is some great feat spirit desires to accomplish, then soul mates are called upon to unite. Although an individual soul might be able to accomplish some very great things by Itself, when two soul mates come together, their combined chemistry will always seem to create miracles.

The masters are not saying you should give up all hope of being with a true soul mate (for the love and burning romance created is totally unbelievable), but what they are saying is that if you desire to be with your soul mate, then you must be prepared to accomplish some fantastic things.

Even though the two may never come together in this life, both will be contributing to the higher self. As already understood, all of the good that both may do will be recorded and kept in the higher self, but anything thought of as bad will be corrected and passed off (forgiven!).

When one of the souls leaves the physical, he will spend most of his time in the astral until it is determined he should return to Earth to clear up some problem, or advance into one of the higher worlds. If the soul is to return to Earth, he will still often be taken into a higher plane to learn needed lessons. He will even find himself visiting the higher self, even though he will not be able to fully understand at what level he has been taken.

When such is the case, the soul will find comfort and solace in the warm, glowing yellow light of this super consciousness. While he may not understand where he is, or what this light is, one thing is certain. He would never guess in a million years that this Face of God was himself!

When the time comes where the two soul mates are able to reunite, the forces they are able to manifest are such that nothing in the lower worlds would be able to resist them. The love that pours forth from them, through this higher self, is one of the most powerful forces in all of the universes.

After this final union of soul is completed, we find we are better able to continue on into the still higher planes. With this movement, there is only peace and contentment, for when the two lost halves are again whole, neither has the desires and longings so familiar to the earthbound mortal. Now that the male has found the female and the female has found the male, they no longer need to yearn to be in the company of an opposite sex. Both are able to satisfactorily quench the eternal thirst of the other, developed while being alone in the world.

This also explains why the Initiate that resides in the fifth plane is better able to work and associate with the Paramahansa, than one who still resides on Earth. The fifth plane initiate is complete and whole and no longer needs to follow the dictates of the cruel master lust. The earthbound, on the other hand, still has not reunited with his soul mate and his desires (both spiritually and physically) are so enormous they are all that dominates his mind.

Another interesting teaching about the higher self is that there can be more than two souls coming from this one singular monad. While it may not be common, it is a possibility if the higher self feels the two that have gone forth are inadequate and are contributing virtually nothing toward their cosmic bank account.

We would need to take into consideration the time period the two souls were in and the extent of their potential abilities. Multi-souls could have been a strong possibility during very ancient times, where most were merely peasants who performed the very same duties every day, never traveling more than a mile or two from home their entire life, and never being exposed to any great opportunities. In that case, the higher self would need to manifest other personalities to assist in Its spiritual development. These personalities though, would still be only a further extenuation of this particular divine soul.

In physical terms, we might look at it in the same light as a man and a woman having the normal two children, but they could also have ten, twelve or even more children. These children would not be coming from any source outside of this particular union. They would all be coming from the very same genes as the original two, but each and every one of them would have their own awareness, intellect and emotions.

Carrying this interesting phenomenon one step further, we would have to stop and ask ourselves the very obvious question, that if our higher self has created these additional souls in a previous time, then what has happened to them now that we are in a period of time where there is an abundance of opportunity to learn and grow? If the multitude of souls are no longer needed to spiritually advance, do they cease to exist, or are they in this world still contributing to the higher self?

The answer is that they, too, will continue to advance with us and will forever continue to be a part of our divine soul.

That would also mean it is very possible we may have more than one soul mate. That would not necessarily mean we would ever be with any of them while on Earth – unless such a thing was seen as an opportunity to achieve some great thing.

This is another reason why some teachers are so quick to deny the soul mate teaching. To them, it is just much simpler to avoid something not only complicated and complex to explain, but something that could probably offer no comfort to that love starved man or woman, who would search their entire lives for that divine loving mate.

A more important fact is that our higher self can bring one into our life who may not be a soul mate, but is one who can love us as a soul mate. Through the process of spiritual evaluation and the magnetism created from our karma energy units, we can draw this love to ourselves.

We only need to open the door to spirit, let go of our problems and emotions and permit spirit to carry out Its divine plan unimpeded by our crazy actions. Once we let go of our problems and let the spiritual essence that surrounds each of us protect us, we find all we need in this life will come to us – love included.

THE TREE OF LIFE

By the time soul enters the seventh plane, it will have reached a degree hardly similar to anything the half soul had been.

There is no longer a need for any physical anchors such as landscapes and desires. Here, soul will reside in a state known as Omnipresence.

It can be active on this plane, but will find it is able to work, communicate and teach on the six other planes all at the same time.

The multi-consciousness introduced on the third plane has fully matured at this stage. There is no longer desire because soul can attract whatever it might want. There is no longer loneliness because there is no place (up to and including this plane) that it cannot go and there is never even one second where soul is not living in a state of sublime ecstasy.

This is also one of the homes to those who are known simply as Silent Ones.

While it is accepted that the Silent Ones are the highest one could ever hope to escalate, we can see they were also once only mortal students in the physical worlds.

Even though they were previously subject to the governor forces and laws of the various planes, when they were accepted into the ranks of the Silent Ones, it can be seen that all governor forces now offer assistance to them when one enters into that force's field of activity.

This is due to the fact these Silent Ones make their eternal home in the Heart of God, and when they give a message to any governor, it is understood they are speaking for God.

The major duty of the Silent Ones is the maintenance of the spiritual energy giving life to all planes. Where the spiritual masters offer the education needed by soul, the Silent Ones offer the energy and dimension needed to carry out that education.

Another amazing aspect of the seventh plane is the phenomenon called the Tree of Life.

Every religion that has ever had the ability to reach into this plane, speaks of it most devoutly and there is no soul that has not seen it on its journey to the physical worlds. This was one of the education stops the monad engaged while preparing soul for its education.

Many travelers have tried to describe it for the benefit of the followers of a particular religion, but there have been very few who could fully understand what this tree stands for. They had no idea why there was a tree, an isolated single tree, located in a place where there is absolutely no other landscape of any kind.

Drawing from the general knowledge released to the explorer, the only answer offered was that this tree is known as the Tree of Life because It gives life to all beings and planes below this level. But to the true inquiring mind, this answer leaves a lot to be desired. It still does not fully explain what this tree is doing, and why it is here serving as some mysterious sentry in the midst of a world where it seems quite out of place.

It is only upon our approaching it that we can see that it is not a tree at all!

What we interpreted as a trunk is a tremendous flow of spiritual energy so concentrated and so powerful it pounds downward in such abundance that it forms itself into a wide circular beam, resembling something like a body of a tree, although the circumference of that beam is not able to be measured in physical terms. It could be hundreds of millions of miles around, or it could be many times larger.

What was recognized as branches are countless sources coming in from different directions, from the different planes still above, supplying the life force known as spirit, and forming great beams (or branches) that reach so high into the heavens that it falls beyond the vision of any of these explorers.

What was seen to be roots are the powerful off-shoots at the base of this apparent trunk, that reach down into all worlds of creation below this point.

This illusion of looking like a tree is only due to the duty of this plane which is to serve as the major collecting and distribution center for all spiritual energy reaching into all lower worlds.

As this duty is performed, the branches come together forming the trunk, giving even greater impact and strength to the collective sources. This force is known as the Voice of God. This Eternal Voice, or Energy, is separated and sent on into the different sectors of the spiritual worlds through what was seen to be roots.

Even though these roots are as numerous as the branches from which they sprang, possibly numbering in the hundreds of billions, each and everyone is so powerful that, although billions are sent to preserve life, it could take only one to destroy all life below the fifth plane.

We only need to remember what we learned from the Mountain of Light located in the capital city of the astral. At that time, we were made aware that although there could be no school and no life without spirit, if we were exposed to the pure, powerful source of this pounding, condensed energy, uncut or unprepared in any way, all life could be swept away in an instant!

This is another reason all beings are so quick to hold the Silent Ones in such high regard. They are the Keepers of this Eternal and Awesome Power.

Since the seventh plane is the distribution center of the universes and since the Silent Ones are the maintainers of the universes, they can always be contacted (by those who so desire), by concentrating on the seventh plane during a contemplative exercise.

This is also the plane one must reach before he can be considered as a candidate for entrance into the ranks of the Silent Ones.

UNDERSTANDING REINCARNATION

One of the most misunderstood and debated items of conversation is, if there is reincarnation and how it would operate.

Even though this is a topic related solely to the physical universe, one may not gain a true understanding of it until they have spiritually progressed to the status of a seventh plane initiate. Although there is enlightenment at each of the levels reaching up to the seventh, it will not be until this time that the individual fully comprehends the workings of both physical and spiritual worlds. This is because the seventh plane provides the dimension, force, and intelligence necessary to maintain life and the laws needed at the lower six vibrations.

When we can control the cosmic force of the seventh plane, we also discover our intellect has greatly expanded. More than likely, you will have a complete understanding of all things leading up to this level.

At this level we can see that the foundation for one's reincarnation actually began long before they even entered the physical for the first time. One also gets a better understanding of the soul and how it is educated.

Shortly after the monad is divided at the fifth plane, the two half-souls spend a certain amount of time on each of the three levels above the physical universe. While in the etheric, they are assigned a certain celestial classroom to start in. This can be comprehended by studying the zodiac.

Under the zodiac, we become aware that certain signs have certain characteristics which help define the character of that particular sign. From there, we discover that each of these classrooms is divided again into another twelve sections. This helps define the soul's identity. While the first division gives a very general understanding of a particular sign (as we experience when reading a horoscope), in the second division the soul develops deeper personality and character.

At this point, we can see we could experience any one of the one hundred and forty four general groups or classes (twelve divisions each being divided into twelve more).

Seeing these one hundred and forty four classes, many shamen have declared we must spend some time in each of these classes to become truly enlightened. But that is not so. We do not need to learn all the lessons of the zodiac. It would be like going to college to gain a certain diploma in a certain field, but once we passed, were told we couldn't graduate because we hadn't studied all the courses offered.

It is not necessary for us to experience everything this world offers to become an effective force in the cosmic. When we were plucked from the cosmic ocean, it was for a definite purpose. We were given a heightened awareness so that we could carry out a certain duty when we graduated by returning to the twelfth vibration.

So, the first incarnation is very basic. The only requirement is that it offers a general foundation for that which you will one day become. Before that first incarnation takes place though, other stops need to be made.

Traveling to the third level, the causal plane, we are actually "loaned" cosmic energy which activates our education. Some call this "primal karma". This is the karmetic energy we use to develop our own karma. Regardless if we use this primal energy to build good or negative results, it is the means that triggers the flow of lessons and forces around us when we finally do enter the physical.

It is also at the causal level we become "farmed-out". Although we belong to the true spiritual worlds, here we become special. While our understanding is of a childish nature, we are placed in the care of a particular spiritual society.

It is the duty of this society to aid us in the regulating and balancing of karma. Viewing us from their standpoint, they observe what we can accomplish, where we may be heading, what we need to learn, and try to help save us (as much as possible) from our own actions. This, they do by providing necessary lessons which will burn up negative karma. Although we may not always welcome these lessons with open arms, we should never forget they are only lessons and not punishments. For example, when we do a grave injustice to another, perhaps the only way we may be able to open our eyes and hearts to what we have done is to literally walk in their shoes by experiencing the same pain we created for them.

Another aspect of the seventh plane is that many of us become very moved and feel a warm glow when we see a certain type of ancient church or temple. This is because deep in our subconscious we can still remember being among the loved friends of our particular society. Strangely enough, most of these societies are usually located at places that resemble temples.

Leaving the causal, we next enter the astral. At this level the two half-souls come to a better understanding about who and what they are. Here, guardian assistants help us discover what it is we will be better at than probably anyone else. From there, the soul will be given a general game-plan, but how we approach it or carry it out is entirely up to us.

Finally, we are born in a particular physical world, one that abounds with what we need.

From this first birth, using our primal karma energy, we begin to carry out actions and start making decisions which will further define what we need to learn.

At the conclusion of the first life, we make a most startling discovery. We now find that each of the one hundred and forty four possible classes seem to be divided further. Twelve is considered a sacred number because when there is a division it is usually into twelve parts.

Now, we find a selection of one thousand, seven hundred and twenty eight different lessons we could engage in. This is not the end of it though. In all probability, each division can be divided as many times as necessary to zero in on a very specific experience needed.

With this understanding, we can see we do not need to experience every spoke of the wheel in order to graduate from the physical. If this were the case, we would never progress to the true God Worlds.

Although some ancient teachers taught we must experience many physical lives to become enlightened, that is not necessarily so. Simply knowing the purpose of this world and doing the best you can, will trigger a release from this harsh world. Why would spirit insist on keeping anyone a prisoner here when they already understand why they were created and hunger to move on to spiritual worlds?

So, although reincarnation is a fact, it does not mean we need to spend excessive time here. As explained elsewhere, I could have been released after my last incarnation had I not desired to return to teach. You have undoubtedly already experienced enough to release you from another return. This can be demonstrated by your actions and interest in researching esoteric material.

WHEN WILL I DIE?

Again, since the seventh level provides all knowledge needed to fully conquer and master physical matters, we understand our lives are not cast to us at random. There is a definite and basic direction laid out for us before we enter the physical. It is so precise that it even includes the day we will return back to the astral. As explained though, that does not mean it has to happen as programmed. There is nothing that "needs" to happen in this world. While a general plan is placed before us, it is up to us what we do with it.

When we enter the physical it is much like buying a round-trip bus ticket. We have a destination. We have a certain reason for going there. And we have a specific date we leave for home. But that in no way means we have to go all the way to the end of the line, nor does it mean we must leave on that special day for home. We could go to a host of other localities which we pass through on our journey. We could choose a detour by staying longer than anticipated at a random stop or even decide to take another bus and head off into an entirely different direction.

That's pretty much how our incarnation operates. Plans are placed before us but as I said, nothing is written in stone.

For that reason, we should be skeptical about anyone who claims to be capable of giving a reading about our future. Since there is no definite future, at best they could only relate what might possibly happen. Even then, if they weren't a fake, they would know this was only a possibility and not a true prediction.

Several years ago there was a psychic society held in high regard that claimed to read past lives, predict definite futures and said they could tell when one would die.

Examining what they might be saying to the naïve, I put them to the test. Yes, I told them, "I want to know who I was in a past life. I want to know what is in my future and I need to know when I am going to die."

The first reader related a story that wasn't even close to anything I had lived. At the end of the letter he wrote SR 251 and told me if I would like to know about other lives I had lived, to be sure to include that number with my request (along with another fee). He explained I should not lose that number because it had special spiritual significance for me. Of course what he really wanted was a classification number he could check to avoid tripping himself up by contradicting dates.

The second wasn't any better. He was so bold as to tell me I needed his assistance if I were to avoid some things coming my way. This he could do, of course, only if I offered a thank-you check to God (but made out to him).

The third said in order to properly predict my departure date, he needed to know where I was born, the date and if possible, the time of day. Of course, his only interest was the date. It certainly wouldn't look good if he told an eighty-year-old man he had a good forty or fifty years ahead of him.

Then, feeling safe with my age at that time, he allotted me another forty-three years. That pretty much placed him in the clear. If I lived, then he was accurate. If I died, well, what was I going to do? Ask him for a refund?

The reason I emphasize this episode is to make it clear that frauds abound! If you really would like to receive a reading, you should first understand your true records are sealed! Even if someone were legitimate, they would at most only be able to read your aura.

Second, you can instantly detect what they really are by what they say. Anyone worth their salt will never say that this thing or that thing is going to happen. At best they would say "might happen" or "could possibly happen". But even then, the reading could be questionable. It is doubtful such a thing would be in your aura if it were not directly related to your health.

And third, watch for the hook. Once a minimal price has been agreed upon, there should be no more talk of money. If all of a sudden, he needs more money so that he might help you – WALK

AWAY! Aura readers read the aura and that is all. There is nothing more they will claim to do or are able to do.

THE SECRET OF TIME AND SPACE

One of the strangest secrets of the physical universe is that everything curves. Everything has a curve, even that which we conceive as empty space.

While we may think the physical has no boundaries, there are definitely some strange laws at work around us.

It is conceivable we could never travel the full length or width of physical space even if we traveled at the speed of light, but we are taught there are limitations.

From the physical consciousness, this is difficult to understand, however once we are able to operate from the seventh plane, we gain a more profound observation.

We have heard that if we took off from Earth and shot through space, never once departing from a straight line, even though an astronomical amount of time would pass, we would one day approach Earth at the opposite side.

It would be quite obvious we had gone around a great circle, but at no point would we be able to identify where that turn occurred.

Another surprising thing is time curves. This opens a whole new dimension of understanding.

While it may be difficult to understand space bending, we are able to get a slight grasp of it when we conceive the circle of space as a solid thing. But how can we take something as abstract as time and come to an understanding?

Even though the physical consciousness is totally unable to come to a satisfactory explanation, it does start to offer a foundation to some of our other great mysteries.

The day will come when we operate in an atmosphere beyond time and space. Moving beyond time or space would mean we would need to escape the dimension of these particular elements.

Even if we can't see or sense how they are contained, we need to escape both if we expect to move beyond the physical level. In a higher consciousness, we can see that some sort of wall must exist when one level of vibration meets the next higher one. As each plane merges with the next higher or previous lower, it must develop a shield to protect its particular rate. Through this process we see there are very specific limitations.

Mentioned before, time is also different from one vibration to the next. What might seem like a great deal of time in one level could seem very brief in the next.

If time can be different in each level, that gives positive proof time also vibrates. Our observation of a particular vibration is what we actually interpret as time. So, while space is limited at its borders by the next vibration, we find time is confined by these very same vibration walls.

THE ULTIMATE SECRET OF THE SPHERES

When one becomes active in the lessons of a particular spiritual institution, they are programmed in the strict limits of that special path. While it might offer some enlightenment as to the true workings of the physical and lower astral, it hardly ever aims at anything higher than the astral. Very few know of anything beyond that.

Even those institutions that teach about the division of higher and lower vibrations, who admit there are many planes existing beyond the astral, and are fully aware of governing forces controlling these divisions, are still at a loss to understand these forces. Just as all religions, they see a higher intelligence as a personality and give it human characteristics.

As for the lower governors, the teachers understand they are saturated with negative energy and are very careful about any engagement with them. They also realize that the most awesome of these governors is the one located balanced between the fourth and fifth dimension.

One of the more advanced of these institutions has even given this governing force a name to go along with the personality attributed to it. Next, they warn students the negative side of this governor will make every attempt to disrupt their spiritual journey and actually halt them if given a chance. They say while it is good to love and worship the positive side, the negative side must be avoided at all costs.

This is hardly anything more than believing God is a man. A man that must be carefully approached. An angry and vengeful man.

Then we hear about spiritual masters who met with horrible conditions when they dared bring true knowledge into this world. This supposedly because it was against the desire of the negative side.

If this were truly the case, then how is it so many travel among the spheres and openly talk of it?

The ultimate secret of true spiritual co-workers is they have a better understanding of divinity. They realize they are never alone. They have given spirit permission to use them as a vehicle and since spirit is in everything, it is also in that negative charge. Through spirit we see negative does not mean bad. It is nothing more than an opposite pole so a spark can be created. Also, since spirit presents this governing force to us as something similar to ourselves, the co-worker easily offers love and assistance. It is this love, offered at each of the governing force levels, that literally opens the door so spiritual and physical blessings take place for us and those near us!

Simply by putting ourselves in the hands of spirit (letting spirit touch others through us), we find we develop a true and sincere love for each of these force personalities. In turn, we find there is abundant love for us from them!

Offering love instead of fear and mistrust, we find we are not blocked, challenged, or disrupted, but actually assisted by these governor personalities.

117

CHAPTER FIVE:

BECOMING A CO-WORKER WITH GOD

THE SPIRITUAL GOD FORCE

The ancient science was based on the Light and Sound of God. It is from this understanding all religions come, either directly or indirectly.

The basic teaching was (and is) that "All Life comes only from that which is called the Voice of God (Spirit), and this Life Giving Force can be seen and heard'."

Moreover, this sound or this light can be altered by either the curve of the various planes or by those who have become Coworkers with God.

Each plane can be positively identified by the manner in which it reflects spirit, i.e., by its particular dominant sound, which could be similar to a waterfall, thunder, or other natural phenomenon – or to the sounds of specific musical instruments, such as a violin, a flute, or even a bagpipe.

Although the plane will alter or bend this spiritual force to meet its particular needs, we find it lacks the ability to form the God force into anything other than required by the laws laid down for that plane. It can manifest what the mortal mind would consider to be miracles, but those miracles and abilities would be found to have their plane limitations.

The Coworkers, on the other hand, are found not so limited. Not only can they reach any plane they desire, to partake of what it might offer, but can also transform the appearance of the spiritual flow to meet his special demands and needs.

Once he is aware of his abilities and stature, he will be found to constantly surround himself with whatever cosmic flow that serves his needs or that bring miracles into the lives of others.

A true Coworker with God will be found changing the lives of hundreds of people everyday either consciously or unconsciously.

It is said that a Coworker will be able to completely change the life of a person for the better, bringing miracles into his or her life simply by passing through a room they are in, or by passing them on the street.

They do not need to know that person and they do not need to know their situation. All that matters is that spirit knows, and it will be according to the karmetic energy flow of this unknown person, and whether spirit will be able to offer assistance or not – often completely oblivious to the awareness of this God channel.

This also helps us to better understand the teaching of the positive and negative karma spin.

It is for this reason that even if the Coworker were to attempt to give a blessing to a specific person, it might not come about due to the openness of the one in need, perhaps having too much of a negative spin of karma energy in the aura. On the other hand, even though the Coworker would know nothing about it, a spiritual flow could encompass him, being much like a great flame, reaching out to all who would pass him or her on a busy street, offering a blessing to those who are prepared to receive.

For those who desire to become a Coworker, offering this spiritual energy flow, bringing miracles and fantastic healings into the lives of others, only need to open themselves to spirit using the most holy of all of spiritual lights, the white light.

It is also necessary to point out that for those who choose to serve in this manner, not only are they experiencing the tremendous thrill of walking among the masses as if they were an unknown Saint, bringing forth miracles and blessings of God, but the positive spin of the units in your own aura will cause your cosmic bank account to soar.

Never forget how simple it is to change this karma spin. Every action, every thought, every desire will affect the spin. Even the fact that you are reading this, has already altered the spin, changing countless numbers to a positive spin.

This can even be verified by yourself, if you so choose. Simply lay the book aside for a moment and permit yourself to look at the excitement produced in the Heart Region, by the concept of "You" working mysteriously and unknown to help others, being a channel for God.

We hear of miracles and healings that occur everyday that baffle the doctors as well as the afflicted.

Most will say these miracles have come about through prayer or faith, but that is precisely the same thing presented here. First, the person must be open and balanced enough to receive the healing and then there needs to be the channel to supply that blessing.

Over and over again we hear how this thing or that thing will change our lives. We are told if we do exactly what another wants, our lives will just simply never be the same again. The list goes on and on – everything from us calling some psychic, to reading a very special book. But the truth is that their real desire is only to make their pocket a little heavier, while yours becomes a little lighter.

Granted, this ordeal about changing your life has been played to death, but possibly for the first time in your life - and definitely for the ultimate experience of your life - if you choose to join these ranks of Coworkers, your life will never be the same again!

It is this select group that are exalted above all others and they discover the meaning of being the Sons and Daughters of God. It is said of them that they walk with their feet on the ground, but with their heads in Heaven.

Those that walk among us that have chosen to become Coworkers are very quick to understand that what they are offering is nothing like simple Christian charity.

Where Christian charity is a matter of offering good will from their heart, the blessing of the Coworker is directly from God.

Good will falls into the category of "Do unto others as you would have them do unto you." It is an extension of and subject to the physical level of ability. Although the practitioner will improve his karma energy flow, it is still only the individual acting on his own. He is not really opening himself so spirit can flow freely throughout his entire body. He has not opened himself to be a channel.

Becoming a channel is a very definite endeavor. He is not just merely walking around, feeling good. He has given spirit permission to flow through him – through his personal space in order that spirit may go as it needs.

A very interesting concept of the ancient times was that God cannot enter into this world except through one's Soul.

This can be easily understood by looking at the Law of vibration. We have seen we cannot enter any plane unless we have a corresponding body that vibrates at that same level, and we have seen that the true essence of God has no negative charge. Thereby, if God were to enter into this world, it would have to be through a vibrating body that has a negative charge.

A person's private space is a very sacred thing and spirit will not enter into our lives without receiving special permission from us. This is why prayer is held in such high regard by so many. It is not a plea for help as most think. Spirit does not regard us (as we regard ourselves) in the light of being little children. It sees us as we really are, a distant kingdom that is either giving spirit permission to enter into our land to carry out the Will of God, or not.

We need to emphasize the words the "Will of God". Spirit is ready and willing to supply miracles not only to you, but to all that you come in contact with, as long as it does not violate any of the prearranged plans of a student's education.

You may be aware of an individual that has some severe handicap and you may desire to assist them (either known or unknown). But you might find that nothing has come about after offering them a blessing, even though you made the proper preparations, opening yourself, giving spirit permission to use you as a vehicle.

Meanwhile, someone else that may have a serious affliction is all of a sudden well, leaving their doctors quite baffled by what has happened.

Spirit should be given permission to enter into your "Kingdom", but It should never be limited by what you think should be done.

The first person may have chosen to have this handicap in this life to pay off some heavy karmetic debt or perhaps to learn a very special lesson. He and spirit may have agreed to this arrangement prior to this life, so that the individual could receive a much greater reward later.

The second one may have paid off a debt, opening his aura to receive a cure.

It is never up to the Coworker to change anything. He is simply making his kingdom available. The Coworker may offer a special cure to pass through him, but it is done only through the understanding that if it is God's Will.

The Coworker never takes any illness, impediment, or other bad karma (what is considered bad karma) unto himself.

Karma is a lesson that needs to be worked out. It must be dissolved. It must be erased. We never agree to take it on to ourselves.

All karma energy units are created for a very specific reason -to assist in our education. It is not just some vague thing in our minds. These units are very real and once they are created, they must run their course somewhere.

Many religious historians believe this was the reason for the anguish and torment of Jesus. He absorbed the negative energy (the sins of man), from those who turned to him for assistance, much faster than he was able to pass it off, having it dissolve in the cosmic.

This was the meaning of taking on the sins of others and dying for the sins of man. It would most certainly appear the sins of man were forgiven when He took on their negative karma.

It is true that Jesus was a great and loving man, but it is also true that those who are in despair in this world will panic and force their pain on another. It was a simple matter of His choosing to not say no.

He took all of this horrible karma unto himself, but even He may have been surprised by the great extent of it. This helps to explain His eternal question, "Father, why hast thou forsaken me?"

Historians agree He did have every intention of coming down from the cross, but much too late discovered His aura was so infested and eaten up by so much of the negative spin, that spirit just could not assist Him. Spirit did not abandon Him, It just was unable to pass through Him any longer, using Him as a channel.

The true Coworker will never pray, "Let me take on this sickness, so that they may be well".To be a perfect channel, we must understand that spirit is taking care of everything.

Everything we see in this world is only an illusion – we must never forget that.

To be a perfectly clear channel, we should try to remain as detached from the healings as we can. It is one thing to let spirit flow through us and it is quite another to try to restrict it, by trying to force our will into the actions of spirit. By making a specific request or demand, we not only hinder spirit, but could be going deep into something we know nothing about.

The request could be ignored because of that prearranged agreement, but just as important is the fact that most of us are not doctors. What we think is wrong could be entirely off the mark. If we were to request a special healing for a pain in the back, and that pain was only a byproduct from a more serious problem, it would have been far better for us to let spirit do what should have been done.

When one is a Coworker, it can be something that someone may choose to do only occasionally – or it can be a twenty-four hour a day job, if we so desire.

The nightly Coworker will permit spirit to use his personal energy to assist others while he sleeps. This was discussed earlier, showing how we would travel with spirit offering our love and assistance to those who may be ill, or are hopelessly lost in their own private sea of misery.

Then, of course, during the day we travel about carrying the essence of spirit with us, which to a true psychic, would look like a fantastically large sword of flame reaching out for twenty or thirty feet in every direction, swinging with great force back and forth.

The Coworker will find he is never without spirit. It will be with him during the day, and he will be with it in the evening.

You only need to offer an affirmation and you will discover you are that Coworker.

THE AUTHORIZING OF SPIRIT

The affirmation offered to spirit, giving permission to use you (your spiritual essence) as an open channel, will closely resemble the technique that was used to open yourself to volunteer dream travel.

The singular difference is that in the affirmation to dream travel, you are addressing the subconscious, giving the order to make available an adventure. And in the affirmation to spirit, you are authorizing the sub to open the doors to spirit and are giving full cooperation in making sure that nothing is impeding its flow.

Just as with the previous affirmation, you should take several deep breaths, holding each for a couple of seconds. Then, when the breathing is again stabilized, repeat the command slowly and clearly three times. Remember, the first time is to record and file the order. The second is to classify it, bringing it to the full attention of the subconscious. And the third is the authorization for it to be acted upon.

An affirmation proven to be quite effective is: "On this evening, I offer myself and my spiritual essence to be used as a channel by divine spirit, to carry out the Will of God!" The affirmation is clear, concise and specific.

THE WHITE LIGHT

In becoming a channel for spirit to pass through, the Coworker will immediately become aware of the White Light that always accompanies him or her as they progress through their daily activities. Sometimes it can be felt and very often it can be seen, but until that ability is developed, the individual can take solace in knowing it is always with them as they move among the masses, remaining totally unknown as they perform their secret acts for the benefit of mankind.

One only needs to picture the white light shining down on them, covering them completely to activate the protective and magical abilities that are vibrated forth, passing from the light to the individual. To be able to fully enjoy the impact to the consciousness though, a proper exercise should be engaged whenever the opportunity is afforded.

To perform this exercise, one can be in bed (such as when performing the affirmation), but to establish the maximum in consciousness awareness, it should be performed while sitting upright in a comfortable chair. The back should be fairly straight so the Coworker can make full use of the spine and the latent Spiritual Force asleep at its base.

The arms should be comfortably placed on the arm rest (or on your legs) and the feet should be placed flat on the floor.

Next, picture a beautiful white light shining just a couple of feet above your head. See it entering into the top of the head. Feel it as it passes through the head and down the spine. Visualize it as it expands and vibrates outward, going into both arms and shooting down both legs.

Continue to feel the flow. Feel it as it moves down both arms and both legs. Feel it as it moves through the hands. Feel it and see it (in the mind) as it flows out from the tips of the fingers.

At the same, time see and feel the flow traveling through both legs and into the feet. See this energy flow come pouring out from the tips of your toes.

Visualize yourself being completely covered and bathed in this awesome white light, as the energy, which is pouring from the fingers and toes, again reemerges into the light that has surrounded you.

Once you are able to stabilize this impression in your mind, see your aura literally saturated with this God Light, with it continuing to pour down from above, passing through the body and then returning to its Source, in an eternal flow that will forever be with you. Then offer your affirmation:

"In the name of the Most Holy, I offer my body as a channel and my soul as an eternal protector to divine spirit, so that the Will of God may be done!"

Once the exercise has been performed, the Coworker should attempt to place the mind in a peaceful state. He does not need to strain the mind to see what is happening. All he need do is simply relax, wait and gently watch for what might come across the blank screen of the inner mind.

This white light meditation is the highest form of meditation. The white light is pure spirit and is the same force that gives life and substance to all worlds of God.

The top of the head is the connecting spot where spirit merges with soul even when there is no special exercise being performed.

From the moment of birth, spirit has made its connecting union with the earthbound traveler through what we call the soft spot located at the rear of the skull.

We only need to look into the eyes of a child to be able to see the flow of spirit. This is one of the reasons the world looked much different through our eyes when we were children, than from when we reached adulthood.

It is this linking spot that Jesus spoke of frequently, but which most have not been able to understand. The statements that, "You must be as little children," and "You must be born again," are direct references to the linking up of spirit and soul.

Actually, "being born again" means the awakening of your awareness. Once you can again be aware of the spiritual flow that surrounds and passes through you, then you can again start to live in spirit.

This is the true purpose behind the ceremony of Baptism. It is the sprinkling of Holy Water onto the soft spot in order to keep it open for a child, or to open it up for an adult. With the passage of time though, the meaning has been lost.

"Straight is the path and narrow is the way," is also a reference to the area where spirit connects itself with our individual bodies.

Light is the Inner Master and the Inner Temple. Both are forever with us and both can assist us in our attempt to be an effective channel.

The Inner Master is the manifested intelligence that comes forth to assist and guide us, and the Inner Temple is the place that our awareness will aspire to when we perform any kind of spiritual exercise.

Once we are able to picture ourselves completely covered by the white light, we should turn our attention toward the third eye (located at the bridge of the nose, between the two eyes), and imagine that we are standing before a glorious, majestic temple.

As the flow of light continues to move through and around you, picture yourself walking up the tremendous marble steps that stretch out before you, rising up perhaps hundreds of feet to a white and golden temple.

See yourself floating effortlessly up those beautiful marble steps. See the great double door begin to open as you now seem to be soaring in that direction, much like a bird, who is not flying but coasting along.

By the time you have coasted to the entrance, see the doors being wide open. Once you float through this entrance, merely settle to the floor and from that point on, simply watch and listen for what may come to you.

What the Coworker experiences in his own temple will be a private matter. It is not possible for one individual to tell another what they will experience. Soul's journey to God is an individual path. It is possible that no two are going to have the same awareness.

There is an old Buddhist saying, "One hundred monks, one hundred religions." All of us are different, and for that reason, whenever we see an incredibly large following of people all bowing to and following the dictates of some self-appointed leader, it will more than likely lead to disaster for the people, as well as the one who tried to control them.

Once you have made this contact with your inner temple, you will find such great joy and love in your heart that you will find you are now not able to survive without it.

This inner master and inner temple are also anchor points for the seeking student. Where we might not be able to fully realize the power and love that comes from the white light, we are able to relate to a Holy Being and to a Sacred Temple.

Spirit has created this channel for us, supplying us with both a holy place that we can escape to, and with a protector whose sole duty is to guide, love and protect us.

THE MYSTERIOUS BLUE LIGHT

As far back as recorded history can go, there has been mention of the Mysterious Blue Light often accompanying one who has entered deep meditation.

Many cultures of the American Indian included a teaching about the blue light, or the blue star that would come to their Shaman while in communion with God.

This blue light, seen on the inner mind, will usually then change into the blue star and following this, may seem to change into a golden ball of light which can be accompanied by a host of smaller, but just as beautiful, yellow lights.

This is the highest possible blessing one could be fortunate enough to receive while still remaining in a physical body. The spiritual masters refer to this as the blessing of the Inner Master.

Those who become aware of receiving this blessing are the most blessed of all, for great changes will occur in their lives, so fantastic it will often leave their mind boggled.

Often, problems or illness that has plagued an individual or his family for years will all of a sudden be gone. Financial disasters are altered and personal setbacks will now seem to straighten themselves out. But, still, that should not be the reason for seeking the blessings of spirit. It should be sought because of the deep love blossoming in the heart, and because the individual desires to be with God and desires to become a true Coworker, offering his or her services to spirit for the betterment of mankind.

The benefits that come are a gift to you due to your undying love and devotion. Although these things may come forth, they should not be sought. Being that they are gifts, they should be appreciated and not expected.

As great as God is, if we were to seek out any single thing or place considered to be the concentrated area of God's Awareness, then this blue star would be that thing and our inner temple would be that place.

In ancient times, the masters often referred to the white light as spirit and the blue star as being God Itself.

They also taught that God could not enter into this world except through the inner temple the Coworker had awakened.

Without a spiritual awakening in this very dark and dismal world where people had forgotten about their inner temple, God would be closed out. It has been only through the efforts and divine love of those who have kept alive the ancient teachings, that our spiritual evolution has been able to make such progress as we are beginning to see in this day and age.

What the masters consider as the true dark ages was when these teachings were brought under attack by those who sought to enslave mankind by cutting out this light.

At the death of Pythagoras, his three strongest and most prominent schools were destroyed in the hope the knowledge about the flow of spirit would die also. The established rule of that time attacked and destroyed the schools of Crotona and Metapontum, then the Temple of the Muses.

The Agents of Darkness failed though, because there were still many more, lesser known mystery schools that simply went underground with their teachings until the time came for them to come forth again.

Attempting to disrupt and destroy the knowledge of the powers alive within you has never been fully successful. There has always been and always will be some channels through which spirit can bring its blessing.

While the blue star is God and the white light the life giving spirit, the yellow lights often in attendance are recognized as being assisting masters.

Another amazing thing about these lights is that they can manifest into your physical vision using your inner temple as a springboard.

Even when you are not engaged in a spiritual exercise, you will often see bright splotches of white, yellow or blue lights attract your attention. When this happens, know you are receiving a Blessing at that particular moment.

The most amazing manifestation of all is the physical ball of light that may appear before you. While it may not seem to be an everyday occurrence, there are thousands upon thousands of individuals who have experienced it.

Unlike the quick blinking of the colored lights, the large ball of physical light will be very clear, and will not disappear once you look at it. It may continue to radiate as long as a minute and will usually be seen shining just a foot or two above your head, or it may be seen at a distance. There will be no difficulty in identifying it though. It will be easy to see that it is not a reflection or a man made light. It will be round, floating independent and will be either clear or white.

When this occurrence happens, the individual should attempt to remain calm. If the Holy Light is to determine you are frightened or startled by its appearance, it will immediately withdraw. It comes forth as a blessing and will never expose you to anything it considers invading your sacred space. The masters have assured their students though, that if this light does manifest before you – and you do become excited to the extent that it withdraws – that in no way means your blessing was withdrawn. The blessing is a gift and it stays even if the light leaves.

OTHER POWER LIGHTS

When performing the spiritual exercise, although we most commonly use the white light, we do have the ability to isolate certain powers by selecting a ceremony using a particular colored light.

Since we know all things vibrate, if we desire to obtain the abilities from a certain power, we will need to raise our vibration to that particular vibration. Since colors vibrate, we need to choose the appropriate color having the same rate of vibration we are seeking.

When we desire to link with the flow of spirit, we use the white light. If we desire to make Holy Communion, we flood ourselves with blue light. But in cases where we are seeking something very definite, we will use other colors, picturing them flowing through us during our contemplative periods.

The following are some of the most common colors called upon, and their corresponding vibrating powers we might need.

RED

Red is a very strong and emotional color having three powers found active within it. It is the color of war, healing and protection.

When we need a healing, we only need to do the spiritual exercise as previously described, except in place of the white light flowing through the top of the head, picture it as a bright red light entering. Next, wherever the particular area of illness is, feel the energy building there. Concentrate on that area especially. Although the red light will be flowing through us as though we were a fountain spewing brilliant red beams, we will picture additional flow to the afflicted area.

Say we received a wound or a pain in the hand, we would direct our attention toward that area, instead of toward the inner screen of our mind. As we concentrate on that wound, we should see the red light working on it. We should feel the activity being carried out, and we should never forget that, although the red light is treating us, it is still spirit working within us.

If we should be coming under an immediate attack, we would immediately surround ourselves with the red light. Since it is quite obvious we would not have time to perform a ceremony, all we need do is picture ourselves being completely covered in a ball of red light. Once we have done this, we have set two other forces into action. First, the vibration of this red light will protect us by confusing and diffusing the aura of our attacker. Next, it will draw the powers of our defense system into full power, giving us far more power than we probably ever believed we had.

Caution should be used here though. You should never call upon the red light if you are already angry. When used for protection, it helps to overcome fear but it will ignite anger.

That is precisely why we say such things as, "It makes me so angry I see red." But, if anger is added to anger, you will have difficulty trying to regain composure.

YELLOW

Yellow is also a high vibrating color and will bring piece of mind, due to the fact it removes us from this Earth and places us on the etheric plane.

A golden yellow indicates one has a very spiritual nature. All of the great Saints had golden halos around the head.

This pure golden yellow needs to be cultivated, which assists us in keeping our thoughts and intentions pure.

GREEN

Green is the color of healing, teaching, physical growth and money. We can concentrate on it before we prepare to speak or teach. We can direct the energy toward our plants once it has passed through us so our essence is imparted to that plant. Or we can even picture money on our inner mind while the green light passes through us, placing our vibration to that of money, so it will be drawn to us.

This is not in contradiction to what has been taught earlier, although it may seem to be. Earlier, we were making it clear we should not be seeking money as an ulterior motive while falsely displaying ourselves as assisting spirit. Here, though, we are not approaching spirit with any false pretensions.

Drawing money is a lower vibration, but there is nothing wrong with performing the ceremony if we feel it will sincerely be of benefit to our life.

VELVET

People who flood their auras with velvet are people who have deep religious convictions and are not those who just profess to be religious.

Velvet will also assist individuals who suffer from heart trouble or stomach disorders.

ORANGE

Orange is often paid homage by some religions due to the fact that it is the color of the Sun. Flooding our aura with orange opens our vibration to the level of humanitarian. This color helps us reach and maintain the level of power needed for us to be able to do good for others. If that orange has a golden yellow in it, it helps us to not only do good, but to serve as a shining example for others.

BROWN

Brown is the same vibration as business. If we are to perform the spiritual exercise using brown before a business deal, we can usually assume that presentation will not only be profitable to us, but to all parties concerned.

However, if there is to be an upper hand in the deal, that benefit will be attracted to the one who has the proper vibration. Which will be the one who knowingly adjusted their aura to the vibration of business.

USING NATURAL FORCES

We have always heard that twelve o'clock, midnight, was the witching hour. This was not due to the religion's desire to perform only in darkness, but due to the fact that at precisely midnight, the ability to perform any spiritual act (magical ones included) are at a zenith.

But why is this so? In being a Coworker we should know not only where, when and how to perform our acts of assistance, but we should know why these acts are more beneficial at certain times than at others.

Even the Rosicrucians tell of offering members special assistance between midnight and two o'clock in the morning. They speak of a Celestial Sanctum where members are taken for a healing while they are in a dream state.

While we are on the subject, we also need to take a look at night births. We are told that it's the pull of the moon which affects not only a mother's ease in giving birth, but also the tides of the world, and aids in the growth of crops.

Looking at this overall picture we can see there is some great and mysterious secret at work here that can somehow tie these events together.

First of all, we must back up and take a look at this on a much grander scale. It is not the pull of this lone, little satellite affecting our lives so greatly, as it is the effect of a force reacting on other forces. The moon is only one small aspect in the much grander play.

It may be this discovery of one force acting upon another that will enable us to become more adept in our space travels in the near future. It may help us to also understand how a UFO can be traveling at a tremendous speed across the sky, and then sharply veer off to a ninety-degree angle and still maintain incredible speed.

This would also explain the Biblical "Wheel within a Wheel" that our scholars have such difficulty understanding. This wheel would be a reference to a surrounding force, which would be encased inside of another force.

Here, we will take a moment to lay some groundwork for what is being shown.

Let's imagine a circular force moving at a high speed from east to west, then within that force would be another – preparing to travel in a northerly direction. Now, let's say some form of vehicle had committed its center of gravity to this inner force. When the inner force engaged its new direction and sped forth, the vehicle would also change direction with it.

You might ask what happens when we exit the first force. Wouldn't we be victim to the primary force movement? The answer is yes, but the whole secret is that we don't leave the first force. Although it may appear that this UFO has left the first and engaged in the second, it has not. It has merely been riding ahead of the center of gravity of the first.

When the second force is brought into action, it will appear to be unaffected by the first movement, simply because by the time the first force has dissipated, the center of gravity will just be reaching the center of the secondary force.

To simplify this, let's draw a straight line on a piece of paper, then toward the end of the line draw another line at a nincty-degree angle. Now, run your finger along the horizontal line fairly fast until you come to the vertical line, then try to maintain the same speed as your finger changes direction, following the vertical line.

You will easily see that the finger will need to slow and nearly stop before making the change, or it will be forced to leave both lines as it makes an arc, going beyond the vertical line and then back to it.

This is our physical understanding of the forces around us. But, now, let's do it a little differently. Place the finger of the other hand on top of the finger that's going to zoom along the horizontal line. When the one finger reaches where the two lines meet, simply push the second finger up as the first finger begins to slow.

To give ourselves a visual aid, glue a small piece of paper to the fingernail on the top finger and we will look at it as if this is our visible UFO (while the two fingers, which are only forces, would be invisible).

With our observing only the piece of paper, we will see how it could be shooting along in an eastern direction and then shoot north, with no apparent difficulty!

137

While it may seem we have gotten off the subject of spiritual forces, we have not. This is only to prove there is still much we need to understand about physical science. Remember, we are laying the groundwork to help explain the much broader concept of how using the center of gravity and the Earth's movement will affect our spiritual development and our ability to perform miracles.

Forces working inside of other forces do not need to be working in different directions though. Regardless if they seem to be in contrast or not, there is one thing they all do that affects us. And that is to create a magnetic reaction that affects everything from our aura to the levels of the tide.

Next, let's pretend we are the Sun, and we take a strong string with a ball tied at the end and imagine the ball is Earth. As we spin around, we see the string stretch out as the ball tugs hard on it.

When we held the ball in our hands, its center of gravity was at its core, but now with the force we have added, it's easy to see the center of gravity has moved to the surface of the ball on the far side.

This enables us to see the first point to be made, that the center of gravity is not at the Earth's core but at the surface on the night side of the Earth.

Now, if we should take a slender pole and push it completely through the ball, and instead of the string being tied to a stationary point, we tied it at the top and the bottom of the pole, we would permit the ball to spin freely.

When we spin around, we see the center of gravity continues to stay on the surface which is furthest away from us, but now that the ball spins - we can see that the center of gravity moves along the surface.

The moon is pulling, which we have always been aware, but now we can see it is pulling in direct relationship with the Earth's center of gravity. Between the moon pulling and the Earth pushing, a magnetic reaction has been set up that moves slowly along the surface of the Earth as it rotates.

This magnetic reaction is found to be at a vibration identical or almost identical to certain cosmic forces and spiritual abilities.

If you would happen to be doing a spiritual exercise at this time, your spiritual vibration would vastly increase due to that magnetic reaction passing over you, between the Earth and the moon. This is also why there has always been such great success for those who practice "Moon Magic".

Being that there are few able to perform their ceremony at this late hour, we can see that performing a spiritual exercise earlier in the evening would have opened us so spirit could pass freely through us when the time was ripe. In this case, when the magnetic reaction passes over us, we will have some sort of spiritual experience.

We must always remember that when something seems strange to us, it is only due to our own inability to step back and look at it in a more complete picture.

Even when we consider something to be supernatural, we should understand that what we call supernatural is really only cosmic principles and laws we just don't fully grasp yet.

CHAPTER SIX:

OTHER METAPHYSICAL ASPECTS

THE SPIRITUAL HIERARCHY

When we speak of a spiritual hierarchy, most think only of angels and such, but that is not what is meant. Actually, there is not one, but two spiritual hierarchies set up for the sole purpose of giving soul an education.

The most recognized is the one composed of spiritual masters giving instruction guiding soul back to its true home.

The second is not composed of master teachers, but great celestial Beings who make their home on the seventh through the twelfth planes. To us they are mysterious and distant and known simply as Silent Ones.

Their duties are vast and varied, but one important duty is the maintaining of all planes. This is due to their being the Keepers of the Spiritual Force, as explained earlier.

The one hierarchy gives us the education and the second one supplies us with the place to receive that education.

Without either, the atomic structure known as soul would never progress, and would remain for all eternity as a dim light with only a semi-consciousness. Just as a lump of coal can be changed into a diamond under the pressure of time and force, so the two hierarchies are able to forge our atomic structure into the Gem of the Universe.

Outside of knowing that the Silent Ones maintain all of the planes, very little else is known about them.

Perhaps so little has been written about them simply because an author chose to not stretch his credibility with explanations about their strange abilities. Regardless, it is important for the Coworker to know that these Silent Ones are always nearby, and they will choose to aid a Coworker quicker than any other.

Although offering blessings is not considered one of their primary goals, they have been known to offer their love, compassion and assistance to those they feel are dedicated to their ideals of total unselfishness. One other interesting discovery about the Silent Ones is that they are not an automatic creation of God. They were once human just as you and I. Although they are far superior to anything we can conceive, they were once just like us. Which shows that we, too, can become Silent Ones if we so choose!

THE TEMPLE OF THE VIRGINS

If someone were to ask if you were a virgin, some might be embarrassed, some might laugh, but about 98% would finally say they definitely were not a virgin.

But they would be wrong.

Every religion has what the spiritual teachers call "dragons". This term was taken from the time mapmakers used to draw "Dragons are here" in the corners of their maps, meaning this was uncharted territory, and they really had no idea at all what might be there.

Some of these dragons in religion can be called "beautiful dragons," because although that particular concept might not be fully understood, they really do no one any harm. On the other hand, some of these dragons were created in an attempt to control followers.

This concept of virginity is one of those dragons.

Being a virgin has nothing at all to do with the physical body. In the spiritual works, we are saying over and over again that the soul is all that matters. We have shown that the physical universe is only a school, our lessons are only illusions and that our physical body is nothing more than a vehicle or a coat we are wearing to help us adjust to the vibration of this world.

Now, all of a sudden, why would it be so important to know if a person has united with another in a Holy Bond of Love and Affection? Even in the Bible, this was supposedly what God had instructed His souls to do.

Then, how could one be considered dirty, stained or shameful if they have not abstained from sex for their entire life? And what purpose would it serve?

No, being a virgin has nothing at all to do with anything about the physical body. This concept (or dragon) was introduced only so that the ignorant masses could be controlled by those who were little more than Fear Merchants in ancient times.

We only need to look at the early stages of religion to see the horrible things carried out in the name of God. There were thousands upon thousands either slain in battle or as prisoners simply because they would not bend to the dictates of the few, who proclaimed themselves as the law, speaking for God.

Control was the key being sought. Without control (and fear) the large body of disorganized individuals would hardly give their dedication, let alone their support to such a small group of controllers. What they were doing was an example of the oldest form of mind control known. First, they would instill fear and then attempt to convince the masses they were sinful, that they were living outside divine dictates and God was displeased with them, and that He still might burn them in some eternal damnation.

That is not to say that all priests of the time were evil, for that is completely false. It is important to understand that these leaders were very unenlightened, compared to today's spiritual evolution, and some had some very serious hang-ups (with sex at the top of the list).

When the true teaching of spiritual purity was being reformed in 60 AD, they quickly chose to use the term virgin soul and simply left it virgin, then attempted to insinuate this was a reference to the physical body.

Actually, though, the term "virgin" as it is used in the Bible, means "One who acts in the name of, and on behalf of Divine Essence." We don't even necessarily have to be so pure in our actions as we might think, even when we do conceive the true meaning of the title.

We were sent into this world to experience. It is only through our experiencing this world that we are able to awaken ourselves to the higher worlds. If we were not confronted by the passions of the mind that need to be overcome (greed, anger, lust, etc.), we would have nothing to conquer and this would not be a school. It is highly unlikely that a parent or a teacher would condemn us for becoming involved in a test we were sent here to learn.

It would be only through our indifference, or our addiction to the passions of this school, that we might be considered a poor student.

A child permitted to play in the mud cannot be punished for becoming dirty, and a student sent into this world to expressly become involved with things of low vibration, cannot be considered as bad or impure.

So, the virgin is not only one that engages in physical sex – but also one that may have many faults. To be a virgin, one would only need to have a deep love in his or her heart. This love might stem from a love for their child, to a love for something they just cannot fully comprehend. But that love will be the spark that will unite soul with Divine Essence.

Can you be considered a virgin? Most definitely. If you were truly not a virgin, you would not be reading this. If you were not a virgin, you would have no interest in any spiritual matters, and would have no convictions in regards to anything that had a higher vibration than money. You would be interested only in how you might lighten the pocket of others – by whatever methods available – without any feeling of regret or remorse.

Those that are able to raise their vibration above the most heavy, are well on their way to becoming a spiritual virgin. The mere fact they are progressing while still residing in this school, has enabled them to attract the powers and blessing of the virgin vibration.

When there is any mention of the temple of virgins, this is a reference to the celestial state of combined effort and ability of this brotherhood of virgins, available for all men and women struggling in the Earth world.

This means that those who would consider themselves to be virgins would be able to draw spiritual force and assistance to themselves.

It was no wonder that the true meaning was hidden from the masses in those dark times. It certainly would serve no purpose to permit the peasants to see themselves in any light other than sinners, and that they could never hope to touch the robes of God except through the priests.

The Divine Essence would forever attempt to preserve the true teachings through the use of symbols and parables hidden in doctrine. Thus, any with a sincere heart and open mind would be able to decipher these truths, once they were able to think for themselves, instead of accepting the limited vision of others.

When a person could question what their sexual activities had to do with their spiritual love, or their dedication to their beliefs, or their assistance to their fellow humans – then they should be able to also question why they should be denied receiving spiritual blessings and miracles.

Since the ancient teaching made reference to the virgin being able to draw forces and assistance to themselves, we can see this is a direct reference to performing the spiritual exercises we have been discussing.

By choosing to become a Coworker, one would engage in these exercises which, would raise their vibration – which would open their eyes to the fact they are a virgin and always have been.

To carry this study a step further, let's take a moment and take a look at it in the physical aspect.

What if a person who has never had sex was actually a cruel and greedy person? Could they be considered a virgin? Strangely enough, by spiritual standards – no! They might be considered a physical virgin, but that is only because of what we think a virgin should be. In the true, pure sense though, their vibration would not be at the rate of a virgin.

Meanwhile, if there was a woman who could be considered a scarlet woman, could she be thought of as a virgin? The answer here would depend entirely on what was in her heart. If she had developed a bad reputation because she had been misused, perhaps by placing her love in a series of bad relationships, loving those who were really unworthy of her love, she could still be considered a virgin. However, if she had developed a reputation due to a desire to get money, drugs, or favors, her desires would be extremely base, which would lower her vibrations as low as they could go.

Making one last observation, we might ask if she could ever hope to regain her stature as a virgin again. The answer to that is a positive, yes. In fact, not only can she become a virgin, she ultimately will become one, as she progresses through this school.

Unlike the physical concept, where we start out as a virgin and then lose it, we have learned that being a virgin is a step up, not down. Once we gain it, it is ours to keep. One can never lose their virginity as long as they keep their eyes turned to the heavens and their heart to spirit.

Always remember that having a sexual encounter based on pure love and desire for one another, raises your vibration – which creates the state of virginity. Love can only progress us – and sex can elevate us to the vibration of a true virgin.

TALKING WITH THE ANIMALS

Most of us have had pets during our life. If not now, more than likely we did when we were young, and without even trying, we developed a communication with that pet that went far beyond words. We didn't need to know what each pitch of their bark or meow meant (although we probably did), and this pet could probably understand only some very basic key words spoken to him, but there was a deeper, more spiritual language the two of us spoke.

This beautiful language hinged more on our being attuned with one another then it did with verbal sound. This language, this attuning, this telepathic communication was based squarely on our adjusting our vibration to that of the pet.

Vibration is always the key – regardless of what we are attempting to do.

While the usual pets are dogs or cats, we find there are many different types of vibration that must be used if we are to communicate with other life forms. Even the rate of vibration between a cat and a dog are vastly different.

Where a dog can be playful, rugged and devoted, and the two of you can roll around on the floor – a cat would be horrified and utterly disgusted by such an undignified spectacle. In fact, cats look down on dogs. They consider the dog to be a very inferior creature, and one that is hardly worthy of being in a cat's company.

A dog's vibration is based relatively high with very active currents and is probably the most easy to attune to because all we really have to do is become playful. Once we decide to play or become active, these currents begin to show in our aura and the dog will quickly sense it.

The cat, on the other hand, would avoid us at this time. If we chose to communicate with a feline, we would need to pull in our excessive energy and enter into an almost meditative state.

Where a dog is worldly like a man, a cat is more spiritual, like a woman. Where a dog can be easily approached, a cat will choose to be distant – until it is ready to receive you.

A dog will do leaps of joy to see you return home, but a cat will greet you with a simple little "hello" sound, which probably is a signal that it is now ready to be pampered.

Communicating with other animals can be just as wide a swing in vibration. Animals that are not domesticated have an inborn fear of man and usually this fear is justified. So, for them, they will not be looking at our actions as much as the vibrations in our aura.

Animals of all kinds are very psychic and especially those of the wild that cannot count on man for protection. We are aware of people such as St. Francis who would enter into a wooded area and the animals would come right up to him. This is not at all unusual. One only needs to place himself in a spiritual state, and as long as he does not make any sudden or threatening moves, the animal may come to their very feet, or to where they are sitting and sniff around.

There are many accounts where wild animals have assisted and even saved the lives of humans. One such account was when a spiritual master was in the wilderness and he became exposed to very harsh weather conditions. When he awoke, he found he was being warmed by two large bears that had laid tight around him and by keeping him warm, saved his life.

We will not go into any great detail here about the many instances where animals have been able to know that they were needed and then offered their assistance, for that subject alone could fill many volumes. It will just suffice to say that we can offer our assistance to any creature, or any animal can attempt to assist us whenever we perform a spiritual exercise.

To do this, we will take a comfortable position in the wild. Make sure there is a good flow of blood to all extremities, (not everyone would find a yoga position appropriate).

Next, we will perform the "fountain exercise", where we picture the white light above us. Feel the flow through the entire body and once we can feel that the flow is strong, feel it flowing out from the fingertips and the toes. See yourself completely covered in this white light. See it pouring down, around and through you.

When you are able to feel it, you can know that the animals around you can see it.

If you perform the exercise for some time, you may become very surprised when you open your eyes. You may see one or more creatures of the wild, standing, approaching, or laying near you.

One should not get their feelings hurt if it seems to fail at first. It may take a few times to completely flood the aura with this peaceful, unthreatening and spiritual flow, especially if we are highly exposed to a great deal of activity in our daily lives. But with practice and time, the aura will send the message that we want to send.

Since it would be very difficult and confusing for us to make a complete study of the different vibrations of the different species, we simply let the white light adjust the vibration for us. This spiritual light is already adjusted to all forms of life, so the animal will recognize and relate to that particular pitch to which it is attuned.

To be a perfect channel for spirit, we must try to change our outlook on many things. If we desire to communicate with animals, we will need to communicate with all life forms, even those we might consider less desirable.

We must remove preformed opinions from our minds. If we sincerely want to commune with nature and develop powers over it, we must understand there really is no such thing as a "disgusting" life form.

Many things may seem that way to our minds, but it is only because we are distant from them.

149

How often someone may have jumped when they saw a mouse run across the floor, but later, when we have trapped the little creature on a mouse glue strip, we hardly see the vicious beast that sent people screaming and climbing on chairs.

Now, while it looks up at us with those sad, soulful eyes, all we see is how cute it seems to be.

There is actually a great deal about mice that most people don't know. Did you know that when a mouse is happy, it will sing?

They sing in much the same way that a cat purrs when it is content. Under careful studies, the technicians have said that at times mice seem to be singing for others of their kind. Often, a mother mouse seems to be singing to her young. And when alone, they sing just for the joy of it.

They have also proven that the ones most active in this singing are our common field or house mice.

We must draw definite lines between the space we occupy and the space of the creatures, but we must still be able to understand their true natures if we ever hope to speak with their spiritual psyche.

Here, we might wonder what all of this has to do with our spiritual development, but we must remember that when the sun shines, it shines on all life, not just a select few. If we are to love spirit, we must love It in all of its forms, for like the sun, it touches all things.

Spirit will carefully guide us into these lesser worlds that we know little about, if we have a true love for all life.

There is only one source, one spiritual power and it is this essence that gives life to a giant or to an ant. It sustains you and me and it even gives life to that which we see as horrifying.

Spirit will always guide us, and I personally find that It is always right at my side when a lesson is to be learned or a point made.

One morning I happened to be on a subway platform in the very early hours, before there were hardly any people around.

Down on the tracks I saw a rat hopping along, heading in my direction.

At first I was disgusted, but then a strange thing happened. The rat stopped and just stared at me. As we carefully watched one another, I could see close behind her was her baby. They were on an early morning forage to avoid the dangers of being seen by too many people.

When the baby was safely at her side, she raised up on her hind feet, as if asking if I could help. There was none of the fear for people she had learned to develop and as for me, what had been disgust on my part, now turned to compassion.

We were no longer a man and a rat. We were spirit. For that one brief second, we had made a connection where we both had been removed from the illusions of this world to the reality of spirit.

People are usually very surprised to find that most life forms are willing to make a "psychic" connection with humans. Often they will even go out of their way to do so, but it's our lack of communication that drives us apart.

Two other life forms I have always abhorred are considered devoted pets by some people. Who could find anything good about snakes and spiders?

Many an actor or an actress about to play a part where they were to have a snake crawl across them, or have it slither down their shirt, have had to spend a little time with the snake ahead of time, so they could "get to know" one another.

Later, they would say, "Well, that snake was alright, it's not like other snakes."

Not true. This snake only seemed to be more acceptable because the actors "opened their consciousness" to it! Most snakes will show a form of compassion as long as they are at ease with the caretaker and not frightened.

However, "snake love" might not be for everybody. If the snake really loves and cares for you, it will desire to display this by going up your shirtsleeve to rest against your bosom. Spiders are the other one. Who could love a tarantula?

Well, it turns out that they are kept as pets too.

I don't know how much love a spider might be able to display, but I have been moved by the trust they will put into their owner.

Even though it can sense the danger of being exposed to humans, the spider will display itself on the arm or hand of its owner, putting complete trust in that person, feeling that individual will protect it.

As for other types of spiders, many writers have written about them and they have been the center of many sermons – praising them for their endurance, stamina and determination. The human race could only benefit by displaying such qualities.

We have now looked at the lovable, the wild and the repulsive, which brings us down to the lower kingdom, that which is the foundation of nature's chain, which would include everything down to ants.

Communication with the lower kingdom is quite different from communication with the higher life forms. In the lower section we are not actually seeking to relate with the intelligence of a lone bug, for that intelligence (to us) would be practically nonexistent. Everything that goes to make up this kingdom does not "think" or "plan". All of these different varieties of life respond only to a vortex which is found to be similar to our higher consciousness.

What they lack in size, they make up for in quantity. Their duties are many and varied, but each of these species are extremely important to our ecology.

Instead of just running around helter skelter, such as they seem to be doing, under a close observation we can see they are engaged in some very specific goals.

These goals are not planned by the individual insects, but by their vortex which will show to have a limited consciousness.

A vortex intelligence will be limited to the area of a single colony, unit, hive, or such. When we break through to what we think is a little spiritual interaction with a lone unit, we actually

152

are communicating with the vortex of this particular insect.

Some of the obvious benefits of forming a spiritual bond with a particular vortex could be anything from having it remove itself from your home to requesting its aid, using the specialty that a particular vortex has been created to cultivate. But mostly, we relate with a vortex simply for spiritual reasons. When we choose to place our mind into the swirling vortex, or for that matter, into the intelligence of the higher animals, we will have done this to bring peace and tranquility into our lives.

The ideal condition is to strike a balance between mind, body and soul. What is good for one is good for all

By our desire to communicate with all life forms outside of ourselves, we are bringing that perfect spirit and physical balance into play. We will not only be enjoying a loving relationship with nature, but are insuring our physical health.

Just as we can leave fingerprints behind wherever we go, we also leave some of our spiritual essence in these lower kingdoms as we pass through them.

Although we place this essence into everything we touch, from a spoon to a stone, we are better able to witness "this *reflection*" in the things that move or function in some way (i.e. appliances, automobiles, etc.).

There are millions of people that talk to some object when they are trying to convince it to assist them, or they might be thanking it for a job well done.

Whenever we speak of divine love and spiritual communication, we should always remember that this spiritual essence reaches into many deep and mysterious places.

TIME TRAVEL

Whenever anyone becomes interested in the aspects of "Inner Movement" knowledge, one very prime topic is the matter of time travel and if such a thing is actually possible.

First, we must clear our minds and take a whole new look at what we are discussing. We must clarify what we think time travel is.

If we are looking at it in the light as it is presented in the movies or on television, where we can use some machine, adjust a few dials and then take off, flying into the future or the past, then we would have to say this is not practical. It is impractical for many reasons, but the obvious one is that even if we were to travel in such dimensions, we certainly wouldn't need to drag along some bulky machine with us.

The only thing we would need to use would be our soul body, which is comprised of our four vibrating bodies held in our aura. With these bodies, we would be able to not only travel in time, but to check the time on other dimensions as well.

Next, when we think of time travel, if we are thinking that we can adjust or change the future or the past by affecting that time period, the answer would also have to be a definite, no. The belief that someone might be able to travel back in time, carry out some act and then return to find an entirely different world is simply impossible.

And if we wonder if we can find out what is going to definitely happen in the future, the answer is again, no.

Now, with these three fallacies out of the way, we can say that there is such a thing as time travel. Our society is simply unaware of our ability to experience this phenomenon because we are looking at it in the wrong light.

Or to put that statement more accurately, our society is unaware that they do time travel because they don't recognize it for what it is.

We swim in an ocean of time, much like a fish swims in an ocean of water. We are in it - it is in us – and it will be found to completely surround us.

To the analytical mind, time is nothing more than a measured span, which is regulated by the rotation of the Earth in its relationship to the Sun. To this mind there is no such thing as yesterday or tomorrow. There has never been a point where we have been able to say, that right now is yesterday or that right now is tomorrow. We only live in the present, so to this mind, traveling in time is not possible.

All we have ever lived in is now. Jesus walked the Earth now. All of the events of history have happened now. Even the mysterious and powerful civilizations that were said to exist even millions of years ago, existed now.

Well, with this outlook, which most people are unable to view properly, we have actually opened the door to time travel.

As stated earlier, if we desire to perform a certain act, and that act is not within the realm of our physical laws of possibility, all we need to do is adjust our vibration to that particular plane whose laws do correspond to our present needs.

By concentrating on the time track, our vibration will become adjusted to it automatically. Because this time track is located on a higher plane, we will find we are no longer limited by physical laws, but now by the laws of that plane.

Since we have full exposure to the time track, we find we don't have to move the track (since it is always stationed at now), we find we can easily slip into any part of it we desire.

This can be done by performing the white light spiritual exercise. We can perform it much in the same manner as we have the other exercises.

Just as before, picture the flow pouring out from the fingertips and toes and uniting with the white light that will be completely covering us.

When we feel that the flow has completely saturated our atomic vibration, we will move our consciousness to the blank screen of the inner mind.

If you are able to control the mind to the point that you can keep it blank, that is ideal. However, if this turns out to not be the case, you should try to form an image of the time track.

To the physical consciousness, the time track looks like some kind of long round tube that stretches out into infinity.

All of the tube to the left will be vibrating with endless brilliant and beautiful colors. Meanwhile, the tube to the right will seem to be sort of grayish with no flashing colors. There is also something moving slowly along this tube that looks very much like a giant black dot.

The beautiful colors to the left represent what the "probable future" will hold. These colors are constantly flickering and changing. There is no such thing as a "definite future", so we are watching the future change.

The very fact they are flickering is due to the constant changes being fed into them, caused by the choices and actions we carry out on a moment to moment basis. What we may consider to be some minor act, could create a major change in our future.

Where you will be twenty years from now and what you will be doing then, could change so drastically that what your future may have been just this morning, could turn out to be entirely different by evening.

Even if this may sound far fetched, you should understand that every action and every thought will have a reaction, and with each of these actions and thoughts, our life will be changed. This is why you could never know a definite future.

The tube to the right, which is grayish and has no movement, is the past. There is no flickering and brilliant color dancing, because these things have been solidified. These events are now frozen in time. They are no longer a probable future, but now belong to the realm of definite fact.

That which you see as the black dot is the eternal now. As it moves along the tube, a metamorphous is seen to occur below it. The bright colors enter from the front and then as they leave, they seem to be little more than a dead substance.

What had been pictures of the future are now pictures of the past, and will continue to play throughout the balance of eternity.

As we view this time tube from our position near or over the black dot, we can either choose to see the pictures to the right or to the left.

If we move to the right, we can see the very accurate account of what really happened in history.

The traveling soul can read these pictures in one of two ways. First, would be the fast display of events which would be similar to watching television.

Second, would be the "emergence technique", where we are right in the center of everything. If we would happen to be visiting a battle site, we could hear and see the clashing of metal swords against shields and we might even become terrified to be directly in the path of a charging chariot – then to only see it pass right through us.

The timid should never place themselves in a battle unless they are looking for a great deal of excitement. It will appear to be just as real to you as everyday life.

It is for this reason the reader will be shown the events first, so he can more carefully decide where to investigate.

Traveling to the left though, will be found to be a little different. Events are not quite so realistic, since they barely have a life of their own, due to the fact that nothing has been solidified. There are no solid lines as far as fact versus fiction goes. What you may see could be a fact. It could be exactly what is going to happen just a little further down the trail or the whole thing could be blown away like a puff of smoke in just a few hours.

This is also another good reason why we must always be thinking about the "law of karma". We know that every action must have an equal and opposite reaction, and if we are going to so easily keep changing what our future is going to be, then we must make every attempt at insuring that these changes are always going to be for the good.

Another form of time travel most of us use on a daily basis is spiritual time travel.

Every dimension has its own time. When we leave one world and enter into the next, we will definitely be crossing from one time to another.

157

To show a good example of this we don't need to go any further than to the astral. The time in the astral is nothing like our time. A period of time that may seem like two weeks there could be a hundred years in the physical – or even vice versa.

This also shows how we can have a long and informative dream that may have seemed to last a long time but when we awaken, we find we may have been asleep only a couple of minutes.

Time travel is not difficult to perform, nor is it weird or strange.

It is something we do sometimes in the day while we are daydreaming and it is something we do every night while asleep.

THE DREAM INITIATION

Perhaps the most erroneous idea in this world, is that we must belong to some particular religion, institution or spiritual group in order to progress or to get a spiritual foothold in the higher worlds.

Nothing could be further from the truth.

We already belong to a brotherhood society far superior to anything created in this Earth world.

To be more clear, it is really the higher self, the over soul, that belongs to this most wonderful and dazzling society. But since each of us is a part of the higher self, we are able to receive most of the blessings that are endowed upon the higher self, having them passed directly to us, instead of them being "filed" and kept at the monad level.

This society (for lack of a better name) is a celestial linking of all units (or monads) that have emerged from the twelfth plane.

Just as we receive our spiritual strength from this higher self, It gathers its strength from this linking which is sustained purely from the flow of spirit. It keeps all of the parts of the body of God in direct communication and assistance with one another.

In this active linkage, we are able to see some of its activities on a daily basis, provided we pay attention.

In the very minor experiences, we may get a hunch or some great idea that may help us in our financial or spiritual difficulties. Or we might develop some sort of craving, which is our body, with the assistance of this energy, telling us that we need to correct some health problem.

The list can go on and on and we would still never comprehend the magnitude of it, because we are so much a part of it.

The thing we are most interested in now though, is how It assists us as individuals and, not just the monad.

One of the teachings in the ancient schools was that man can, not only advance into the higher worlds while he is still in this school, in a physical body, but that it is *expected* of him to do so.

This society, this link, is always very aware of our intentions, our capabilities and what we will do if we are given a chance.

We were not necessarily sent into this world to experience each spoke of the wheel of life as some religions teach.

If we are sincere and attentive, such a delay would be a total waste of talent. Our schooling system was created only to teach. Would we leave a very advanced student, perhaps one that could function at a high school level, in the first grade simply because he hasn't taken each step that the system has provided? I think not. So, why should we do so at this much more elevated status of "God trainee"?

Putting our trust, our actions and our promotions into the care of spirit, we will find we move rapidly up the scale in spiritual rank, and may very well find we never need to return to this school. We may not even need to spend any considerable time on any of the other planes below the true God worlds.

We become aware of our advancement during our dreaming state.

Over the years, you might remember some particular dream where everything seemed to be so beautiful and wonderful. Even after you awoke, you could remember the wonderful feeling that you had and you could still feel it in your heart. It was so moving you may have even told others about it.

This is what is known as receiving an initiation in the dream state. Such a dream is a sign of spiritual elevation on your part. This spiritual society has endowed you with greater concepts, broader awareness, and grander abilities than you previously had.

These initiations can take on many different forms. The surroundings can change. The ceremony can change. Your state of mind will definitely change.

Because the dreaming consciousness is very flexible, the changeover will be so smooth that upon awakening, you may be sad to think that this wonderful experience was only a part of your dream.

The initiation usually occurs after midnight but before two a.m. This is most likely due to the magnetic enhancement allowing the two planes to have a better link (remember the lesson on forces acting upon other forces), than at other times of the night.

During these initiations, people have said they experienced being on top of a majestic mountain, where distant celestial music could be heard. They saw and became part of an incredible sunset while a host of loved ones and angelic beings looked on in reverence and great joy.

Others have said they seemed to be in a gigantic amphitheater, being honored as if they were a king or queen. Tears of joy could be seen everywhere while they received a robe of velvet and gold.

Some have experienced the initiations in gardens, on beaches, in temples and even on other planes where they seemed to be encased in a myriad of gorgeous colors.

Regardless of the manner in which an initiation is given, there will be three components easily recognized in these initiations – sight, sound and feeling. When these three seem more magnified than a regular dream, you have undoubtedly received an Initiation.

The sights are always brighter and more colorful. The music you hear will seem sublime, coming directly from the music of the spheres. And the feelings that pour forth from the heart region will soar you to spiritual heights.

At the conclusion of an initiation, the dreamer is usually so elated that he will wake up. There are two reasons for this. First, the heart beat has increased, drawing the soul back to the body and second, so the soul will be able to remember as much as possible of the event, which might become lost to the physical consciousness without a dream break.

If you take a moment to look back, you will undoubtedly remember some such Initiation. It is nothing new. It has been going on for millions of years, and you have been a part of it ever since you began this journey.

You can now understand what you were experiencing and more important, you can now recognize and understand what is happening when you experience it again!

Perhaps this study may even aid you to accelerate your next initiation. Your vibration has already been increased due to the consciousness expansion that has come through your comprehension of the grander concepts of the cosmic, and through your ability to know what you really are.

Once the exercises presented are put into action, the atomic vibration will elevate you to such high states, that you will find great changes coming to you, to those around you, and to your surroundings as well.

If Jesus were to walk in this world today with the divine spiritual energy and vibration He would emit, what kind of miracles do you think He could do on a daily basis?

Well, this is the same power and ability in your hands right now!

Use it well. Use it wisely. And walk with the Gods!

CHAPTER SEVEN:

MOST ASKED QUESTIONS

In February of 1991 an international experiment was begun to gather the documented results of individuals interested in taking part in the spiritual meditations presented here. Although it was felt many would have some results, the response of reported miracles was overwhelming. It was not only the number of miracles, but the magnitude of these blessings, that caused the door to a whole new understanding of life to be open.

The response was so great that the experiment was expanded into a monthly discourse where we could learn more about the true nature of spirit; how to master the forces that surround us; and how to share our blessings with the world.

This study, called Pealer Group, placed ads in *Fate* magazine and grew to a membership that included seven countries. It then endeavored to learn more about the many levels of humanity. It was soon realized that it was not enough to simply look at ourselves as mere humans any longer.

It was not enough, any longer to go by a code of understanding laid out for us by those who were either attempting to control us, or knew very little about the true teachings that had survived for thousands of years.

Presented here, are some of the most asked questions coming from these seven different cultures, which were answered through spiritual intervention – by our being able to function in (and draw wisdom from) planes existing beyond our Earth world.

Q: Do we still eat food in the Astral world?

While we are in a physical body, we supposedly eat primarily to keep the body alive. The bodies we use in other worlds get their life directly from spirit. However, I think most people will agree one of the primary reasons we eat is because we enjoy it. If that were not so, we wouldn't be interested in having such a great variety of foods in our diet. So, eating is also a pleasure - and pleasure is what the astral is all about.

So, yes. Not only will we find that we eat while in the astral, but we find that food there is far more delicious than even in this world.

Also, not only is there an abundance of food, but we can have anything we desire. Those loves and attractions we developed on Earth are more often than not, carried over with us when we leave. Whatever pleases us here, will be permitted to please us there.

As the soul slowly evolves into the higher vibrating worlds, certain desires will cease to exist. But as long as there are some desires within the soul's makeup, it will continue to share in these joys.

Q: If you are married in this world, are you still married after you die? And what if a mate dies and you marry again? Which one would you be married to in the next world?

Such things are not even considered in the astral. First, let's take a look at it in a much broader view. We know we are not a complete soul, that we are only half a soul. We were divided into two (or more) separate divisions at the Fifth plane, before we were permitted to enter into the lower vibrating worlds. Each of these divisions are called Biocentrics. Each of these Biocentrics may draw to themselves all they may have ever loved. That's what spiritual development is all about – love, not jealousy. There is no personal greed and a need to "own" another. Instead, all will find they share in a grand and wonderful spiritual love. When the two Biocentrics (the male and the female) of a particular soul come together, they will undoubtedly find they are very closely tied to many other "Reunited" souls that they loved and cared about while on Earth.

In the higher worlds, when the soul is reunited, it is no longer two different souls, but one grander soul. To love the Biocentric of any particular soul, is to love that whole and complete soul. An example of this would be an out take from the book *The Occult Life of Jesus* written by Rev. Alexander Smyth in the 1800s and published by the Progressive Thinking Publishing Company. In that account, he related how Jesus so greatly loved the youngest daughter of Lazarus, that he almost gave up his teaching to be with her. While religious accounts do not give the complete story of their love, it was said to be such a burning passion it could be called one of the greatest love stories ever told (or untold). But Smyth carried the account even deeper. He actually told about their love in the other worlds. This information was made available to him through astral records.

He also explained that when she was reunited with her Biocentric, becoming the complete soul that she had previous been before her journey into the lower worlds, Jesus was elated. The love the two of them shared was not limited to only their personal experience, but was expanded to engulf the two souls completely.

Q: Is there still sex after you die?

The answer is a definite, yes! Actually, sex belongs to the astral. It is a bi-product created from the vibrations of that plane. Our understanding of it (or enjoyment of it) can only take place after it is filtered through the physical realm and then through the bulky physical brain. That means we are receiving only a small portion and a limited enjoyment of the actual act. It is like trying to collect rainwater dripping through the ceiling for drinking water. Not only do the droplets pick up dust particles as they fall to Earth, but then become contaminated as they slide down the roof and through a bacterial infested hole. Hardly the pure element it started out.

When the physical body heaves in pleasure and the brain is filled with ecstatic explosion, what we are experiencing is a "limited" astral vibration passing through us.

Many people that have had a real out-of-the-body experience said it was like having sex – only better! In the astral, it is a pure and spiritual experience.

Q: Where do we live when we leave this world? Do we have homes we can go to?

Yes, most definitely. Would you desire to live in a palace? Or would you prefer to live in a humble abode in a forest setting? Perhaps you might even desire to have a classy retreat alongside a sandy beach by a magnificent astral ocean. Or you may decide to have your home in one of a million other ways.

Whatever you can conceive and desire, will be yours. Usually, it's not even necessary to ask for it. Spirit already knows what pleases you the most, and will furnish these things during your stay (vacation?) in the astral. However, it is your privilege to receive something else, other than provided, if you so chose. I have even heard of a sea captain that only wanted to return to the sea. For him, a ship was provided (similar to his physical one – because that was what he wanted) and he spent his time there sailing on a fantastic astral sea.

Q: When in the astral, do we work? Do we have jobs?

Not in the same sense as you think of work in the physical. You do not get up and go to a job where you toil at something that doesn't please you, just so you can get money to pay your rent. There are no obligations laid on you there, such as you find on the Earth world.

Instead, you are either relaxing or being shown the miracles and wonders of spirit. Even your lessons are wonderful, fun experiences.

When the time does come for you to move on into the higher vibrating worlds where you will receive a job to do, even that could hardly be considered a job because it will be something pleasing and exciting to you.

Q: Using the powers of spirit that come to us when we become Co-workers, can I make my life better by drawing money to myself?

There are ways to draw money, but we must always remember that everything in this world is based on balance. For every action that we take, there will be an opposite and equal "reaction." If we want to receive extra money (money other than what you will normally receive), we must understand it is the same as taking out a loan.

You should realize you will probably have to pay it back, and sometimes even with a little interest. That should not be scary though, since it is spirit we are dealing with, and not some loan shark.

That also does not mean the payback has to be monetary. It could be through giving aid and assistance to others, when the opportunity arises. What we are drawing money from is our cosmic bank account.

There is nothing wrong or evil in performing a ceremony to bring money to ourselves. In reality, it is nothing more than contacting proper channels to draw money already available in our account – or to apply for a loan.

So, that means that sometimes it isn't even necessary to pay it back. It all depends on how much you wish to draw and how much you have available. A person that does some good everyday could be a very wealthy person in his available funds.

As far as the amount of interest you will need to pay (assuming your needs may outweigh your balance), that is determined by what is in your heart. If the money is used for physical needs (medical, debts or to help others), the rate is minimal. For the frivolous, it may be slightly higher, but still be in the bounds of reasonable acceptance.

The ceremony to receive money is the "green power light".

Take a position similar to a "white light ceremony" except the power light will now be green.

Picture it flowing down into the top of your head and completely filling your body. Then, picture the green energy flowing out of the fingertips and toes, joining the entire green light you see yourself bathed in.

Performing the ceremony while totally nude will not only enhance the flow, but bring a tremendous sensuous message to the subconscious, whereby It will open many doors to levels of power that the physical consciousness seldom has access.

This is also the secret to "sex magic".

Sex is not only one of the most powerful forces in this world, but is the most powerful force known.

When you can feel the wonderful drunk-like effect that will come, place the image of money (or the things you want to do with this money) on the inner screen of your mind.

If you want a certain amount, to pay off some very definite balances, then picture that amount in your imagination. If you should need twenty four thousand dollars, picture a large sum of bills spread out on a table before you, with a sign above it that says twenty-four thousand dollars.

If you want a new car, picture that car. Not some vague picture of any car, but a very clear picture of one particular kind you want.

If you want to travel around the world, then see yourself, or you and your mate, on a ship or in an airplane, completing this dream. See the Alps. See Rome. See London. See the things you are intending to visit.

Let the subconscious know exactly what you want. It is through the subconscious that the loan application will be presented to the higher self, which is the keeper of the cosmic bank.

The subconscious is very literal. If you should simply ask for a new car, It could interpret that to mean only a car that is new to you. You could end up with a piece of junk coming your way, and we certainly don't want to waste any of the money we have in our account for something like that.

This is the reason some people came to the conclusion that performing magic was evil. They would ask for something and it would come true, but not in a way they expected.

There was nothing evil in what they were doing. It was their right to do it. But the fault was with themselves (and not some prankster devil), because they simply could not form a clear picture of what they wanted.

The subconscious is not out to trick you. It is totally incapable of carrying out any such intentions or jokes. It is very explicit because it is trying to please you.

Neither the subconscious nor the higher self will question your judgment on anything. They are only geared to carry through on your requests, provided such requests are not detrimental to you, or to anyone else. And provided it doesn't create an awesome debt to be repaid.

With this in mind, you should not be too concerned if such a loan application is (for the time being) turned down.

Q: How can I cast a spell to make someone love me or do what I want?

You Can't! You must never, never, try to control the actions or mind of another. Not only is there a terrible retribution that must be paid for such actions, but also any such request would be denied.

Just as we have constitutional rights, there is also a code of spiritual laws that regard our rights while we are attending this school. At the top of that list of rights is our right to freedom of choice.

This is the primary purpose of this school. We have been sent to it to learn to regulate and control ourselves. It will never be the privilege of another to use us as a puppet in any way.

Q: Why do bad things happen to good people?
This is one of the most asked questions and probably one of the easiest to answer.

We always underestimate the power of our minds. Each and every one of us can send out forces that have the power to build a Rome – or to destroy one. Then, when a large number of people all start to concentrate on a singular thing, this force will continue to grow to unbelievable heights.

As far as the disasters among the famous, this is caused by too many people all concentrating on something detrimental to them. When the public becomes involved in some story about a famous person (such as might be dramatized by a tabloid), it will affect that person. This is why we hear so much about their being drunkards, drug addicts and the such. They simply cannot handle the endless bombardment of vibrations, and often even think they are going insane.

For those who are not in the public eye, but still experience some bad things in their life, it is simply because they are breaking some spiritual law.

These spiritual laws aren't just random rules passed down from God, but are the natural rules that govern this physical plane. However, we will find we are able to dissolve some of this karma into the white light when we practice a spiritual exercise.

But, that in no way gives us atonement. Instead of washing away the karma, we are elevating ourselves, which will elevate our goals, achievements and ideals.

We should always approach a spiritual exercise, or ceremony, in an attitude of reverence. If we think we can use it only as a means of escape from responsibility, we would be acting as if to say God will pay the debt. We must never try to pass the buck or attempt to let another pay for our debts. We must always try to act as the Little Gods we are.

Q: Since even the Creator (at the Fifth plane) came from a Higher Source (the twelfth plane), is it possible there is anything beyond the twelfth plane?

To those of us in the physical world, spiritual knowledge seems to be an enigma. In our world everything is either black or white. Something is either a fact or it is not a fact. This is not the case when it comes to the higher worlds.

The teachers of the ancient mystery schools often referred to the knowledge that comes from the true God worlds as being similar to a double-edged sword. All of the things we learn as the sword swings forward, can easily be contradicted, as the sword swings back again. That is not to say that either of the lessons are false, but that at the same time both can be true.

When we operate in dimensions beyond time and space and in places that do not have to answer to the logical laws we understand, we can become very easily confused, trying to measure infinite knowledge with a limited and finite brain.

It is true that the twelfth plane is the highest that soul could ever hope to reach, being the source of all that we know, but it is also true that there are planes beyond the twelfth.

The actual teaching of the ancient schools said that soul was created so God, the Holy Essence, could "mirror" Itself, to better understand what It was.

To manifest this mirror so that it would give a proper reflection, It needed to give the full powers of God to these reflections.

Once this was done, the Holy Essence discovered It still could not comprehend what It was, because every time the soul would evolve, so would the Holy Essence. No matter how close the soul would come to the perfection of God, this God would be evolved even of Itself unto a next higher step.

As the souls finally were able to return to their home at the twelfth plane, God discovered that It had evolved to another whole plane previously unknown. Then as these souls would attempt to follow the Holy Essence into yet newly created dimensions, they discovered that even they were not what they had previously been. These great ones would become greater and greater and with each advancement – God would become even more.

So, it is true that the twelfth plane is the home of God, and that it is the highest state that soul will reach – unless it chooses to become more than a soul! While we can become what God was, we can never become what God is!

Q: Where is Jesus? Can we use a spiritual exercise to meet with Him?

All Saviors, regardless of religion, are more or less tied to the lower worlds. This is because if they chose to advance on to the higher planes, they would be moving beyond the range of assistance they could offer to their followers.

There is really no point in debating that statement, because that teaching is already older than any known religion we have. So, while they are doing us a favor by sticking around, we are certainly doing no favors for them by constantly begging for something, acting like little children.

All heavens do exist and they are located in the upper part of the fourth plane. We, as individuals, have extremely easy access to these heavens. Purely through our dedication and love, these gates have swung open wide. We don't even need to die to journey to them.

This can cause some obvious lower world situations and problems for those who are still in service to their followers – such as Jesus. If Jesus made Himself literally available in the form of the man that He represents to us, He would be forever receiving visitors. It wouldn't make any difference how dedicated these followers were, there would be virtually no end to still another demand made upon Him.

So we offer our love to Jesus (or other savant or savior) in the name of the Holy Spirit. It is in this manner that He, or they, can always be with us.

Q: How can I know that God really understands my needs? How can I overcome this dreadful feeling of emptiness, never knowing if I am attuned to God?

Although we speak of heaven being located on the fourth plane, we should never forget that the kingdom of heaven exists also inside each of us. The spiritual masters teach that the path lies within you, in the depths of your consciousness. You will find it nowhere but within you.

When we make complete contact with spirit, all our needs are met on all planes and we only need to be aware that this is so.

It is taught that it is God's desire for us to have whatever may be in our hearts. This comes not as a reward, but due to the fact we can realize our contact with God.

When we engage in a white light or a blue light ceremony, we will create a flow we can strongly feel. We are never cut off from God or from spirit. Sometimes spirit may act like a mother standing nearby, just out of sight, so that we can develop self-confidence, but it is still watching out for us.

No matter how difficult things may appear to the physical consciousness, we will discover that somehow, we always land on our feet.

Never permit yourself to become doubtful or negative to surrounding conditions. Always keep a happy and joyful attitude regardless of appearances - and you will soon discover you have a great deal to be joyful about.

Q: Every country, especially those in Europe, have stories about or a belief in "Little People". Why is there such a widespread belief in such beings? Does the physical plane have subdivisions that we are just not aware of?

Those, which are called gnomes, leprechauns, trolls, etc., do not exist as they are presented in children's stories, however there are "nature spirits".

Nature spirits serve as links between spirit and the regulation of nature. They will assist, correct or bring a balance back to those things that have been destroyed, usually due to some action carried out by an unwitting human society.

The majority of humans will never see nature spirits for a variety of reasons, but the most obvious is that these spirits operate from the lower levels of the astral, meaning they really do not belong to the physical.

It is usually only those who are Coworkers, who become aware of their presence at any given time.

Those interested in making friends with a nature spirit, can practice a combination of the white light and green light ceremonies.

For this exercise, leave the home. Go out into the woods or at least to some secluded spot where there is either no one around, or where the presence of people is scarce.

Take a comfortable position under a tree, next to some pond, or someplace that greatly impresses you.

First, perform the white light ceremony, permitting it to enter through the top of the head, fill the body and then saturate your aura with its divine light.

After a few minutes have passed and you feel the vibration building within you, do the exercise again. Only this time, use the green light. Perform it in the very same manner that you performed the other.

With the combination, you will probably become surprised at how easily the mind will be calmed, which opens the door for these nature spirits to make contact with you. Since they come only to those who they feel they can trust, you will have established a channel between yourself and them.

At first, these intelligent forces may be drawn to you purely out of curiosity.

Since you will have tapped into their main source, the source that not only gives them life – but through which they communicate, they may very well believe that a divine being has come to commune with them.

After you have permitted the green light to flow through you for a few minutes, simply continue to sit there, moving as little as possible and watch for what messages may come to your inner mind.

It is not necessary to open the eyes because nature spirits, except for very rare occasions, never appear to the physical consciousness through the eyes.

Once you are able to feel a calm and loving presence, either watch to see what kind of impressions you may receive, or you could offer some information to them.

If you were to simply offer your love and blessings, they would quickly realize that you are a Coworker with God, and would be quite eager to establish a bond that could last for the rest of your life.

The fantastic and mysterious magical results that pagans have been able to demonstrate was due to this very secret.

The next life form down are called the elementals. There have been many children's stories written about them also.

They are neither as intelligent nor as dedicated as the nature spirits, but there are some people that like to make contact with them simply because they are very playful and quite funny.

In some stories they have been presented as devilish forces or naughty spirits, but this is also quite mistaken. They could be compared more to an otter. Their entire life seems to be one of gayety and joy as spirit passes through them, to carry out the most basic of Earth's needs. They are able to be used by spirit to spread spiritual essence, much in the same way a bee unwittingly aids nature by spreading pollen.

In the spiritual exercises, contacting the elementals is probably the lowest and the least beneficial of all. Seekers are not encouraged to do this exercise simply because the time could be better spent by contacting a more elevating source. However, to do it just to compare it with the other exercises can be very educational.

For this, you would use the white light ceremony. After the flow has started, simply chant the name "elementals". This would be broken down as el-e-men-tals.

Again, while this exercise has little redeeming factor, it is highly encouraged that you do perform the previous exercise of nature spirit contact. Although the elementals are unable to offer anything, the nature spirits can open many mysterious and powerful worlds for you.

Q: If one does Inner Movement (or astral projection), could they spy on someone?

No! When one is prepared to leave the body, it is a religious thing.

To leave the body means we have committed ourselves to divine spirit. We are agreeing to work with it and perform whatever duties It may desire of us, for which we shall be spiritually rewarded. There is no room for any evil intent during this most holy time.

In addition, there are very strict cosmic laws in place that are intended to protect all people of this world and to guarantee their right to privacy is insured.

A person that might be bathing or dressing could never be spied on by some invisible visitor. In fact, the laws are so strict that if a person who was extremely adept at leaving the body should attempt an invasion of privacy, he would be stripped of his ability.

It is true that some governments have engaged in secret projects to do just this, by trying to spy on certain people (either their own or people from another country) in the name of national security, but all such projects have been met only with disaster and failure.

Spirit is never swayed by any form of justification. Spirit sees things on a much grander scale. What we may think is a good cause, could be just another way to invade the rights and privileges of another.

This is another reason the spiritual exercises are so very important to us. Since it is a law of spirit that nothing can come to us unless we give our permission, that would also include the blessings of spirit. We must open ourselves and give our permission for spirit to fill our lives.

For this reason we should perform the exercise of volunteer dream travel in the evenings as we prepare to sleep.

Q: What is the Akashic Hall of Memories? Is this anything like the "Day of Judgment"?

First of all, a very important point that needs to be made here is that there is no such thing as a Day of Judgment.

It's important for you to understand this was a creation from sick (but clever) minds to control you. You have undoubtedly been told you would need to stand before some great and majestic court where you would have to answer to God for all of your acts. Balderdash!

Your akashic records are for no one but yourself. No one will ever see them except you.

This teaching is another example of the Dragons of Knowledge (erroneous teachings) that are so much a part of our daily lives. The purpose of the akashic records is only so you can get a full perspective of the many lives that you have lived, what you accomplished in them, and how that may be applied to your present lessons.

One of the ancient laws is that our personal space is a private and sacred thing. There are strict cosmic rules in place to insure our right to develop at our own particular pace, without any outside interference or without it being anyone else's business.

Now, all of a sudden, why would it be everybody's business? It's not.

There is never any need to be embarrassed at the place called The Hall of Records. To your consciousness it will seem pretty much like you are in your own small, private booth.

You can see all life that has already passed, a part of it, highlights from previous incarnations that have an affect on your present life, or even get a slight glimpse of what the future "might" hold for you.

All of this is only for you. The only time anyone else might be able to see even a little of this record, would be if and when you gave your explicit permission. Even then though, maybe very little or possibly nothing at all would be revealed to the researcher. This is why it is so difficult to get someone to do a reading for us while we are still in the physical world.

The Hall of Records is located in the astral at the capital city known as "the city of a thousand names". Endless cultures that make contact with it all seem to give it a different name. The most widely accepted name by the spiritual teachers is Aga De, "Place of the Sacred Spirit".

Q: Is Inner Journeying a Christian Teaching?

That which we call Inner Journeying has never been a mystery to the Christian religion. It has been demonstrated and revered over and over again throughout the Bible.

Revelations is exclusively about spiritual journeying. Without the ability of inner movement, we would have never received any information about anything that exists outside of our mundane world.

St. Francis Xavier, a Jesuit Saint, was responsible for spreading Christianity throughout the Far East, and not only practiced spiritual journeying, but taught others of it. St. Anthony of Padua, a Franciscan monk and his close contemporary St. Francis of Assisi, both spoke of it and were noted for taking journeys together.

There are also many Abbots, Clergy and at least one Pope that have openly displayed their abilities to perform spiritual movement.

Q: What is the difference between a ghost, a phantom and a poltergeist?

Actually, all three are very different. First, a ghost can be considered to be an entity, or just an etheric reflection.

If it's an entity, it will be a fairly new disturbance to a surrounding and is one that won't last very long. Regardless of what we may think about ghosts, it is just not possible for them to hang around. They no longer are operating at this vibration and it is highly unlikely they will desire to stay – once they can comprehend the higher planes.

The ghost is usually trying to console a loved one, or maybe trying to give a special message. There is nothing scary or malicious about their intent. Their mission is one of peace and love. There is certainly nothing to fear. Our fears probably stem from stories or movies we have grown up with.

Three important things to remember about what we call a ghost is that first, spirit does not want our lessons to be interrupted by any outside forces. Second, since the departed no longer needs his physical abilities, having left this vibration, he is not permitted to venture here without your permission. And third, the most interesting thing of all, is that if you loved them while they were in a physical body, why in the world would you be afraid of them now.

Unfortunately, we have a primitive and superstitious attitude when it comes to spiritual matters. If your mother loved and protected you while she was alive on this world, do you really believe she would desire to scare, tease and torment you now?

The other form of ghost is really only a picture that was captured by the etheric and played over and over again for all eternity. This too, can bring you no harm, except the harm you may do to yourself while trying to run away. Anyone that may have tripped and fell, or broke an arm or a leg, would probably feel very foolish to find they were only running away from a movie.

A phantom is also no way as scary as it sounds. Phantoms bring miracles and messages. In fact, that would be a better name for them: messenger. Angels are an example of a phantom and everyone loves and adores angels.

A phantom can be hazy due to the great space that might exist between its cosmic atoms or it can become very solid, depending on what is needed to carry out the particular duty they are now engaged in.

It has also been discovered if you should be blessed by having one touch you, your health can become greatly improved.

Last, the poltergeist is probably the most misunderstood force of all.

Contrary to what you have seen in movies and on television, a poltergeist has no intelligence, no anger, no evil intent and no score to settle with anyone.

What we call a poltergeist is really only unbridled energy created from accumulated sexual energy and is being released in much the same way that a safcty valve works on some hot furnace.

Until fairly recent times, there wasn't even a serious interest in the poltergeist, believing it was only a prank.

Over the centuries, whenever there was a report of objects being thrown around a room, it always seemed there was at least one child in the room when it occurred. But, to make the matter worse, when there were reports of a poltergeist operating in two rooms, there were usually two teenagers in attendance. Not only the law, but the church, believed these children were responsible.

The strange thing is that they were responsible, but not in the way the church and the others believed.

When a child enters into the stage of puberty, that child not only suffers from the very obvious physical changes taking place, but also from mental changes that have suddenly invaded their world of innocence.

Their aura becomes saturated with energies totally confusing to the teen, and they develop a shield completely covering them – which is known to have incredible forces therein contained.

The child not only has no control over the forces emitted from this shield, but the child himself, will become terrified by the results of this force.

Sexual energy is the most powerful force known in the physical world. While other forces, considered powerful, may seem to be able to do far more damage, sexual energy is the basic building stone of creation. Therefore, it will be this energy that creates a clashing of emotions and electromagnetic energy that causes otherwise stationary objects to take flight.

As said, it has been television and movies that gave the misconception of what poltergeist means, but they could hardly expect to make all the millions they feel they should with a title like, "Electricity / The Legend Continues".

Q: You hear a great deal about Magic. Are there Magic Words, Magic crystals, and so forth?

Magic is one of the oldest of all religions. In fact, even in the most primitive of cultures, you will find magic plays a large part in not only their basic beliefs, but in the activities of their daily life.

The definition of magic is that it is the use of a technique presumably assuring human control over supernatural powers, where that individual can exhibit extraordinary or mystical influence. To break that down into a more common understanding, so we can see how to develop these powers and skills for ourselves, we need to return to our old friend, vibration.

The major theme of this lesson is that everything vibrates, so all we need do is adjust our own vibration to match that which we desire to achieve.

Once we find we have made such a contact and are able to demonstrate it, we will be able to attract these forces, manifesting them into physical awareness. To those functioning on a single

181

plane of awareness, they will see the spiritual forces we have drawn and in their superstitious ignorance, call it magic.

Yes, there are magic words, crystals, ceremonies, etc., due to the fact they can bring some obvious changes into our very limited, everyday awareness.

Just as colors have very definite vibration ranges, they are also able to demonstrate magical abilities, bringing about certain results, such as demonstrated in the light ceremonies.

Words also carry a very dramatic and tremendous influence on our physical awareness.

Outside of the obvious results that the use of proper words can bring, we should realize that words are sounds. And sounds are the most powerful of all magical components.

Abracadabra is a good example. Many centuries ago it was used in certain ceremonies, because it offered a good, smooth sound and it attracted results from its vibration that could be physically seen.

As the years passed though, it became overused and lost its position of any longer being considered a sacred word. It is for this reason that most practitioners are not too obvious about the sounds or words they will use in a magical ceremony. It is felt if these words should enter into the mainstream of everyday life, they might lose their powers.

While these words or sounds cannot possibly lose their vibration, it is true that overuse will cause it to become less effective. It is for this reason when you practice a spiritual exercise and you choose to use a personal power word, you should keep it to yourself unless it's a commonly taught word, such as those used to attune yourself to particular planes.

The next question might be how each of us might find our own personal power word. Actually, it can be quite a simple matter. Since all words have vibrations, it doesn't matter which word or sound we choose. Regardless of what that word may be, it will offer a certain vibration pitch and if upon practicing a spiritual exercise, you find you are achieving greater results with one word over others, than you should stick with it. These words could come from any source. You might choose to pick one from the Bible or other religious scriptures. You might even choose a certain musical name, as long as it isn't in common use.

As for other magical things, crystals are known to carry an extremely high pitch or vibration, and so do certain shapes.

In our study and examination of crystals, it has become quite obvious they all have their own particular range of vibration activity. It has also become obvious that these vibrations will affect us if we choose to carry some sort of crystal around with us.

As for magical shapes, the pyramid is the front runner. It is known to take spiritual energy and transform it into many practical physical uses.

It was by no accident that the ancient Egyptians adopted the shape of the pyramid to honor and preserve their Pharaohs.

When we take into consideration the positioning of the pyramids, along with the strange and mysterious inner tunnels, an immediate assumption is that the Egyptians were not alone in this design and planning. It has been discovered that the pyramid offers an extremely high vibration, that can be targeted using high tech equipment. Many scientists have suggested that the pyramids are serving as some kind of cosmic lighthouse.

Q: Why don't Miracles, like in the Bible, happen anymore? It is actually very surprising how common a question that is, especially when we take into consideration that more miracles are happening now than ever before in the history of the world!

First of all, we must determine the magnitude we are looking for before we can classify something as being a miracle.

We know that Jesus, as well as many others of His time, had the ability to call upon certain vibrations, bringing them to the attention of the people. But, we must never forget that even the most insignificant of things happening around us, should also be classified as being a miracle.

When we take a moment and think about it, we are faced with two modern day problems in trying to detect miracles. First of all, if something isn't earth shattering, making the evening news, then we fail to even notice it. Second, when these miracles are produced by some holy man, we are quick to condemn him, calling him a fake and a fraud. Also, when we add to this the fact that we have entered into a highly evolved society, where we see quite impossible things being done by magicians on television, we lose much of our sensitivity in being able to appreciate miracles coming to us every day.

A miracle doesn't have to be something that is going to change our lives forever, for us to appreciate it. More often than not, all of us have had some form of miracle in just this week alone coming to us. All we need do is open our eyes and pay attention to our surroundings to see what might be happening.

One of the greatest of miracles this ministry has taught its members, is to watch for the Blessing of the Lights, but this is only one of five ways for us to detect that a miracle has occurred.

Take a moment, and see how many miracles or possible miracles, have taken place in just the last few months.

Miracles are often classified as being good things happening, having an unexpected turn of events, having something bad removed from your life, an improvement in health for you or your loved ones, and the list can go on and on. You only need to make yourself aware of what you have already received and show your appreciation – and your cup can be filled again.

As stated, there are five ways for the physical consciousness to detect the presence of a blessing. They are by Sight, Sound, Smell, Touch and Vortex.

In Sight, you see the white or colored lights that often visit when you are at rest or watching television. If you are at all attentive, you will find that almost on a daily basis, you will be able to detect a light in the corner of your eye. When I was taught about the visiting lights, I was told to never look directly at them because they will vanish. It seems that the human eye was not created for looking directly at something spiritual. The masters aren't saying the blessing goes away, they are just saying you will lose your physical awareness of the presence.

By Sound, reference is being made to how we can measure our spiritual development by what sound we hear during a spiritual exercise. These sounds will usually manifest during contemplation or meditation, and can range from anything from the sound of birds singing to the sound of a waterfall.

The blessing of Smell is well known, especially in the Christian religion. Many associate certain Saints with a particular aroma. When we receive this type of blessing, we usually feel pretty good from the aroma, but we may pass it off as something physical and unfortunately, simply dismiss it from our consciousness. Just as with the lights, we should not be too quick to think that it's nothing and then forget about it. The rule of thumb is if you are not sure if what you experienced is real, you should accept it as being the real thing. This, because spirit is in everything.

Touch is very often used to drive the fact of a miracle home. It is also a very effective way of removing undesired karma energy from our aura.

It will usually come from a spiritual encounter between us and a secret master where he elevates our vibration. It can also come from one of the Coworkers with God, such as yourself. Spirit may bring blessings to us through touch or it can just as easily use us to pass a blessing on to another.

When the blessing of touch occurs, it is a sign of a new birth in your life.

The last of the five, Vortex, usually affects the equilibrium. You may feel a little dizzy for no apparent reason, but it never lasts long enough to be frightening. Plus, it usually leaves a feeling of well being.

The reason for an unbalancing of the equilibrium is that your low rate of vibration is receiving energy from a higher vibration. This process never takes more than a second or two though.

Miracles and contacts are a part of our daily lives. All you need do is look. Never forget if something could have been a miracle or a contact – then it probably was. Give thanks. Show your appreciation. Always accept an "if" for an "is" and the blessings will flow.

CONCLUSION FOR PART ONE

Sometimes we get so involved in the illusions of this world that it's hard for us to remember what our true reality is.

While we are in this world, we must constantly remind ourselves of the things we know. We can be aware of the workings of spirit. We can see the many wonderful things manifested from It purely for our enjoyment and assistance, but it is still so easy for us to lose touch with It while we study in this daily school.

Granted, it's hard to love God when you don't know who or what God might be, but it does seem to be easy to love money when we fantasize about the peace and joy it might bring to our lives.

You might say life in this world is like playing a character in a movie. We start playing that part with such gusto and feeling, that we show we are very good players. However, just as in the case of regular actors and actresses, we lose touch with what we really are.

One day, just as in the case of all of us, I had become a little too involved with the irritating story plot of this sad world. There was a problem on my mind that seemed to bog me down. No matter how hard I studied the situation, it seemed to lead to a dead end. It was like trying to run in mud up to my knees.

As I walked along I finally decided to surrender the whole problem to spirit.

"Alright," I said, "I give up! There is something I'm overlooking. Show me what it is I've forgotten."

Then, up ahead I noticed several women talking together on the sidewalk. Nearby several children were engaged in play.

As I approached, one of the young girls looked up and a glorious smile spread across her face.

It reminded me of when my children were younger and they would come running out to greet me when I came home in the evening. It was that same marvelous and beautiful smile.

As she began to run toward me, I immediately believed she must have mistaken me for her father.

Just as she came to a stop in front of me, she looked up and said, "Wave at me, God!"

At first I was a little dumb-struck at the statement and wasn't sure if that was what she really said.

"I recognize you! Wave at me, God! Please wave at me!" she pleaded as she held up her tiny hand, waving at me.

I held my hand up and moved my fingers up and down at her, thinking what a wonderful game she must be playing. As I began to walk away, wondering if this might have been something she had learned in Sunday School – that God is in everyone, I heard her yelling to her mother, "God waved at me, Mama! God waved at me!"

It seemed that she wasn't interested in anyone else. For some reason she had singled me out and seemed to see something I may have temporarily forgotten.

My gloom changed to a big smile. My old friend spirit was always there, to help me get back in touch with reality when the illusions of this world became a little too much to handle.

This time spirit gave me a lesson through a wonderful and beautiful child.

I continued to walk along noticing for the first time what a truly beautiful day it really was.

SECTION TWO:

THE SCIENCE OF TRANSITION (DEATH)

CHAPTER 8:

SPIRITUAL ASSISTANCE

A MYRIAD OF HOSTS

One can only wonder where such information as presented in this book comes from. It is true I have carried a great deal of pre-birth memory, and been able to open further channels of esoteric information using this memory, but one should understand that memory alone isn't enough to gain such in-depth understanding of life beyond the physical as is shared in this book.

When we visit the astral (or higher) it might be compared to a visitor coming from a foreign country, sailing up the Hudson River for a short distance, observing not only the Statue of Liberty, tall buildings and massive hustling of cars and people, but many other aspects as well, and then returning home and attempting to write a book explaining everything there is to know about this exciting place. Simply by seeing a great deal of activity and being able to remember, would hardly give him the ability to write about the activities carried out there. Nor would he understand the work and home life of the multitude, their basic

191

laws, their beliefs, their schooling system, their economic status, or anything else relating to the people or the city. Not only would he have great gaps in his presentation about this particular place, but he certainly couldn't speak with any authority about the country the city is in.

I would like to take a moment to thank those who have helped me, filling in with spiritual knowledge where gaps have existed. While there have been a myriad of assistants, there are four I have personally identified, and with whom I have been permitted to become familiar. They are Eve-Annibelle, Dap Ren, Antaris, and a spiritual teacher known only as EN.

By far, the longest running relationship has been with Eve-Annibelle. We are from the same Monad (Soul Body) and both of us entered the physical realm at the same time. Sometimes we have been together and sometimes only one of us at a time has been in this world. At this time, which will be our last incarnation, I have served as the physical vehicle while she has guided. You've heard of Guardian Angels? This is precisely what our relationship is all about. We all have at least one individual taking care of us at any given moment. If your soul mate (Bio-centric) isn't presently in this world, chances are he or she is acting as your personal Guardian at this time.

Dap Ren, Antaris and EN are all spiritual masters often known by other names by the endless tens-of-thousands they assist and have assisted. Dap Ren has been my spiritiual guide for more than forty years and for many years, served as spiritual leader teaching dimensional science (laws of the higher vibrating planes). Both Antaris and EN are historical figures who entered into my life primarily to teach the importance of the relationship between us and the higher spheres.

I have been asked how this knowledge is passed to me. While most has been through physical communication, some has been through a process called cosmic intervention. There has previously been an explanation about this. When this occurs, there is seldom any doubt about what is being related. Sometimes it's as simple as being able to adjust ones awareness, or as explained, being taken and shown.

As for the endless hundreds of assistants that can be called upon for help, it's important for you to understand there is absolutely nothing special about me. You are able to call out for spiritual assistance and instantly be surrounded by those who can relate to your own problem.

On the surface, with all the millions of people who might be calling out for assistance in one matter or another, that might seem a little incredible. However, we need to understand that we are in the lower worlds to gain experience. The more experience we get, the better our grade, and the better our grade, the sooner we graduate to an exaulted position of a little God.

Another thing we need to understand is that only the physical can provide all of the experience we need. It's true the astral is dedicated to peace and rest because that was the reason for it to exist, but with all of this peace there is little opportunity to spiritually progress. Those presently in the astral have the opportunity to progress only when they interact with those on a physical world. So, while they would be doing you a favor, you are also doing one for them. You would be giving them the opportunity to work off some of the less desirable karma they may have picked up previously.

Another point to be made is that our conception of death is greatly in error. For some strange reason, most of us believe that when one passes away from this world they instantly gain a vast amount of knowledge. Some practitioners of magic actually believe that the newly departed have some mystical knowledge of all things. Many attempt to call on these assistants for selfish reason, such as to learn what numbers might be coming up on the lotto.

While it's true that one does absorb vast amounts of knowledge about a new dimension where he will be making home, that in no way implies he will have any more knowledge about the world that he just left than he had while being there.

In fact, once one leaves this world it is as I described earlier. A newly departed is pretty much like a child literally led around, having little awareness of where he is, where he's going, or what might be going on around himself.

So, you might ask what is it that these departed can do for you? As far as making you rich, or fully solving all of your problems, probably very little. But what they can do is offer moral assistance and "be a channel" for spirit to flow through to you.

THE UPPER AND LOWER HOUSE

Anyone who has done a basic reading of esoteric matters have heard of something called "the Second Grand Division". What this means is there is a division between the higher worlds and the lower ones. (And again I emphasize that means higher vibrating and lower vibrating worlds).

The beginning of all things is the upper house, the higher vibrating worlds, also called the God Worlds.

This is comprised of eight levels or planes. Observing these planes from our position, the first of the God worlds would seem to be the fifth level called the "Soul plane" and the last would be the "God-head" or twelfth plane. But once we can understand that we are not the center of creation, that we are not the first plane but the last, we can see we are really an outpost located way out in a wild frontier.

The first plane of the upper house is the one we refer to as the twelfth. It was from here your pure essence was taken and like a small child, sent off to gain an education. This was done to awaken you to your true heritage.

From there, you were taken one level at a time to fully explore the spiritual worlds as you moved away from the center. At certain points of your awakening you were withdrawn back into the highest vibrating world to keep you attuned to that awesome world. Even though that was and is your true home, it can be very frightening to someone familiar with the lower vibrations.

In that first vibrating world, the forces and sights are overwhelming to one who has become disassociated with this world. Even though you were and are a part of it, each time you re-enter, you again become overwhelmed for a period of time.

The Twelfth plane is pretty much like being in the center of a vast whirlpool. You see forces greater than can even be imagined, swirling about you and then cascading into an indescribable crevis. On a closer inspection you see this great gaping hole passes down into the center of all creation; all of the worlds down to and including the physical universes.

When we saw the Mountain of Light on the astral plane, which is the receiver and distributor of this cosmic energy, we learned that this spiritual power was so great that if it were not absorbed at that level, it could completely wipe out the entire physical universe. Take into consideration that by the time this spiritual energy reaches the astral it has lost most of its impact. This awesome force that can destroy every planet, every star, everything in our known and unknown physical universe, is only one twelfth of the original power you witnessed in your home world!

The balance of the upper house is dedicated to spiritual lessons and spiritual matters. There is absolutely no negative energy in any of these worlds. So, while this energy is so forceful, it is comprised entirely of positive movement. While it would be devastating to a physical body, once the soul can readjust to it, it becomes an enjoyable (and usually soothing) experience. Once readjusted, the soul can even find extreme enjoyment in "riding the current" as it passes down and through all planes.

The lower house is pretty much all we have been taught about while in this world. The lower house is comprised of all physical universes, the astral, causal, and the etheric planes.

No matter how advanced one's religion might seem, none is based on any world above the etheric. For anyone wondering if there really is a heaven, the answer is definitely, yes! Every religion regardless of its size or following has its own private heaven. Even if an individual decided to create his own religion, a personal place would instantly be created for its manifestation on the etheric level. That means he would also be able to draw from the energies manifested at the etheric level.

Surprising enough, this is why when a misleading cult created purely to gain money or power suddenly has a show of power, it is because of those innocent individuals who put their faith and trust in it. Because of their combined faith, they often experience various miracles. Even though some individuals have attempted to set up a con, the faith of the followers have actually created an energy field. That by no means relieves the con from his ill intent though. We must always remember we are surrounded by etheric atoms that control our karma flow. While the con must pay for his misdeed, the pure-at-heart can actually reap rewards from their intent.

Of course, the larger a religion is, the more energy its members will generate on the etheric level. But that in no way is to imply that one needs to belong to a certain religion. Many have become disillusioned with controls certain religions have attempted to enforce on its members. In turn, they have found a reliance and a faith in themselves which has not only established an opening on the etheric level for themselves personally, but advanced the positive spin of the karma units to a point of acceptance into the soul plane.

THE GOVERNORS

Each of the planes is controlled and maintained by a certain vibration and a certain force. While the vibration of each is different, the force manifested at each level is also a different nature and complexity.

In man's quest for spiritual knowledge though, he is unable to fully understand these manifestations. Spirit at its highest level realizes that its physical outlets (physical awareness) are totally incapable of understanding the source from which they sprang, or the workings that brought them to this station of development. It, therefore, has manifested a series of intelligent sources that life forms throughout the physical universes can relate to.

Since we can only think in terms of God being a man, each of these great oceans of intelligence will relate itself to us as being a man when the occasion calls for us to be in the presence of one. Thus, when we start to spiritually advance, we may have the opportunity to find ourselves in the presence of one. While this force wants us to absorb certain aspects of knowledge, instead of it being done through a process of osmosis, we often receive instruction from something we can easily associate with.

Sometimes this instruction may seem verbal or sometimes through thought, but it will always be a deep understanding seeming to come from one human form to another. This will continue until you have entered into the true God worlds. At that time, when you can see that you are really something more than a low primate, the appearance of the Governor will also change. When you can see you are pure spirit, the Governor also manifests as pure spirit.

To the physical awareness, the structure greatly resembles a massive schooling system where each of the Governors is like a teacher in a classroom with the ultimate lower world force being the principal.

As you will remember, when spirit needed to create the lower vibrating worlds, it had to divide and create a negative and positive pole, since there is no negative charge in the God worlds. This combination of negative and positive created a force that none above it had. It could now create not only several levels of vibrating worlds, but all physical manifestations as well.

This is the governing force that also gives life to the governing forces below it.

Naturally, if each of the plane forces needed to manifest a human appearance, then that would be especially true for this force, for in our human awareness we look at this combination of

197

charges as God.

Even with this understanding, when we are allowed to explore the various dimensions, we discover it is carried even a step further.

For example, not only do we find a governing intelligence regulating our entire physical universe, but discover there are particular force fields for each planet. These, in turn, offer an intelligent connection between itself and the life forms there. This also helps to explain how all life forms, regardless of being fish, animal or even insect, are regulated by a higher intelligence called a vortex.

The name given to the intelligence of our Earth world is Jot. This force is like the first link in a chain-of-command. A petition to this intelligence would likely receive more favor and attention than one at the highest level.

A good experiment would be to submit an appeal to Jot and then watch for what might come. But remember, the Jot life-force is mainly interested in maintaining life and balance on our planet. That's the reason all creations in a certain vortex can so easily work together without understanding the over-all picture of a project. So, if you feel your petition is of a selfish nature, more than likely, there will be no results. However, if you lean toward the welfare of others, there may be a very good response.

To do this experiment, use the White Light exercise while chanting the name Jot.

MORE ABOUT THE PARAMAHANSA

Very little is known about the Paramahansa in the physical universe. Outside of my own remembrance of them, the only other place where they have been mentioned is in the ancient teachings called "the religion of light and sound".

As mentioned, they are the only permanent residents of the fifth plane and serve primarily in the duty of preparing the divided monads (male and female counterparts of each soul) for their journey into the worlds of lower vibration, but they are also the direct agents to the governing force of that plane.

This governor is one step above the governing force we call The Creator.

In our limited ability to expand our spiritual awareness beyond our insignificant speck of dust in the galaxy, a great portion of our population would accept the Jot force to be the ultimate god. The rest would worship the governing force on the fourth plane, which is the true creator and maintainer of physical matter. But the governor of these people is far superior. It speaks for the ultimate source of all manifested vibration.

Being that these individuals are that force's agents, their abilities are virtually unlimited. They could travel into the highest of realms if they chose, although all others are permitted to advance only to a level where their awareness has unfolded. Also, at their discretion, they could travel into the depths of the physical universe to perform a miracle – if such a desire should enter them.

It is conceived they may be approached with a petition (spiritual exercise), but one should understand their goals and ideals far exceed our interpretation of what we need in our life. Besides, there are governing forces between them and us that are already providing what we need for our education.

They are primarily interested in the workings of the two units to advance to a stage where both half souls can be reunited, reactivating the monad, with it continuing on until it advances itself into what is called the Golden Universe. At this point the soul's ability is expanded to a point where it can be united with all other advanced souls. It is here we finally become a Little God! For all eternity we have total and complete power. We will have finally achieved the ultimate goal spirit has been preparing us for.

When we realize the power of spirit, we may ask why we couldn't have just automatically been advanced into this state of consciousness within a wink of an eye. Spirit certainly has the ability to pluck the lowly consciousness from where we resided before our development. It could have instantly given us these positions, awakening us to the wondrous worlds, but it hasn't done it that way for a very good reason. Such an awakening would have no compassion, no true enlightenment, and certainly no love.

That's the primary interest of the Paramahansa. They *are pure love*! That is what they demonstrate most and what they bring into the soul's development. They have been charged with the responsibility of training soul that spirit can only exist in an ocean of love.

Unlike our understanding of a cruel, vengeful, angry, and frightening god, they show us God is love. If spirit had angry and violent atoms, these atoms would fight one another and blow themselves apart. Only pure love among these atoms keeps them and holds them together. With love, the force of spirit is united and flows forth with powerful energy. If it were negative and violent, the atoms would repel one another, causing an explosion and an end to life.

So, instead of approaching the Paramahansa with a greedy petition, if one were to instead ask for a blessing of love to our small planet, the results could be a lot more effective.

However, one thing we must never forget is that even though they are pure love, that love can enter only into an open and enlightened heart. Only until men of power can understand the true wisdom of the universes from which we come, will they be able to cultivate that love.

CHAPTER NINE:

READING THE ASTRAL
&
SOUL RECORDS

The following readings are based on astral records open and available to everyone. They have been read and translated through the efforts of Eve-Annibelle, Antaris, Dap Ren, and EN.

One might wonder when we explore these ancient records what it has to do with exploring higher worlds, but we should understand as much as we possibly can about what these worlds offer. These worlds open doors to great knowledge. Not only when we are there, but while we still reside in a physical body.

Also, this section can better assist us in understanding the higher worlds by enabling us to go beyond what we might believe came from religious teachings.

THE ASTRAL RECORDS
AND THE DEATH EXPERIENCE

Everyone's experience of death (transition) can be different, but for the most part, the individual's awareness at that time is at a limited level. It's true the astral awareness is far greater in ability and scope than the physical, but it will return to us slowly in stages. Just as in the physical, when we first enter, our awareness is restricted to our immediate surroundings. It can be so limited we may not even be aware of those who are near us. As a baby, our attention can be confined to the one individual taking care of us. Even as we begin to move about in the astral vibration, we are still like a young child led around by his mother, hardly aware of what might be going on around us.

The astral plane is a place to relax, refresh and heal from possible emotional scars received while in training in the lower vibration. There is not always a flurry of activity as one might suspect. Perhaps it's for this reason it's so difficult for us to remember much about this brief period of occupation.

However, our astral records is the major training tool during this time. It's sort of like being able to have a more expanded understanding of who and what we are, where we are headed, and how our spiritual evolution can be accomplished with the most ease.

An important point to understand is that your records are sealed! No one but yourself is permitted to view them. There is never a reason to feel embarrassed or ashamed. In fact, anything that wouldn't go directly to help you in your quest to become a spiritual being would be deleted anyway.

What you see will be more like a glorious account of each life you have previously led. Outside of that, most of the time is spent in beautiful, relaxing vibration.

As for the open records, these were also closed until that particular individual (who the account is about) gave permission to have them opened. This is usually done so the facts of what really happened can be better understood.

Usually, the astral accounts you become familiar with are limited to your own particular section of universe, but every world, every universe, every insignificant speck of space (such as Earth), will have its own astral account.

While the astral records deal mainly with happenings in the physical realm, as we spiritually move along, we discover another great set of records. The soul records exist on the fifth plane and will cover all the training you have gone through enabling you to enter the true God Worlds.

THE TRIAL OF JESUS

One of the greatest mysteries is the study of Jesus. There is so much we think we know and so little we do. In 1880 an old parchment roll was found in Alexandria in an old building formerly used by Grecian Monks, in a forgotten and abandoned library. It had been written by an Essene brother of Jesus. He was writing to an Elder belonging to the Alexandria sect of their Brotherhood to explain the true story behind his brother Jesus. Even two thousand years ago, lies were already being distributed about his brother. The intent of the parchment was to clarify the true actions and teachings of Jesus.

Although there was a great deal of mind-blowing revelation, at this point we are going to concentrate on only one small aspect of his life taken from that scroll and which has been verified through Astral recording.

When we hear of the trial of Jesus, we picture in our minds a place in some small, candle-lit room with only three or four priests and a couple of guards in attendance. However, that is far from what actually occurred.

The court of the Sanhedrim temple was an enormous and magnificent chamber. It easily held all of the seventy members of the holy council. It not only had columns but, also, a massive marble floor covering hundreds of square feet.

On this occasion when Jesus was being tried for blasphemy, all seventy members of the Sanhedrim (the ruling body of the priesthood) were in attendance. Their leader was referred to as the president of the council or Nasi, and he sat in the center of a long, impressive, horse-shoe shaped table with thirty-five to each side.

When Jesus was dragged before them, it was this leader who addressed and informed him of the charges of being a blasphemer.

After the charges were read, Jesus had a great deal more to say than has ever been recorded.

He informed them it was not his intent to defend himself against the likes of them. With lack of fear, he exposed them for what he saw them to be. He accused them of being closed-minded bigots living in superstition and attempting to rule by keeping the people in fear. He said a mad dog would be a better priest than any of them could ever be.

*(Author's note: In this account, dialogue is not presented in an Old English format for quite obvious reasons. Jesus did not speak Old English or any other kind of English. Thus, the translation has been presented in a simple and clear manner.)

The Nasi rose from his seat and proclaimed to his brothers in attendance that a great deal of blasphemey had been spread among God's chosen people.

Reading the official list of charges, he began, "First charge is this man Jesus has been heard to deny the divine authority of Moses, saying that much of our history is a lie and that Moses was hardly anything more than a crazed liar!

"Second, this man Jesus has said the people of Israel are not a chosen people and that because of our Brotherhood, they have lowered themselves to being ignorant, wild, cruel, and savage!

"Third, this man Jesus has said Moses was a cunning impostor and all of his revelations were pretended and his conversation with God Jehovah on Mount Sinai was a lie!

"Fourth, this man Jesus has said our God Jehovah was only a creation from out of the mind of Moses, and the attributes we allow to Jehovah were really based on the nature of Moses – which was stern, cruel, and ignorant!

"Fifth, that our Lord Jehovah, being of stated nature, burning and torturing his children, could never be a God – but could reside only with the lowest of men, being filled with hate!

"Sixth, this Jesus asserts that all other of Moses' accounts are nothing more than lies and fables. He has said the stories of our scriptures are nothing but absurd fiction and resemble no truth to our true history and that no parting of the waters took place to assist our people in their escape!

"Seventh, this man Jesus has asserted our sacred Order of Priesthood could thus never have been ordained by any such being as an evil Jehovah. As such, we are not wise, pious, or learned. Instead, he has accused us of being cunning knaves who are only interested in stealing from the people and keeping them living in fear!"

After the charges were read, Jesus was permitted to speak.

First pointing to individuals and then running his finger back and forth at his long line of accusers, he spoke to them in a loud and bold voice.

"You men of Judah, who are ignorant to the true workings of Spirit, hear my true words! You bring charges against me as a child would a playmate. You claim to know all things, but know very little about most things, Spirit being the head of that list. Is there anything in the character called Jehovah that any man of common sense can accept as being divine? By examining this cruel being in the light of philosophical reason, we can easily see that Moses, with his limited knowledge, created this being Jehovah, claiming him to be the ultimate god, but then in the next breath saying he was god only of the Jews.

"Yes, all of this was from the mind and creation of Moses! Let us look at this Jehovah as he is presented by Moses. It is asserted that this god is all-powerful, all-wise, and all-benevolent. Now, taking this into consideration,, let us examine the works and holy scriptures.

"I have not blasphemed against any god, not even your Jehovah. Let us consider the account of the creation. Did Jehovah in the beginning create the heavens and Earth out of nothing?

"Philosophy tells us there never was an atom of matter ever created or destroyed. Did he make the day before he made the Sun, or even any of the billions of suns which might exist? Did he make the Sun to rule the day and the Moon to rule the night? That is impossible, for both are really only from the source of the Sun. Did the Lord feel tired after working six days, then need to rest on the seventh?

"Your scripture says that after working six days on just this one planet, with a mere wave of his hand, he filled the heavens with lights! Today we know these lights are other solid bodies, possibly supporting life as we know here! If this Jehovah was so talented and clever, then why did it take six days for this one pathetic world among untold billions? Why didn't he just wave his hand and create everything at once? This account of the creation could not have come from a wise god, for it shows a great perversion of facts. This only proves that these concepts came from the minds of ignorant men who couldn't think clearly!

"I will pass over endless other ridiculous accounts which leave just as many important questions unanswered, and would ask you about the Garden of Eden. In the Mosaical account, it states God saw everything was good, yet he planted a tree of evil to tempt and tease his children. The consequence was they did what he tempted them to do, especially not knowing any better in their innocent state, there being no knowledge of what was considered good or bad. They sinned and displeased God. That is a most absurd and ridiculous statement, totally destructive to the loving nature with which you wish to present him.

"Would a wise and good father put temptation in the way of innocent children to tempt them to do wrong? No loving father would do this, but in this stupid account he is shown to do even worse. He not only tempts his children to sin, but curses them and all that will ever come from them because they fell into the snare he laid for them!

"As for Moses, we only have his own word about his discussion with God. Any reasoning man can easily see this account was a silly lie! Since he didn't know how to identify God, he used a symbol the people could understand. He claimed he talked with God through a burning bush, and through this bush God said, 'I Am That I Am'. Now Moses knew no more than he did before! This nonsensical statement is held even to this day as some divine conception of the Deity! This is nonsense because it does not convey an idea. Can it be opposed that if the god Jehovah wished to reveal himself to any mortal, he would have given such an indefinite description?

"Moses has said Jehovah was the God of Abraham, Isaac, and Jacob. However, a true God would have been the creator of all mankind, and would not have made such a limited and foolish statement. He certainly would not be partial to any one race of people. If so, then why would he create others?

"The scriptures also say that Moses led the people to the water where Jehovah parted the sea. Anyone with just basic knowledge could see all Moses had to do to take the people out of Egypt was simply head east. There, land stretches between the two seas. This is what was meant by moving between the parted waters.

To need to call upon Jehovah for a miracle, Moses would have stupidly needed to lead the people south, where they would have been enslaved by other enemies!

"So, according to holy scripture, you not only show Moses to be dim-witted, but also present your Jehovah to also be thus! For truly, what kind of god who talked to Moses, wouldn't know the lay of the land he created, would send Moses in the wrong direction and then need to perform a totally impossible act to redeem himself?

"The fact is that there is no such being as the evil, jealous Jehovah. He is a figment of the imagination invented by our ancestors, to resemble their own natures. He was created in the image of themselves both in body and in mind, having the same passions as they. It is said God made man in his own image, which meant the inner self, the soul! But here they have represented their God as being exactly like themselves with eyes, nose, ears and every other body part. If they had tails, then they would have undoubtedly given a tail to Jehovah! To this imaginary god, they gave all human passions including hatred, revenge, vindictiveness, cruelty, fear, doubt, and a love of praise, flattery, and adulation! This is not a god. He would be no better than a mere mortal!

"That there is a great and wise power existing in the vast expanse of the universes is as true as the god of Moses is false! But you can only know this great power when you can open your eyes to the Spirit that passes through you, bringing life to you and to all things about you! You can only know truth when you open your eyes to the true miracles that are about you! Close your minds to the ignorance you have created!

"I have always said we are all the children of God, meaning each of us is a divine entity who has been given the opportunity to be placed in a particular physical body to help us learn more of the nature of the lower worlds.

"While I have said we all are children of God, it has been your very own agitators, those who are only interested in keeping the masses in darkness, that have said I claimed to be a son of God. I have not said this! It has been you who has said I am the son of Jehovah! I would not stain my worth with such ignorant teachings!

"However, I challenge you to let all know what I have said here today; that every man, woman, and child comes directly from the ultimate life force! We are never separated from the true God as you feel you may be separated from your Jehovah.

"As for the charges that I have claimed to be the redeemer of mankind, I have given no sanction or encouragement to these things and again lay the blame at the feet of my accusers.

"Now, men of Judah, my accusers and judges, I have made an end to my explanation that I have felt necessary to clarify. I do not ask for your pity or mercy, for I know such things do not exist in your heart. I know you thirst for my blood and therefore patently await my doom, and let the blood be upon your heads!"

Author's note: Although the teachings of Jesus were presented crystal clear more than two thousand years ago, isn't it strange we still cling to ancient superstitions? Jesus denounced Jehovah as a fictitious, blood-thirsty beast, yet his enemies claimed he was the son of Jehovah.

Jesus taught that no true God could have an evil nature – but how many still use the phrase "I'm a God-fearing person"? No parent would *roast* their children over a fire and certainly no divine being would. Still, in our highly civilized, high technology world, not only do many still believe some wicked god would roast us, his children, in a fire, but an eternal hellish one at that! One has to wonder how so many have blocked Spiritual knowledge for so long. Unfortunately, we have been programmed to believe we are evil if we dare question anything deemed religious, regardless of how illogical it may be.

OF EARTH AND MARS

The following account is given to show how astral records can be used to help us better understand not only our own world, but our sister planets.

Up until about 100,000 years ago, Mars was almost identical to our world. There were great oceans and the planet flourished in vegetation and animal life. Then, in a distant galaxy a gigantic star, hundreds of times larger than our own Sun, exploded. As billions of chunks shot off into different directions, one chunk, larger than our Sun, eventually made its way into our Milky-way.

As it passed, the vibrating forces created were so great it rocked Earth and neighboring planets for more than eight days. It was like a continuous explosion of nuclear bombs on all planets,

Earth included. This is what really led to the destruction of Earth's great beasts!

The hardest hit was Mars. Almost all vegetation and animal life disappeared, and great bodies of water were either dissipated or literally sucked off into space.

Earth fared a little better. However, earthquakes and tidal waves covered the entire planet. A great continent sank beneath the waves taking with it a very advanced technology. Many areas were scorched creating the deserts we know today. The planet was knocked from a circular orbit into one that is elliptical. It also became tilted on its axis and developed a wobble still noticeable today.

At this time not only were all large animals destroyed, but Uranus and Neptune were also pushed into orbits much further away.

With this better understanding of what really took place, many great mysteries about Earth and its neighbors can be cleared up.

THE SOLOMON SECRET

This reading was selected to show how drastically our understanding of ancient events (religion included) can be altered. Simply because something taught may be ancient, that in no way is an indication it is true. We must never forget that almost everything passed down to us has been interpreted, reinterpreted, added to, and changed. The story of Solomon is a prime example of this. While we have been taught that Solomon was a wise, pious and beloved leader, the Akashic records reflect quite a different story. Many saw him as a cruel and dangerous person. He even sent many thousands of his own people into slave labor, forcing them to work on his projects.

We all know the story of the two women who claimed to be the mother of a particular infant. With both women saying they were the mother, Solomon decided to divide the baby in half giving equal parts to both. While one agreed, the other said, no.

She would rather give up her child than have him killed. Thus, Solomon declared the one willing to give up the baby as the true mother.

But there is something surprising about the story. It was not really about two women but about Solomon himself and was a symbolic story questioning his right to the throne.

Everyone in those days understood that Solomon was represented as the false mother and his half brother, Adonijah, as the true mother.

Solomon was an illegitimate heir to the throne and willing to split the kingdom (the baby) with a civil war.

At the death of king David, Adonijah became king. Behind the scenes though, Bathsheba and Solomon, assisted by a few corrupt priests, claimed that David, on his death-bed, proclaimed Solomon king.

Seeing the kingdom was divided about the rightful king and war was evident, Adonijah stepped down saying he would rather give up the crown than sacrifice the kingdom.

As his reward, Solomon publicly declared no harm would come to Adonijah or those who supported him. Then in private, ordered his death and the death of his friends. Even an old general formerly dedicated to Adonijah, who now gave allegiance to Solomon, was hacked to death while praying at the tabernacle altar.

Solomon became Israel's most powerful king, and as the prophet Samuel had foreseen, laid heavy taxes, took hundreds of wives and worshiped alien gods.

After his death, subjects came to the coronation of his son, Rehoboam. When he was asked publicly by a priest if things were going to change or if they were going to stay the same, he said, "Things will change. My father chastised you with whips. I will chastise you with scorpions!"

This time the kingdom was divided for good. At the conclusion of war, his rule was reduced from all of Israel to the small realm of Judah.

RAISING THE DEAD

Raising the dead is such a frightening thought that it's surprising any religion (outside of voodoo) would want it to be a part of their teaching.

Raising the dead has nothing to do with resurrection. Resurrection is the teaching that the soul lives on. It has nothing to do with putting life back into a rotted and decayed corpse – which is impossible anyway!

This outlandish teaching became popular after Saul of Tarsus saw the effect it had on people when they thought Jesus had done it and Saul attempted to capitalize on it.

Actually, Jesus never raised Lazarus from the grave, nor did he claim to!

The true story goes like this: When Jesus received word that his friend Lazarus was sick and needed his immediate attention, he journeyed to Bethany to see what he might be able to do. He was accompanied by his Disciples.

As they reached the home of Lazarus, they were met by Martha, his eldest daughter.

Weeping, she informed them her father was dead.

"Dead!" Jesus exclaimed in astonishment. Motioning for Martha and the others to wait, he entered the chamber of mourning. Mary, the youngest daughter, rose from her seat and threw her arms around his shoulders and burst into tears. Oh, my beloved," Mary cried, "if you had been here, he would not have died!"

He held her for several moments, then led her gently back to her seat. Jesus then advanced to the bed, removed the cloth, and studied the body for several minutes.

He noticed the corpse didn't display any of the features of death. The body was not cold, but actually quite warm. Also, there was no odor and he looked like he was simply asleep.

When he touched the face, he noticed it was soft, and when he touched the eyelid, Jesus let out a cry of surprise.

The visitors looked at each other in alarm. Jesus noted the eyelid quivered at the touch, and he could see a quivering at the corner of the mouth. "Lazarus lives! He has not left the body!"

Looks of amazement spread around the room as Jesus frantically attempted to revive Lazarus. When Lazarus let out a slight groan, many fled the house in terror. Outside, the Disciples stood in shock as the people pushed by them.

Very little was known about the human system in the days of Jesus. Many aspects were not known about at all. All serious conditions were said to be caused by demons, and when one became cured, it was taken for granted that the demon had been cast out. The state of a coma was often mistaken for death.

Although Jesus did not know the nature of this particular incident, he had learned other men had experienced similar conditions. With the recovery of Lazarus, most fled to the safety of their homes.

Jesus and his group stayed the night to show there was nothing to fear. However, before the Sun rose high in the sky on the next day, the news had spread all over Jerusalem that Jesus had raised Lazarus from the dead.

Later on, when it was assumed Jesus was dead, Saul remembered this event and saw a way that he might capitalize on it.

When Saul arrived in Jerusalem, he immediately attempted to join the disciples, but they were afraid of him, knowing he was in close alliance with the Sanhedrim priests.

His friend, Barnabus, took him to them and attempted to show how Saul had endured a change of heart and now wanted to be one of them.

Saul stayed with them and moved about freely in Jerusalem, boldly speaking in the name of Jesus. Caiaphas, the head priest, believing him to also still be on his side, informed the other priests to ignore these speeches.

With no further attacks coming from the Sanhedrim, the teachings of the Way continued to expand throughout Judea,

Gailee, and Samaria.

Although Jesus was gone, the stories still persisted that he had risen from the dead. Saul was not sure if Jesus had really survived the cross or if this was the result of mass hysteria, but it didn't matter either way to him. The story was too great a golden opportunity to not take advantage of.

With the help from Saul, the priest Ananias, and another lesser known accomplice, Cobi, Peter was prepared to give a public demonstration. It was Saul's intent to give a performance of raising someone from the dead.

The sister of Ananias proved to be the equal to any man when it came to staging a good show.

Tabitha lived in Joppa, near Lydda, so Saul announced to the masses that the Lord had descended upon him and told him to go to Joppa, where he would assist Peter in raising a woman from the dead.

Since this had worked so well before, Saul felt it was time for another resurrection.

Hundreds followed as the group set out to perform the miracle of miracles.

When they arrived at the chosen place, Peter was informed the body of the dead woman would be found in an upstairs room. It was a room which overlooked the street and displayed many windows.

The three went upstairs while many attempted to follow. The door and the stairs were blocked by the dozens who desired to get a better view.

Under Saul's instruction, Peter put his hands on Tabitha and commanded, "By the power of the risen Christ, I command you to rise!"

A tremendous gasp spread when she opened her eyes and sat up.

Saul took her by the hand and helped her up. He then led her to the windows to show the crowd outside she was alive again.

Saul was held in high regard as a great maker of miracles, but more and more people wanted to witness the miracles for themselves.

Such was the case in Troas. To avoid any difficulty and to assist Timothy with the group he had formed, Saul (who had by now changed his name) traveled there under the pretense he had been called to bring a young man back to life.

The story the people had been told was that Eutychus, who in secret was another of Saul's group, had been sitting in an upstairs window when he fell asleep, slipped, and fell to his death.

Arriving at the house, Saul requested the body of the young man be brought down from his room and placed on the same spot where he had supposedly fallen. While suggesting this was done for some magical purpose, the real reason was so the people of the village could get a better view of the miracle.

When the man was properly placed, Saul lowered himself over the supposed corpse, laying completely on him. This was another new twist added for effect.

He put his arms around the youth and held on tightly for a short period of time.

When he stood up, he announced to the people, "Do not be afraid! This man lives again!" That was the clue for Eutychus to begin moving and then slowly stand up.

The entire audience gasped at the sight of a dead man rising and many ran away terrified.

On the other hand, Timothy noticed Saul seemed to be bored. Saul walked inside, broke bread, and ate, while the excitement continued outside.

Many close to him had begun to notice something wrong. Some suggested perhaps his guilty conscious was beginning to catch up to him. Others thought he might be bored. It was very difficult to stage a miracle that would be greater than raising someone from the dead.

MARY MAGDALEN THE VIRGIN?

It was common knowledge that Jesus was deeply in love with Lazarus' youngest daughter, Mary. Jesus had not even tried to hide the fact that on many of his visits to Bethany, the journey was made solely to see her.

This was of little concern to any until it was discovered that Mary was going to become the thirteenth disciple. She would travel with him, and they were planning to wed. It was at this time the enemies of Jesus devised a cruel plan.

Many remembered a time when a prostitute was about to be stoned to death and Jesus intervened to save her, telling the people to let one who was without sin to cast the first stone. Although this woman had been forgotten about, with none remembering her name – if, indeed, any had known it – they now referred to her as Mary with the strong insinuation that this beloved of Jesus was that same prostitute.

As the enemies of Jesus wandered about the countryside, they told the story of how Jesus had saved her from being stoned and they were now lovers.

Judas and Peter, on the other hand, tried to end the lie, telling people where they went that this Mary was as pure at heart as was the Master Jesus himself. This served little purpose though. People were always more interested in some deep, dark secret than in hearing the truth.

They both felt sincerely sad, knowing she was pure and filled with love. She loved him with all of her heart, and they knew she would be there by his side when the end came – whatever that end might be.

CHAPTER TEN:

VISITORS AMONG US

THE PHANTOM ON THE BRIDGE

For some reason, most of my life I have been surrounded by what I call phantoms and ghosts. Perhaps for this reason I have no fear when a contact does occur. In fact, I often call upon spirit to provide me with an answer when I need one, and it might come by some strange messenger. Such answers though, usually come when my consciousness has reached a certain vibration, delicately balanced between being awake and asleep. It is at that point all of us are most acceptable to receive something spiritual.

There is no doubt that everyone receives information or assistance almost on a daily basis. We only need to be more aware of what is going on around us. The light flashes in the corners of our eyes are an example. While we usually pass it off as a trick of the eye, or not even bother to let it register in our consciousness, be assured most of the time you have been blessed with a presence of one kind or another.

There is also another form of appearance. Our contact can be a very real and solid body. There is really no telling how many times you may have encountered this. Thinking back, try to remember some time when something strange happened when in the presence of a stranger, or how they may have rapidly disappeared when you weren't looking. Chances are that was a very significant encounter.

There have been numerous encounters in my life. Often, when a recent death occurred, I would sometimes see this strange man in the distance. He was always walking away from me and regardless of the weather, he was always wearing a full-length black coat, large black hat, and black shoes. The first time I saw him I was thirteen. My parents, sisters and I were on vacation when we were asked to return home as soon as possible. My grandfather was deathly sick and it was feared he wouldn't survive the night.

As we sped along the deserted country road, my father's headlights revealed a man dressed completely in black walking ahead of us. Since there was nothing around and a distance of several miles between farmhouses, my mother remarked how strange it was that this man would be walking down this dark road at two-thirty in the morning. And my father remarked about his being dressed all in black and not even attempting to step off the road from being hit.

As we sped by, I tried to get a better look, but it was too dark and his face seemed to be turned away from us.

The main problem I have with this figure whenever he might appear is that I probably had a better understanding of things of this nature than most, but I couldn't understand who or what this man was. Remembering that when one left this world, he would be escorted by a loved one, along with a very beautiful being that had chosen to be an escort, I fully denounced the concept of a grim reaper or a dark angel of death. Even though I had witnessed him many times, I continued to teach there was no such thing as a grim reaper.

Then, later in life I began to understand this strange messenger. He was more like a guide or sign letting me know things were changing. I finally came to understand he was letting me know changes were coming, and not really notifying me of a death that might cause these changes.

A prime example of this occurred on a blistery, freezing morning one February. Living in Sunnyside, Queens at that time and working in Manhattan, I had fallen into the habit of walking the sixty-ninth street bridge every morning. This particular morning the streets were bare. Everyone had retreated to the subways. It was so bitterly cold that even the normal traffic congestion into the city didn't exist. Only occasionally did a car go past.

Trudging across the bridge, I was even beginning to consider turning back and taking a train myself. I kept going though and didn't stop for a rest until I was almost half-way across.

Noticing a tug boat puffing along below me, I grabbed the handrails and watched it tug slowly beneath me. At the same time, I took a look behind to see if there might be any other brave heart out. Even though the weather was rough, vision was clear. I could see clearly all the way back down the walkway for more than a mile and saw I was the only fool out in this terrible blow.

Looking back down, I watched the tug move under the bridge. Then, turning, to continue my trek, I was suddenly bumped by a large figure. As he hurried past, I wondered from where he might have come. Just two seconds earlier I had noted I was alone on the bridge and now this person had come from virtually out of nowhere.

Adding to this mystery, I saw he was wearing a long black coat, a large black hat and black shoes. Nothing else of him was visable.

Even though he was walking quite fast, I was able to keep up, following about twenty feet behind. One thing in particular I noted was that regardless of the violent wind blowing, it didn't seem to affect him in the least. I fully expected to see his large hat come flying off and sail into the East River, but no matter how hard the gusts, it held firm.

Fully believing I was experiencing a spiritual experience, I told myself to catch up, finally get a good look and maybe strike up a conversation with him. At the time, I had no doubts about who this might be. Because of the strange way he appeared, I felt this must be the man in black I had often seen.

But even as eager as I was, I was also hesitant. Even though I had no doubt about who this was, I held back on just the slightest chance I might be wrong. If this was just some innocent walker, and there being only the two of us on the bridge, I was concerned I might frighten him. Besides, there was no hurry. There was still a long way to go before we reached the other end and even then, I could approach him as I followed him along the street. I certainly wasn't about to take my eyes off him.

Still maintaining a position of twenty feet in front of me, he suddenly stepped behind a steel-girder, disappearing completely from my vision.

I didn't take it as a threat of any kind. If he had been a mugger, he knew I had already seen him and doing a thing like that would only arouse my suspicion. I just took it for granted he was lighting a cigarette or something like that.

When I reached the girder, I took a look to my left and my eyes shot open!

No one was there! He had merely stepped behind the girder and disappeared!

I looked over the side and could see it was still a good twenty feet to the ground and besides that, it was solid concrete. Even if he had jumped, and he did survive, I would still be able to see him. It had only been five or six seconds.

I remembered my previous instincts and wished I had listened to them. I knew I would always wish I had approached him if he should somehow disappear.

However, my previous understanding that he was a messenger of change proved correct. With no deaths occurring, there were still big changes. For the next ten years, I worked closely with many people in our country and around the world helping them open to the true teachings of spirit.

I haven't seen him in recent times, but I do have a message for him. The next time we meet, I'm going to attempt to finally meet "face to face"!

THE NIGHT VISITORS

We are probably offered more protection and assistance than we ever realize. The strange thing is we might avoid much of it due to our internal protection system.

We are like a country with an elaborate system of self defense. Regardless if we are awake or asleep, we have a net of special radar that lets us know when our boundaries have been invaded. Without even thinking about it, in a public place, we will look up at someone staring at us. Or we might suddenly think of someone we haven't seen in a very long time, only to see them coming around the corner a moment later. Many will even know when they are being talked about. All of this belongs to the same network of defense.

This network also helps protect us from psychic attack. That's why it is so important to ask for and leave ourselves open to receive special blessings. The network doesn't know the difference between an attack or a blessing - and doesn't really care. It's sole duty is to protect you from outside influences.

When you are approached by someone, even bringing a blessing, the network will go into a panic mode. That's the real reason behind so many anxiety attacks coming out of nowhere for no reason. It also helps to explain what many believe to be UFO encounters while they are sleeping.

When the brain is at that delicate twilight zone between sleep and being awake, it is most susceptible to receive blessings, suggestions, lessons, or anything else your personal guardians feel necessary for your well being. That also includes healings!

There was a period when I was having nightmares. It also coincided with a period of severe chest pains.

221

A couple of times I could remember the nightmare, but it wasn't like being chased by monsters or anything like that. It was a simple occurrence. All of a sudden, my attention would be focused on the doorway leading to my bed. It was as if someone or something was standing there watching me, but I could see nothing. Then as it, he or they approached me, my internal alarm would go crazy. Even though I could see nothing, I'm sure the hairs on my body stood up.

Analyzing the situation when awake, I finally realized what it was. It had all the symptoms of a healing. First, paralysis took over. Then, I was unable to move any part of my body and unable to speak. Next, my wife seemed to have also fallen under strong vibrations, since she never woke-up regardless of how violently I shook (caused by my own internal defense system). However, when my internal alarm reached a certain level, it would always back off.

Realizing this, I set my mind to accept what was trying to come into my life, telling my internal network that when this should occur, I would no longer panic. The mere fact we can understand something, the easier we can overcome our fears.

On the next occurrence, I instantly told myself to not be afraid. As I felt something or someone coming closer, I kept reminding myself "it's of God".

Sure enough, again I couldn't move, but I now knew something necessary was about to happen.

It was as if someone placed their arm under the bed and brought it straight up through the springs and mattress, through my back and into the center of my being. Then I felt a strong vibration. It wasn't scary and it wasn't painful, but it was very forceful. I could feel my whole body vibrate. It grew to such an extent that the whole bed seemed to shake violently. This was proof my wife was also affected by whatever was cast over me. Although she is a light sleeper, she slept soundly through it again.

Finally receiving the healing, I knew there would be no further dreams of this nature and there weren't. Following up with a complete physical exam, even though I previously had high blood pressure, various aches, and had reached a point where I could barely walk because of back and chest pains, I was now told I had the health of a sixteen-year-old.

The important lesson to be learned from this section is to try to over-come your fears, anxiety, and apprehensions and when you feel you are in a nightmare, simply say to yourself, "I am in the hands of God! I am protected!"

ARLENE, THE LITTLE GIRL GHOST

When I returned home after my active duty training in the National Guard, I didn't particularly want to return to my mother's home. I felt it was time to set out on my own and jumped at the chance to get my own apartment   . It was the downstairs of an old dilapidated building sitting by itself in a grove. Although it wasn't much to look at, it was my first home and it was beautiful to me. The rent was fifty dollars a month, not a tremendous bargain like it might sound in these days, but still, it wasn't a bad price, so I took it.

Having to come up with the first and last months rent took quite a bite out of me. Many people were still making as low as thirty-five dollars a week, and anyone making a hundred dollars a week was considered extremely well-off. So, although I could come up with the hundred, having just received my government pay, I realized it would be at least a couple of weeks before I would be able to have the electric turned on.

My first day out looking for work, I returned home quite late. It was also quite dark. Sitting in the grove in the blackness, what had been my beautiful home seemed more like a scene from a horror movie.

Having just received military training, I quickly tried to brush the eerie feeling away. I had just been trained how to kill, now was I going to act like a little boy afraid of the dark? I started to hum a little tune as if I didn't have a care in the world and approached the house.

Just when I was about to reach the door, a most horrible and terrifying feeling shot through me. My protective network of instincts kicked in and I felt I was being watched! The only way I could advance closer was by again falling back on my training. Even if I was being observed, there had been no hostile actions toward me, so I decided to advance and investigate.

As I entered into the darkness, I literally couldn't see my hand in front of my face. It was only by my earlier remembrance of where the bedroom was that I could make my way along. With my psychic alarm still sending warning signals strongly to me, I fell back on the lesson to never show fear when in a compromising position.

"Alright, my friend," I called out loudly. "I mean you no harm. I'm only here to get a little sleep. You're free to leave if you want. I won't stop you."

The calm sound of my own voice made me feel better. If there was someone physical trespassing, they would realize I meant them no harm and perhaps would take this opportunity to get out.

I finally found my way to the bed and was tremendously grateful I hadn't encountered anyone while probing along. As I moved onto one edge of the bed, I carefully felt the other side to make sure I wouldn't be surprised to find I wasn't alone.

Finally, I curled up on the bed, tried and failed to adjust my eyes to the incredible darkness and gave out one last call, "Goodnight".

I thought it showed how really cool and unafraid I was. However, I must admit I slept with my clothes and shoes on.

I also slept dressed for the remaining week and a half until I was able to have the electric turned on. I also made sure I was home every day before dark for that full period of time.

Prior to the electric, there were occasional noises in other rooms and I could swear I heard giggling a couple of times, but for the most part, whoever or whatever it was, didn't seem interested in me and I certainly was willing to appreciate its desire to be left alone.

After the electric was turned on, I began to practice a spiritual exercise to bring peace and contentment to my home. I was only nineteen at the time and still wasn't knowledgeable about matters such as this. However, I did have my pre-birth memories about the astral and with that, had learned to not be afraid.

The first night of electricity, I turned off the living room light and went to bed. After I had been in bed for about five minutes, the light came back on.

Again, in an effort to show I wasn't afraid I called out for whoever turned the light on, to turn it off. I must admit I was shocked when the light quickly snapped off. At that moment, I wished I had kept my big mouth shut.

After that night I decided I would try to make friends with whatever I had become saddled with.

While in a meditative mood, I picked up what I interpreted as Exfien. Slowly, after a period of time, it seemed to smooth out to Arlene, which I soon identified as a young girl.

As the days began to roll by, I started to sense she was between seven and twelve years old. I went to the landlord to ask him about the history of the house and if there had been any children there in recent years.

He seemed to be uneasy with my questioning, but said he hadn't owned the home long enough to know anything about it. He said he just recently bought his own home and this one just came along with it. The previous owner hadn't placed much value on it, being no renter stayed there for more than a month or two.

While at home, I made every effort to give my little guest recognition. I often talked to her while cooking or cleaning, asked her various questions I knew she had no way of answering, and told her to not be afraid. I said I would take care of her, and try to help her go where she was supposed to be.

Now, when I came home at night, the lights were always on, although they had been off when I left. Often, things would disappear, but when I let her know I realized they were gone, they were quickly returned.

She particularly seemed to enjoy when my two young sisters came to spend the night. Wendy was eight and Debbie six and they quickly made friends with her. They couldn't see her either, but became aware of her presence when she bumped them.

Of course, we didn't tell our mother about my ghost border. Even my sisters realized if she heard such a thing, they wouldn't be allowed to spend the night any longer.

One thing people don't understand is that even a truly haunted house doesn't stay haunted for a long period of time. That would be contrary to the law of transition and change. Everything and everyone must continue to progress spiritually.

Slowly, I noticed activity was decreasing. Once in a while, I would find an item on the bed to let me know she had been there while I was out.

Finally, one night I returned home after ten o'clock and the house was completely dark.

I returned to a dark house every night thereafter. My precious little angel had gone to her own home.

SPIRITUAL INTERVENTION

I have no doubt everyone is periodically contacted for one reason or another. One of the first lessons I offered was that we do not necessarily need to use a spiritual exercise to petition for a blessing; that spirit already knows what we need and has provided a channel to reach us.

In my own case, I have learned to take notice of things around me. Doing so, I can quickly see if I have had a visitor. I do not necessarily always understand the reasoning behind a certain activity, but it always seems to turn out beneficially.

Have you ever dropped something that seemed to pass right through the floor? It is absolutely nowhere, but then a few days later you find the item sitting somewhere in plain sight.

This has occurred so often that I no longer look at it as some great mystery. There are far too many times this has happened to mention. However, I'll give two examples proving it hasn't been imagination.

For example, once in the bedroom I was removing a burned out bulb from an overhead light. I had to remove a specially designed knob to lower the glass covering which protected the bulbs. While on the step-ladder, the knob slipped from my hand and hit the floor.

After I put the new bulb in, I came down and looked for it. I looked for quite a while, but couldn't find it. I covered every inch of the bedroom floor, but it was no longer there.

Finally, giving up, I sat the glass covering aside. There was no way it would stay up without that knob. I didn't get upset because I figured it would come back to me like other items had done. That particular apartment in New York City seemed to have a great flurry of activities of that sort.

An hour later, I went into the kitchen and on the side-board sat the knob! I was alone in the apartment and had been alone all afternoon. I took it as a sign that something was trying to come through to me.

Later that evening, while in meditation, a great deal of information came through that was used in the monthly lessons prepared for my students.

Another time, I was practicing placing a crystal on my forehead at the bridge of my nose, spiritually called the Tisra Til, while I was laying on my back and meditating.

A couple of times I felt it slip and both times immediately it snapped my attention back. Both times I found the crystal beside my head on the pillow.

Then, at the conclusion of my meditation, I felt my forehead and noted it was gone again. I felt around the pillow but couldn't locate it. I got up, looked all over and under the pillow, checked the bed, and even looked around the floor. There was no doubt it was gone.

As I was leaving the bedroom, I finally saw the crystal sitting on the dresser. I just smiled and said, "OK, you got my attention, Eve. I'll be watching for what you're trying to show me."

I attributed things of this nature to my Guardian or what many call a soul-mate. Eve-Annabelle has always been my closest spirit contact, and I attribute the bulk of these sort of unusual happenings to her.

Even though she is usually the one getting my attention, that is not to say she is the primary source of information. My lessons and the lessons for my readers could come from various sources.

This is how Spiritual Intervention takes place. While it may seem strange, you should understand everyone in the world is involved with spiritiual intervention at one time or another.

When you came into this world, there was a general game plan laid out and over-watched by spirit. However, nothing is written in stone. If spirit can see a golden opportunity available to you, it will use whatever means necessary to carry out this intervention.

The primary intervention is during the dream state. While you are having a particular dream, your subconscious is being fed information that it stores and then kicks in at the necessary time. Even without your conscious awareness, your life will lead in a better direction, that is, if you permit spirit to guide you.

As you look back on your life, you may be able to see many cross-roads where if you had done something different, your life would be entirely different now.

Sometimes it was just a simple act; so simple it didn't seem to matter much. But, if you had done things just a little different, you might not have the mate you have now, the children, the job, and even the home you live in. Just a simple, insignificant act (at the time) can really greatly affect your entire spiritual training here.

The subconscious can play a major part simply by giving you an idea from out of nowhere. All of a sudden, you may become inspired to go to a certain place or do a certain thing. Often, this will lead to some greater event, which in turn, will alter your present path.

I have been asked by many about my contacts. They want to know more about how I relate with many of the master teachers. It is true that a great deal is in the physical, face-to-face, such as with Antares and Dap Ren, but a great deal has also been through spiritual intervention. I have had an untold number of lessons and discussions while in that special state where we are most acceptable to receive the next higher vibration.

My father has been gone from this world for twenty-eight years and my mother for twenty-six, but believe it or not, I still see them on a regular basis.

As of this writing, my most recent encounter was with my father just a short time ago. I was asleep, but being a light sleeper, I was brought out of it when I heard a noise down the hall, outside my bedroom.

My internal alarm had focused my attention to the open doorway, and I quickly discovered I couldn't move. While that might cause panic among many, since I had become so familiar with that state, I simply told my inner alarm it was of God and instantly I returned to a deep, hypnotic calm.

A few seconds later, I saw my father standing in the doorway. As he approached, he brought out his arm and waved it above me. A mysterious, black net seemed to spread out from the arm and fell on me, covering me completely.

Through this intervention, I instantly realized it was a medication of some sort. I had developed a nervous condition and it was beginning to block my ability to receive instruction. My life seemed to be affected by some outside sources, and I had the understanding this was the purpose for the healing. Undoubtedly, since my father desired to have contact with me, he had been granted the privilege of bringing it.

As the net settled slowly over me, I heard him say, "I heard you lost."

"Yes, I'm afraid I have," I responded.

Although the wording wasn't correct between us, I knew what he meant. A large publisher was in the process of releasing a book I wrote. I had even signed the contract and received an advance. However, due to a period of financial difficulty, it was taken over by another publisher not quite so enlighted. Not understanding the working of spirit in our world, they wrongly classified me as an occult writer. The old contract was ignored and my work returned..

"It's too important to be ignored," I told my father.

"I know," he responded. "But don't think so much about it. There is a new age of enlightenment coming into this world and although you may never see the full, world-wide bloom, you must understand you are an important bud on that tree."

I tried to raise up, but found my arms and legs to be as effective as mush and could only lie there. "What am I supposed to do next?" I asked.

A smile spread across his face. "It is in the hands of God. You love spirit and you know spirit is all there is in this world. When the time is ripe, those who are ready, will be led."

With that, he was gone.

A couple minutes later, I was able to sit up again.

THE FIRST ENCOUNTER OF THE WHITE LIGHT

I was the first member of the family to see the White Light. It was 1955 and I was in fifth grade.

It was about ten o'clock at night when Mitzy, my dog, started jumping at the door, barking.

My mother came into my room and asked if I had taken her out before I went to bed. Sheepishly, I admitted that I hadn't. I was upset that she made me get up and get the leash, but in my heart I knew it was my own fault. That was part of my regular duties, to take care of the dog and make sure she received her nightly walk before I went to bed.

That particular night the dog was acting strange. Usually, when we went for our nightly walks, she would tug on the leash and drag me along as she excitedly explored the territory, but this night, when she got outside, she seemed to freeze.

I shook at the leash as if it were a horse's reign, but for the longest time, she refused to move. Then with a sudden burst, she jerked me backward as she charged for the door. She began to beg to get back in.

That ticked me off and I literally dragged her back out in the yard to a distance about half way between our house and the neighbor's.

She seemed to be frozen like a statue except for her quivering.

I took a long look around, thinking some big dog was nearby, but finally decided there was nothing out there in the darkness.

Even though I was anxious to get back inside, I was patient with the dog, knowing she sensed something and figured she would get on with her business when she saw nothing there.

As we stood there though, she began to quake harder and harder. I swore she was going to drop dead with a heart attack.

Then, as I was staring at her, the ground around both of us lit up. I could see we were in the middle of a big circle of light. It was as if a gigantic flood light was beaming down on us.

I slowly looked up, being a little nervous about what I might find.

There, about ten feet above me, I saw a ball of light. It was floating independently, not having any visual means of support.

It reminded me very much of the florescent light in my grandfather's kitchen. Just as that light would do when it was first turned on, it shimmered slightly.

As I watched in total amazement, it began to move to the right, back toward the house. It was level with the roof and when it reached the part where the roof rose because of the attic, it followed the roof up instead of passing through it.

I stood in shock for a few seconds, then ran to the back of the house where I hoped to see the light come down the other side.

Getting to the backyard, I saw the light completely gone. Just as it went over the peak of the roof, it disappeared into thin air.

Fortunately, my parents were very spiritually advanced, so when I told them what I had seen, my mother began to ask questions, wanting to know every little detail. She even went outside with me to see if we could recreate it, but it was gone for good. It would be several years before I would see it again.

Twenty years later when my mother and sister, Wendy, were taking a night trip to Pensacola from Orlando to see my other sister, Debbie, they would finally get to see the light for themselves. With Mom and Wendy not caring for heavy traffic, whenever they went anywhere, they usually traveled at night.

On a long, desolate stretch of road, Wendy, who was driving, couldn't see any traffic except for what appeared to be a motorcycle, a long distance behind them.

As she kept checking in her rearview mirror, she told Mom it had to be traveling at a rapid rate of speed. It was closing in on them fast.

She estimated it to be moving faster than a hundred miles-an-hour as it zoomed up to the back of the car.

She screamed and swerved. Instead of crashing, as it reached the car it shot up the back window, and came to a stop on top of the roof.

Wendy ran off the road, slammed on the breaks and both jumped out. But nothing was there! Just as in my case, once it was out of sight, it just disappeared.

Later, as we discussed it, we realized that both times we saw the light, there were major changes in our household.

It was after I saw the light that I became exposed to a flurry of what most would call supernatural events. But it was at that time my training was beginning, and I would learn there was no such thing as supernatural. There is only science we understand and science we don't. Once we understand how a certain thing happens, it becomes a matter of science and is no longer considered strange, unusual or frightening.

When my mother and sister saw it, both of their lives were dramatically changed. There were many things, but one thing in particular – both experienced a healing.

The next appearance was a long while later. My mother and I were at a hotel in Miami Beach attending a convention.

It was Saturday night and after a full day of attending lectures, I was watching the Carol Burnett show in my mother's room.

As we sat there, she called out in a whisper a couple of times.

As I looked in her direction, she carefully lifted her finger, pointing at the window.

We were speechless as we watched a gigantic ball of light move around on the other side of the window. It was easy to see it was a solid object and not a reflection.

This time, it seemed to put on a show for us as it shimmered, changed shapes and changed into many beautiful colors.

After about a minute, it rose above the window and was gone. It was beautiful and calm and this time my mother seemed to understand the message. My mother had been undergoing treatment for cancer for over a year.

She calmly told me it told her to not be afraid. There was no such thing as death.

Two months later, my mother was gone from this world.

THE RETURN OF GRANDPA

I was extremely close to my grandfather. We had a bond that went even beyond the relationship I had with my parents, which was strange because he was quite elderly. If Abraham Lincoln hadn't been assassinated, chances are he probably would have still been alive when my grandfather was born.

Even though he was an old man, he had the spirit of a young one. Having been a railroad man his whole life, he wasn't about to sit in a rocker and slowly die. He had always been a hard worker. He had been a stoker, a fireman who shoveled the coal, and was used to working up a good sweat He usually could be

233

found outside working in his massive garden, and chances were pretty good I would be with him.

One day while picking strawberries, I told him I thought we might have known each other in another life. He just laughed. Spirituality wasn't really his bag. Having been reared in what I call hard-core Christianity, there hadn't been room for thoughts of that nature. His whole life he had been told there was only an Earth, a heaven and a hell.

Where his father left off pounding the fear of god into him, the minister of his youth took over. He learned everyone was born in sin and already on a slippery road to hell. Over and over in his youth, he was told how everyone was headed to hell beginning the day they were born. It would be only through righteous acts, unwavering dedication, and turning his back on things of the devil (which included just about everything that might be pleasurable), that he might be saved.

My grandfather was a very good man, but he was convinced he was a sinner. Being a railroad worker, he enjoyed an occasional drink with his friends and a game of poker. That, he felt, was grounds for eternal damnation.

I remember a friend of his that came to the house all the time. He was what my mother called a Bible-thumper. According to him, everyone in the world, except for a chosen few, were going to hell. I guess my grandfather put up with him because deep in his heart he thought maybe this man was his only chance at redemption.

I was just a child of eight, but when I listened to him besmear my grandfather, telling him how evil he was, while he sat there stuffing his face with grandmother's strawberry shortcake, I couldn't keep quiet any longer.

"Reverend, do you have any children?" I asked, knowing very well he did.

He took his eyes off my grandfather just long enough to glare in my direction. "Why, yes! Yes, I do. I have a daughter a little older than you."

"And would you do anything in your power to protect her?" I asked.

A big smile set on his face, convinced his hell fire lecture about saving people had gotten through to me.

"Yes. There's no way I'm going to let her spend eternity in hell's burning fires. She's going to be with me in heaven!"

I thought for a moment, then asked, "You wouldn't help throw her in the fire, if you felt she deserved it?"

Horror spread across his face. "Of course not!" he boomed.

My grandfather twitched nervously in his chair as he motioned to me, but I refused to let go. "If she was really, really bad, like if she gambled, stole things, and lied, wouldn't you throw gasoline on her and set her on fire?"

"You're a sick, evil child!" he yelled. "How can you think up such evil things?"

"Why are you angry?" I asked.

"Because only a sick maniac could think of doing such things!" he screamed.

"Then," I continued, "what you're saying is, you're better than God?"

"I never said such a wicked thing! You're not only evil, you're stupid too!" he snarled.

I moved close to my grandfather. I was afraid, but I wasn't about to give up.

"You said you wouldn't do such a terrible thing," I said as I put an arm around Grandpa's neck, " but you said God is going to burn everybody except for a few. So, if God would do it and you wouldn't, then you must be better than God."

"You're going to hell!" he hissed.

With that, my grandfather raised his head, sat up straight and said, "Reverend, I'm afraid I'm going to have to ask you to leave."

The Reverend jerked his Bible off the arm of the sofa chair and stormed out.

Giving my Grandfather a kiss, I said, "Don't worry, grandpa. There's no such thing as hell."

Giving a weary smile, he whispered, "God! Let's hope not!"

Four years later, on his deathbed, he still harbored a deep fear of hell. My parents, knowing I was down to Earth and not given to imagination, often listened to the things I remembered about the astral. But my grandfather, even though he loved me with every ounce of his being, was afraid to put so much faith in my memory.

Because of our age, my two sisters and I weren't allowed to be in his hospital room the day he died.

Eavesdropping, I heard my father relate to my mother about the fear in my grandfather's eyes as he was dying. Right up to the end, he was certain he was hell bound for eternal punishment.

I remember how angry that made my mother, saying the world would be a better place if there were more people like my sainted grandfather.

Although my grandfather didn't really want to hear what I had to say about the journey to the other side, he did believe that a departed spirit could contact you if it wanted to.

"If you came back to contact me," I asked one sunny day while he was still able to enjoy the great outdoors, "how would you do it?"

"Why, I guess I'd just give you a tap on the shoulder," he answered.

More than a month went by after his death with nothing happening. I really wouldn't have been shocked to see him in his usual physical body, but it didn't happen.

Then, one night watching television, I felt a slight brush against my left shoulder. I turned around thinking it was my mother, but no one was there. Then I felt something just below the backbone on the left side. At first, it was slight, but then became heavier and heavier until it felt like someone was poking a finger into my back.

I took it to be my grandfather letting me know that he finally found out there was no hell.

The finger-in-my-back phenomenon lasted for quite a while. It didn't stay all the time, it would last only a few minutes at a time, but would occur almost everyday.

My mother told me to let her know when I felt the finger. She would then take that opportunity to talk to him.

The finger-in-the-back became an important event. My mother being slightly psychic, claimed he related thoughts to her during that time.

When the finger contact ended, it ended for good. No matter how hard I tried, it would not return.

A strange thing though, twenty-two years later, when my mother passed on, after about a month, I felt the finger again!

This time, it was under the bone on the right side. There was never any doubt in my mind. I knew it was my mother, but it didn't last as long as the previous encounter. After about five weeks, it also left, to never return.

Back when my grandfather's encounter began, there was also a flurry of what my father called "supernatural" activity.

One evening, I was sitting on my bed tossing the silver dollar my grandfather had given me several years previous. The bed was pushed up next to the wall and on one flip, the dollar hit the wall and slid down between the bed and the wall.

When I pulled the bed out, I saw it had gone down the crack between the siding board and the wall. I tried over and over again to pull it out, but I just couldn't get a grip on it. Using a knife, I was able to move it, but there was no way of pulling it up.

Finally, giving up, I went across the hall to my father, told him what had happened and asked if he could help. He said he would try later.

I walked back into my room, and to my astonishment, found the silver dollar sitting in the middle of the bed.

That shocked me for more reasons than one. It wasn't as shocking to me to know that my grandfather was there and retrieved the dollar for me, as it was to understand how he did it.

Being at a different wave-length, it was my understanding that something astral would simply pass through a physical item. It was easy to understand his hand could pass through a solid wall, but it seemed it would also pass through that silver dollar.

But that was only one of many things happening around me.

Things were forever being moved. It actually went from being miraculous to being irritating.

But something more important was happening. A slow and strange change was coming over me. I seemed to lose interest in things I had previously loved. And when one of my parents would talk to me, I would look right through them and not be able to repeat what I had just been told.

I started to sleepwalk and even sleep-run. I would get up in the middle of the night and run around the house. My parents took me to a physician and he concluded I was going through an emotional trauma, and that it might last awhile until the problem could work itself out.

Then, the most frightening event for my parents took place one cold February night. About two o'clock in the morning while still dreaming, I got out of bed to go to my grandfather.

Even though I was dreaming I was in his old house, trying to go to him in the kitchen, I had actually ventured into a closed-off section of the house. It was common practice for my parents to close off certain sections of the house we wouldn't be using to conserve heat.

While I was seeing only the doorway to my grandfather's kitchen, I had gone into an abandoned upstairs bedroom, had somehow forced the window open and was attempting to climb through it.

Suddenly, in total shock, I snapped awake as my parents came crashing in. My father grabbed me and jerked me from the ledge. Finally realizing where I was, I told dad something had been holding me back. I had been trying with all of my will to go into the next room, but something was refusing to let me go.

Then, they did the strangest thing. Keeping me in tow, we began to search the house. Both had been awakened by someone banging on their bedroom door insisting I needed help. We were all alone in the house, but Mom insisted it was a man's voice calling to her.

The next time I felt the finger in my back, my mother and I went into a quiet room and Mom talked to grandpa. She told him how much I loved and missed him and how I was suffering, but for my own benefit, it might be best if he let me progress through this difficult process alone.

Thereafter, I often felt my grandfather's love, but I never again felt his finger in my back.

ANDERSON STREET:
A PORTAL TO OTHER WORLDS

One of the most active fields of spiritual activity I ever encountered was our home on Anderson Street in Orlando. My four children were all passing through puberty while living there. That was probably a major factor in helping to heighten the fantastic spiritual activity there.

It is an old mansion-like home with a history of which no one is really certain. Some have said a murder occurred there. Others, who are quite elderly and have lived in that area for more than sixty years, said they heard stories suggesting strange ceremonies were performed there many decades ago; ceremonies where ungodly things took place. I cannot attest to either, however, I had no doubt then (and even more so now) that this place was some sort of portal to other worlds.

When I first saw the For Rent sign on the front yard of the beautiful home, I doubted it would be within my means, but jotted the phone number down anyway. The next day when I called, the landlady said she was sorry but it had already been rented out. She asked something I thought to be rather strange, though. She wanted me to leave my phone number. She said as soon as it was available again, she would give me a call. I was amused at her statement but gave the number anyway.

Changing my mind about moving, I stopped looking around. A little over two months later, the landlady called. She said the home was available again if I was still interested.

Not even questioning why it was available so quickly, I told her I had primarily contacted her mostly out of curiosity. The rent was more-than-likely beyond my means. She said if I would take it, she would do her best to keep it reasonable. When I questioned what she meant by reasonable, I almost fell out of my chair when she said she would let us have it for a hundred and forty dollars a month. Although prices weren't as high then as present, the average apartment went for two to three hundred dollars. The rent for a moderate home was from five to six hundred and a place such as this would have easily been from seven hundred up.

Even though I had passed up the idea of moving, I quickly jumped on such an insane offer. Within a week I moved my large family from an expensive two bedroom apartment into a fabulous four bedroom, two bath home complete with many spacious rooms, a good heating system and even a fireplace. The children quickly fell in love with the place, especially enjoying the gigantic backyard to play in.

I cannot say for certain at what point I became aware of strange or unusual activity taking place. When there is more than one person involved, little attention is paid to objects moved around, but as this force (or forces) took greater and greater strides to gain attention, I was forever agitated by things being moved or disappearing altogether, even while I was using them.

I suppose I realized from the beginning that something had to be wrong with this deal, but I chose to not think about it.

As things progressed though, I finally paid a visit to the landlady to find out about our new home. She admitted she also didn't have much knowledge about the home, but her husband grabbed it up when it went on the market at a dirt-cheap price.

Being honest, she finally admitted that although they had owned the home for several years, no renter had stayed there for more than six months.

Circumstances sounded pretty much like the home I rented in the grove when I was nineteen.

With the passing of time, it was quite evident that whatever these particular forces were, they were fond of the children and quite eager to protect them. Realizing nothing was detrimental to my family, we made the decision to stay.

However, I must admit we were exposed to things that contradicted much of what I understand about spiritual activity. If I had seen a movie similar to what we experienced, I would have laughed, saying such things were impossible and sometimes outright silly.

On our first Christmas Eve, I was attempting to get the younger children in bed, telling them Santa would soon be there. They were laughing and playing when John, the youngest said he heard a noise on the roof. I lost control as they all raced to the window. Within a few seconds they were all squealing with delight. As I approached the window located in one of the second floor bedrooms, I was horrified to see some sort of large shadow the size of a deer slowly move by. Seeming to demonstrate moving appendages, it looked as though this shadow was attempting to gallop.

I have never been able to explain this. The only conceivable answer would be that these resident forces had the ability to create illusions based on group imagination and expectations.

John often talked about an old woman who came into his room and told him stories. While such talk was unnerving, it wasn't until Lynda referred to her as the bedroom witch, that John would no longer sleep alone.

On the second floor, there was a linen closet across from the bedroom where Granny slept. It was also right next to the bathroom. As Barbara was putting fresh linen in one morning, Granny came out of her bedroom, passed Barbara, and went into the bathroom, closing the door behind her. Barbara called out a good morning, but there was no answer back from Granny.

Shrugging it off, she rushed back downstairs and was shocked to see Granny sitting on the couch, folding laundry. Barbara asked how she did that trick, but of course, Granny didn't know what she was talking about. Barbara quickly found Lynda and Cathy, told them what she had just seen and bravely, but cautiously, all three slowly made their way back upstairs. The door was still shut. Terrified, but excited, they slowly turned the knob and threw the door open and jumped to both sides of the door. Finally peeking inside, they found only an empty room.

If Granny hadn't been living, it would have undoubtedly been accepted as being her ghost. Since she was sitting downstairs, this was further proof of its power to create illusions.

Even though the entities from this portal enjoyed playing games, they could also be deadly serious about protecting the children. One night there was screaming in the girl's room. As I rushed in, they told me a rat had woke Lynda by jumping on her bed. Everybody but Granny was crammed into our bed that night.

The next evening as I was going upstairs, I saw the rat boldly sitting at the top of the stairs, staring down at me, seeming to challenge me. Freezing, I slowly backed down and quickly looked for some sort of weapon. Finding only a broom, I quickly returned to the stairs and slowly started up again.

Expecting it to have run away by then, I was surprised to find it still sitting there in apparent defiance. I readied the broom, ready to bring it down on its head if given a chance. Moving within a few steps, I finally slammed the broom down. Unfortunately, I missed. But to my shock, it was still sitting there. I seemed to be frozen in time as we seemed to stare at each other. Then it slowly fell over. At first, I thought it was a stuffed toy, but quickly discovered it was a very real rat. A very real dead rat. There weren't any marks on it, but something had killed it, then positioned it there at the top of the stairs where we would easily find it. Without looking up, I sensed something by the bedroom door and I offered it my thanks for helping to protect the children.

I always seemed to have a good relationship with the entities, so did Granny, but that wasn't the case for my wife at that time. Betty was stern and if she attempted to discipline any one of the children while angry, some object would come flying at her.

They also seemed to love playing tricks on her, or making her look guilty when she really wasn't. We had a pool table in the game room and everyone loved playing, except Betty. One day in a fit of anger, she said she should throw the pool balls away. That would teach the kids to pay attention to her when she spoke. That night, I was watching television and was the last to go to bed. When I finally went upstairs, I sat at my desk for awhile writing. After a couple more hours passed, I heard a noise downstairs and quickly rushed down. Everything seemed to be alright. The house was securely locked and at first it seemed nothing was wrong. Going into the game room, I found all pool balls gone from the table. Although it was apparent to everybody the next day it had been Betty that removed them, I was proof she was innocent. I knew she was asleep the whole time.

My defending her seemed to anger the entities, though. Whenever something would disappear, it would always be returned within a couple of days. However, those particular pool balls were never seen again.

Actually, it could take an entire book to openly discuss all of the strange things that occurred there. Lynda, my eldest, wrote a manuscript about their childhood in that house. Called "Growing up in the garden of the mad", she went into great detail about the many entities there. As of this writing, it is being considered for a television movie.

We would have moved if there had been even one person uncomfortable in that house, but by the time we had lived there for awhile, most had developed a gentle bond with the forces. Even Betty admitted she had become much calmer and rational when attempting to maintain order among the children.

Surprisingly, we lived in that house for fifteen years. In gratitude from our landlady, the rent stayed a hundred and forty dollars the entire time.

CHAPTER ELEVEN:

A DEEPER UNDERSTANDING

The following discourses were a part of the training given to those seekers desiring to open their inner consciousness to a better understanding of what has and is taking place around us. Having the understanding "As Above, So Below", we see that by having a good grasp of the physical, we are better able to understand its counterpart, the astral.

LONG AGO AND FAR AWAY....

In this account we will be discussing events based entirely on astral readings. Outside of these readings, it would be very difficult for us in the physical world to verify. There is a good reason for this. What we are looking at supposedly happened many, many eons ago. So distant a time that our planet was hardly more than a gaseous, fiery ball still facing many millions of years of solidifying.

We must never forget our world is hardly the ultimate reality. Physical life is often called an illusion, while departure from here is considered reality. With this in mind, we find another world with its own historical accounts on which we need to base our study on many points. Such is the case now. Supposedly in the akashic records there is a most unusual story about that ancient time; a story which would prove to have an important impact on our present civilization.

This particular account is about five individuals belonging to an advanced civilization so ancient no trace remains of it, even in the most evasive reaches of the universe. Although our world had not yet begun to form, these five had already spent a great deal of time in the physical, and had developed spiritually to such a degree that each had attained unbelievable powers.

However, there is a spiritual rule just as true today as it was then. "Take care once you stand on your spiritual feet, for while you reside in the physical universes, even though a master you may be, you are susceptible to illusion and temptation."

These masters, three men and two women, were no longer required to return to the physical universes, but they chose to remain in the lower universes to assist others in their search for truth and wisdom.

As the reading goes, one of the masters found a great deal wrong in the universes and often found himself questioning the wisdom of the way things were done in this physical school.

At first his observations were based on very humanitarian concepts, but as he began to bend and then break many spiritual rules, the dark nature of the universe slowly began to take over his mind.

He eventually became a prime example of what can happen when we have extremely powerful abilities, but fail to use them in an appropriate manner.

It was almost like a Star Wars movie. The master and the negative energy of the physical became as one. It was difficult to determine if the master ruled the dark side or if it ruled him.

His incredible abilities, intended to give aid and comfort to occupants of the physical worlds, instead brought misery. While he intended to free people from their physical obligations, he had forgotten that experiencing such obligations had been the reason for the creation of these universes and their coming here. The people of the physical universes are here for only one purpose, to develop spiritually. The things he desired to free them from were the very tools needed to carry our their education. So, pure spiritual energy could offer no protection as physical forces (negative energy) attempted to correct his changes.

As he continued to seek a following from others who thought as he did and who had already graduated from the physical school, it was quickly discovered the god-like abilities they had developed were gone and they had become "fallen angels".

Slowly, he and the others fell victim to the illusions of this world. Finding themselves trapped once more in the physical, they became quite angry at the spiritual forces that seemed to abandon them. They openly spoke against any God force that would punish them simply because they loved humanity enough to try to save it from misery.

Turning their backs on previous good intentions, they decided they would first need to establish themselves into positions of power. However, the master only managed to darken his mind as he sought to reach out and control all physical worlds.

While he became dedicated to his ultimate goal of controlling all known universes, the other four attempted to show him the error of his thinking. They continued to make every effort to save not only him, but those who fell from grace with him.

As time passed, most of the fallen were once again raised to their previous positions, but the master seemed to become more and more demented as he slowly turned himself over to the negative forces completely.

They became so dedicated in saving their brother they even agreed to take on physical bodies following him into several incarnations. They made attempt after attempt to bring him back into spiritual light, but although they rescued many, their efforts with him were constantly thwarted.

A surprising thing about this story though, is that these actions and decisions would greatly affect our own distant universe. Because of this episode, these ancient ones have greatly influenced us – even in our present age.

The master called Antares, looked at the suffering of humanity and wondered "why people had to be subject to their own misdeeds". He felt once an individual saw the error of his ways and decided to correct his behavior, he should no longer be subject to the law that he must compensate for his previous misconduct. Such a concept was also accepted by untold thousands who agreed they should not be forced to pay their debts – even though they fully understood there was a law of karma that could not be revoked.

While Antares was the only true master of the rebel ranks, a great number of the following had also developed various degrees of power. Thus, when the entire group presented themselves as a solitary unit, the forces they generated was far too great for an average mortal to resist.

When Antares fell from his spiritual position as a Brother of the Light, becoming the undisputed leader of these thousands, this became the basis for the story of the fall of Satan. Even though he was one of God's favorite angels, once he turned from God, he was cast from heaven, along with all of those who chose to follow him.

In his first incarnation of the new regime, his name was Tyrantis, but he was often referred to as Satan, which surprisingly enough was a title of great respect and spiritual honor at the time. Many temple-like structures were even built in his honor, offering a place for the people to study and learn about the many secrets of the universe.

When he held court, he wore a red cloak displaying several pointed peaks rising up behind his head. He also sported a pointed goatee, adding to his demonic appearance and was always accompanied by his trident, a scepter offering a constant reminder he was in a position of complete and awesome power.

As time began to pass, he who had been known as the new savior, slowly became a god-like man to be feared. He was a prime example of why we should never consider the Essence of God to be considered a man. His mind slowly became demented and eventually his courts of mercy and grace became courts of trial and punishment. His power seemed to grow to even greater heights than he had previously experienced.

Over and over his two brothers and two sisters of the Light entered his universe not to destroy, but to save him.

While there were many who joined them in an attempt to bring him back to the Light, we are going to concentrate on only two of these masters. The reason is that once our planet was inhabited, these two followed him into this world not once but many times, which ultimately affected our concepts in many religions.

These masters, Raphael and Uriel, played a major part in many ancient civilizations. While they were still unable to save their brother, they were able to assist the souls that now inhabited this planet. In the Pleadian universe, from which they came, Antares had been able to amass a great deal of destruction and fear, and these two were determined that would not happen here.

Over and over again, they reincarnated as various entities offering protection and guidance against the destructive forces so closely associated with their brother. Many incarnations were at such a distant time it is doubtful any would recognize their names, however, they also lived many lives we could easily recognize. One of the overshadowings of Uriel was said to be the Buddha. Raphael also lived many important lives. One none other than a man called Jesus!

This is extremely enlightening for us for many reasons. In this greater understanding, we see there is much more to the foundation of various religions than previously believed.

Another important point is that Antares did return to the light with their assistance and this happened during his occupancy on our planet. Suddenly, we see an insignificant speck of dust in the universe now becoming the planet for enlightenment and redemption!

As the various adventures continued, especially between Raphael and Antares, we discover they made their way into recorded history just two thousand years ago. This time as Jesus, he confronted Antares on another level. Even though much of the previous power had been stripped from him, Antares still maintained a position of power and authority. In this strange account, Antares had incarnated as Pontius Pilate, the Governor of Judea. At this time many could see a return of compassion to the previous master as he made every attempt to save Jesus and said he "washed his hands from the blood of Jesus".

Then, we discover an even more surprising event taking place. In the same akashic record, the final chapter of "the great rescue" brings them within the range of our own time period!

Accordingly, the final incarnation of Raphael took place in 1909 on a farm in Illinois. Uriel was born a couple of years later in the southwest. Approximately at this same time, Antares incarnated in the eastern united states. The three came together for one last complete victory of Light over Darkness.

In this final incarnation, we find a surprising twist to the story line. It appears Antares had already rejoined his brothers and sisters of Light back in the higher worlds. The three had chosen to come together to our world for an entirely different purpose.

This time Raphael and Uriel joined their combined powers with Antares becoming a close associate – in an endeavor to save Earth from nuclear destruction.

It is no secret in the 1950's our world balanced on a sharp edge of destruction. Thousands had bomb shelters in their basements and hardly a home didn't have a stockpile of food and supplies.

The akashic records strongly stressed our planet could face total destruction if men's reasoning failed.

For millions of years the spiritual forces were divided against themselves, now however, they were able to come together, offering their combined flow of Spiritual energy to help save the world at this most extreme time.

Raphael left this world for the last time in 1959. Uriel stayed a short time longer, leaving in 1985.

Antares was the last to leave, dying from his physical shell for the last time in the physical universe in 1998. Although I never had the opportunity to physically meet with the two personalities of Raphael or Uriel, I have established a strong relationship with Antares.

Prior to that meeting, I was totally unaware of his strange and exciting story. In fact, I was not even aware of who Antares was supposed to be until much later.

We met in a small town near San Diego, where he introduced me and a handful of other invitees to an institute that promotes writings left behind by Raphael and Uriel. He has also written a few books making an attempt to bring light and golden wisdom back to a new, unfolding world.

As we walked the distant grounds, up in the hills, he related much that Raphael had shared with him, including the potential for the very ground we were walking on.

"In the years to come," he said, "on this very spot, there will be a universal medical and science center. It will be assisted by many of our spiritual brothers, some coming from distant galaxies! When this center is completed, it will offer a cure for almost all known diseases. It will also play a major part in ending turmoil we see in the world today.

"The few 'fallen angels' still remaining here have already completely returned to the Brotherhood of Light and are eagerly awaiting the opportunity to assist their galactic brothers."

THE NEW ERA OF COSMIC REBELS

In this new millennium, we find we are in an age filled with men and women who serve as Advanced Guard to a new spiritual revolution. They no longer cling to terrifying threats and foolish superstitions. They no longer accept rules made by mere men, who suggest that they speak for God, but are only interested in serving their own greed. These rebels have finally awakened to the fact that freedom of worship means their right to come to an understanding about Godly matters, and refuse to let others tell them what must be done regarding religious decisions.

They appear every generation, but in this decade they are more defined in their opinions and can seldom be silenced or controlled by various "authorities". Many so-called religious groups have become closely associated with mind washing techniques and try to disguise their agenda with such names as "religious adult training" or by threatening their members with hell fire.

The new breed doesn't lead an attack against such controlling groups or institutes. They feel all people have the right to their own personal opinions. Unlike rebels of past generations, they do not desire or endeavor to overthrow, dissolve, or otherwise destroy anything not falling into their range of acceptance. Since they demand the right to think and speak as they please, they openly encourage others to follow whatever dictates they desire for themselves. The rebels could hardly be held in high regard if they chose to force others into their line of thinking. The lesson here is that we are all Divine Beings and have the ability to decide for ourselves what is right or wrong for us.

More than likely, the reason for the surge in spiritual evolution is due to "cosmic intervention". Just as the infant will one day become an adult, we find there is no point where we can draw a line when that individual can say, "I am now an adult, and no longer a child." The stages occur, but cannot be so easily identified. It is the same with spiritual development. At one point we are the seeker, at another we become the enlightened and at still another we discover complete spiritual enlightenment. There never was a definite, singular point where these developments could be identified. It is for this reason so many have become enlightened and are not fully aware of it. It didn't come in a wonderful burst of lights and emotions. It was something developed over a period of time and we are aware of it only because we can now see how our thoughts and understandings so easily move and guide us.

Cosmic masters were not presented as mild-mannered beings in the ancient mystery schools. The drawings of that age presented the masters as forceful men, waving blazing swords and riding fiery-eyed stallions. This did not suggest they were here to change the world, but to liberate the enslaved.

For this reason the new cosmic rebel has strong feelings about rights and freedoms, but will seldom attempt to change the world. If we are to step into true enlightenment, it must be our choice to do so and not because we follow the dictates of others.

The rebels do not desire to destroy the school (for we must never forget all of this is only a school), but instead, choose to assist the newly liberated souls who have outgrown this lowly classroom.

That is why they say it's all right for sheep to be sheep (if that's what they want), but the eagle must make its home in the highest peak that it can reach.

By searching, you have become that eagle. You have become that Cosmic rebel.

DIFFERENT FORMS OF SPIRITUAL INTERVENTION

Just as the physical body grows on a daily basis, so too does the "psychic self" mature on a day to day basis.

The physical body develops because of various forms of energy (both physical and spiritual), exercise, and the food we eat. The psychic body develops through experience and pure spiritual energy.

While most of us are well versed on the health and care of the physical body, only a few are aware of "nourishing the inner child".

Your inner self is able to grow through the various spiritual stages only because of the cosmic intervention that comes to it. This form of intervention most likely takes place while the body is at rest. At this time the subconscious can fully absorb energy and convert it into psychic substance, which in turn, programs the

253

higher consciousness. This is carried out mainly in one of three different ways. They are: energy received from the Higher Self, through vibration adjustment, or through implanted codes put into the DNA as the physical body developed.

ENERGY FROM THE HIGHER SELF

We are much more than we have ever believed. In our purest state we were called a "monad". This monad could be considered the same thing as "a spark from God". It has unlimited Divine ability and is credited with being God-like in all ways.

When we ventured out, leaving the higher realms, we did so as a monad. A strange thing happened at the fifth plane though. To enter into the physical world, the monad split into three different consciousness levels. One of these levels is masculine, one feminine and one stays neutral, which remained behind as a collection source, gathering and filing the experiences of the other two. This is the basis for the teaching about soul mates and guardian angels.

All the good either the male or female performs is registered and kept within the third consciousness, now called the "higher self". This consciousness can hold or use the accumulated energy (commonly called karma) to assist one or the other, provided their positive energy is greater in quantity than the negative. This, then, can be fed to the sleeping individual – which not only helps to grow spiritually, but can assist in many physical endeavors.

VIBRATION ADJUSTMENT

Vibration adjustment would be a cosmic master or cosmic teacher bypassing the higher self and administering the frequency change directly to the individual. This can be accomplished only if one was prepared to advance. This would be shown through his or her physical actions and mental attitude. The more mature the attitude and the more spiritual nature they demonstrate, the greater is their chance to constantly receive such vibration adjustments.

Such adjustments can be made in one of two ways, mentally or by physical touch. Neither is as uncommon as one might expect. While mental is the most common, received in the dream state, if greater doses of energy may be needed, a slight touch (either in the dream state or while awake) can be given.

CODED IMPLANT

Just as our DNA is implanted with definite patterns determining our body and inner structure, so too, does the "inner child" have definite coded implants enabling it to know what to do.

According to the DNA implants, we could be blond or dark haired, blue eyed or other, big or small, weak or strong, and so on. But our actions are also highly regulated by similar codes.

These codes can be administered only if we sufficiently open ourselves to receive them. We were born with a complete set of codes. Without them, we would hardly have more than a vegetable existence. But new codes can constantly be added to the previous ones as we progress.

Just as we moved from one grade to another as a child, we are constantly moving forward in this grander school, constantly unfolding and developing.

ENDING THE "FEAST OF BLOOD"!

We have been taught many things throughout our life that are simply not true. Even though this so-called wisdom is quite outrageous to any clear thinking person, we have been taught we must not question what we are told. If we question these things, then we are questioning God – and that will make him very angry. However, even *that* statement should make us stop and take a moment to think.

What we are told is that God isn't really very God-like. According to them, God is an angry and vengeful man not only ready, but quite eager, to deal out harsh and eternal punishment.

Entire civilizations are held mental prisoners by controlling individuals who use fear to feed their superstitions. But we must remember that these lies are pounded into us from the cradle to the grave by those with limited authority who desire to have complete and uncontested power.

While they claim to speak for God, they speak only for themselves. There are so many who claim to be speaking for Jesus – but don't have the slightest idea what his true words were. As it turns out, Jesus actually spoke out against any religion that attempted to control followers. He made endless attacks against the priests of the time, calling them treacherous demons seeking to enslave the mind of man. Jesus was almost killed for saying it would be better to have mad dogs as priests than these hypocrites with their endless flow of lies and fear.

He denounced their man-god, saying Moses created this angry and vengeful beast from his own mind in order to control the unruly mass. He said no such being existed or could exist. He explained such states of consciousness as anger, vengeance, pride or jealousy could not relate a true meaning to the Creative Forces of the cosmic. Such attitudes would only produce an extremely low and ignorant consciousness.

Although he taught this two thousand years ago, you are still fed the same lies so you might be controlled in this day and age. You have been taught God is jealous and angry, and you must pray for forgiveness to ensure you don't burn forever in an eternal hell. Even though Jesus insisted the concept of Jehovah was false, in ignorance, they not only continue to insist the evil god exists, but that Jesus is his son.

Furthermore, Jesus spoke against blood sacrifices, saying such a barbaric attitude was a throw-back to the primitive days of human sacrifice.

What kind of God do we worship if we believe its anger can be bought off with gore and blood? What kind of horrible beast would demand a blood feast?

What if we heard of a neighbor who demanded the death of his son so that he might be appeased? Such a madman would be quickly locked up. Such ranting would not be acceptable among normal, healthy-minded people. However, without question, perhaps out of fear, we eagerly accept such a nature belonging to some fearsome god.

Our society has been controlled to a point where we don't dare question the fear mongers. Here, we lower the God concept to the lowest of low vibrations. This god is nothing more than a blood-feasting barbarian that can just as easily toss a child into a burning furnace as he can slam the Earth with wrath.

Rest assured no such monster exists. The universe is based on love, compassion and high vibrations. It is a universe of peace, not hate.

Unfortunately, our fearsome concepts are a carry over from the ancient worship of Moloch. He was a fierce and vicious god demanding blood tributes. To deny the god was to condemn the people. To satisfy his thirst for blood was their only hope to have good crops, to keep their health and have a peaceful existence.

In the days of Jesus, blood sacrifices were still being made to this beast god, but with some changes. The name Moloch was changed to Jehovah and instead of the blood of females and children, the new reformed god could be appeased with blood from livestock.

The priests were more than pleased with this arrangement. Primarily, it brought in a continuous tidy sum. The only acceptable tribute was one purchased from the priests, and their price was two to three times greater than original cost. In addition, the priests then feasted on these sacrifices.

Did you ever wonder why Jesus was so adamant in his attack against the priesthood, or why he was accused of turning over the temple's change tables? Jesus was attempting to put an end to making priests rich by paying tribute to an evil god demanding blood. It's believed Jesus would have been abhorred to any teaching suggesting he became a blood sacrifice, similar to the ones he spoke against.

Most Christians know his predominant teaching was that Spirit (God) is in all of us. God is not something external, far away or foreign to us. He explained that we are all sparks from this same Divine Essence.

Due to our fears and superstitions, we have closed our awareness channel to such a degree we could never see ourselves as the Divine Entities we are. We must understand we are Divine Beings with all the blessings and abilities of our true God Source. We must stop thinking of Divine Essence as something terrible, frightening and angry. We must also stop thinking of it as being something outside of ourselves.

The very nature of existence is that all parts are drawn together and work in harmonious balance. This is evident in every aspect of science. If there was some angry and vengeful god, it would be a display of disharmony, causing a rendering and tearing apart of natural environment. All things work in harmony to such an extent we can see everything we know about our essence would have to be based on love. While hatred blows energy apart, love draws all units together.

To carry this a step further, let's take another look at our madman neighbor. If we were to read that this demented man constantly teased and tormented his children and forced them to kill one another in his honor, we wouldn't be the least bit surprised to hear he was committed to prison or a mental institution. Then, why do we take for granted that a superior life form acting in this manner is acceptable?

In the physical concept, we read this evil man teased his children by leaving candy and fruit out in plain sight, but forbid them from touching any of it. While he hid and watched, if he saw any give in to temptation, they were punished by having their hand held over a burner on the stove, and then thrown out in the snow, told to never return. We also read that he often beat his children for no other reason than to constantly remind them they were evil, sinful beings.

To make matters worse, he taught them they could only repent from their sins by offering blood to him. Anything less would only bring more wrath.

Then, we finally read how he encouraged and delighted in the murder of one of his children, whose dead body and drained blood so greatly pleased him, that he forgave all, with the promise he would absolve them of their sins. But even in this stupid account, the children were still threatened with the punishment of being thrown in the oven and roasted – regardless of the human sacrifice!

Only by breaking away from irrational teachings can we build a new and better life, and finally understand what is meant by "the spirit within". It is time to end the lies, the fear and enslavement by those who seek to blind us from our unity with God.

CHAPTER 12:

INSIDE THE CAPITAL CITY

THE UGLY DWARF OF AGA DE

I remember the first time I saw him. He was totally horrifying. Most certainly, I would have ran away if it weren't for the fact my Guide was beside me.

"Did you see that!?" I gasped after he passed by.

My Guide said nothing. He just smiled and continued to walk along.

I had good reason to be shocked. It would have been surprising enough to engage him in any of the lower worlds, but I couldn't understand how such an evil-looking being could gain access to this wonderful city. Some call it Aga De, but most call it the city of a thousand names. The Buddhists call it the Lotus with a thousand petals. Many believe it is heaven. The Christians call it the Golden City, or refer to it as the place where streets are paved with gold. Here, there is only the most glorious and beautiful landscapes. Instantly upon entering, the most sublime and peaceful feelings fill you with a form of ecstasy unknown in the physical world.

So, it's quite apparent I would be dumbfounded. I couldn't understand how he got there, or why he was there.

Not being satisfied with receiving only a smile, I continued to probe. I was fully aware everything that happens below the Soul plane occurs only to give a lesson. However, if I was expected to come up with an answer on my own, I wasn't able. I wanted to know beyond a shadow-of-a-doubt who and what this creature was.

Carrying a silver lantern, waving it back and forth, he looked like a troll that had just stepped out of a child's fairy tale book.

Finally, the Guide responded by offering only that the dwarf had lived in the city for a long time and was now a permanent resident.

While it was evident the Guide felt he had said enough, it wasn't enough of an answer for me. Seeing he wasn't willing to offer more information on the subject at this time, I began to mull it over in my mind. After awhile I felt I had come up with the perfect answer. Perhaps he wasn't an ugly dwarf at all. Maybe he was some sort of master in disguise, taking this opportunity to test an individual on what might really be in one's heart. Satisfied that was the answer, I quickly passed over it and then forgot about the incident completely.

A long time later, when I returned to the beautiful city after another physical sojourn, I again saw him. Remembering my previous conclusion, instead of cringing, I approached him. I felt if he wanted to pretend he was an ugly troll-like being, I would go along with it.

As I approached, a strange thing became apparent. With the astral awareness being more highly refined than the physical, I could instantly see this was no master. Not only was he not very intelligent, but was actually quite dim-witted.

Facing each other, I looked into his face and asked, "Are you good or evil?"

His eyes opened wide and his face filled with surprise and confusion. We continued to look into each other's eyes for a short while, neither of us saying anything. Finally, he made a wide step to the left, to by-pass me, and then quietly continued on with his secret mission, waving the lantern as he walked away.

Remembering the encounter in this incarnation, I have to smile when I think about my question to him. I'm pretty sure I would look shocked too if someone came up and out of the blue, asked if I was good or evil. I probably would also just walk away. However, I continued to wonder what it was I had experienced. I still didn't have a satisfactory answer.

Taking the question to Dap Ren, he chose to answer by asking a series of questions.

"What do you remember of the little man?" he asked gently.

"Pretty much everything," I answered. "He had big brown eyes, messy dark hair, an enormous nose covered with bumps, and a head that seemed too large for such a small body."

"Well, it sounds like you have a very vivid picture of him. Do you remember what he was doing?"

"Yes," I answered. "He was carrying something like a lantern."

"What did it look like?"

Thinking for a second, I answered, "It looked like it was made of silver. It had holes all around. They were little star-shaped holes."

"And what do you remember about where you were just before you saw him?"

I was shocked at the question. I had to think. After a moment, I told him about my walk through a beautiful forest with loved ones.

"What about after you departed from the dwarf?" he continued. "Where did you go next? What did you do next?"

Instantly, I could remember a great deal about the beautiful astral city and seemed to explain to his satisfaction all of the events that followed that encounter.

He then asked, "Do you think maybe this ugly dwarf is important because he serves as a door for your memory when you are ready to teach about the city of Aga?"

It was as if I had been in a dark room and someone suddenly

turned the light on. As I looked back on various encounters at different levels, there was always a plus factor, an anchor, that I could use to open memory channels. Often, by meditating on these anchors, my physical consciousness would slowly merge with the higher awareness, and I more easily remembered events leading up to and departing from that particular anchor.

Just as the city has a thousand names, perhaps this little man has a thousand purposes. For me, he was a door to memory. Perhaps, for others, his purpose may be different. But one thing is certain. Once one has seen him, the event will certainly stick in your memory.

I NEVER REALIZED……!!

"I'm so young and beautiful!" the radiant soul exclaimed. "And the weight of the physical strain on my mind is finally relieved! It's like I've recovered from some terrible sickness, where there was constant and horrible pain!"

Several of her friends stood by, smiling on the scene.

As she spun around, soaking in the beauty – the long forgotten beauty – of this incredible place, her attention was suddenly drawn to one of the individuals in particular. It was her long time friend and teacher. A bright smile crossed her face as she continued to sing praises to this place called the astral. To her physical awareness she had been away from this place for more than eighty-seven years, but as she stood among her friends, it seemed like she had been gone for only a couple of years.

She spread her arms wide apart and turned her face skyward, looking much like a young girl dancing among the flowers. She could feel a loving vibration that passed through this world from some distant and unseen source, and which could hardly ever be felt in the physical.

"How wonderful! How loving! How peaceful!" she sang to the sky and distant range of mountains. "Why couldn't I feel you while I was on Earth? Why do you remain unknown to those who are filled with fear?"

"Sometimes it does seem unfair," the teacher interjected, "that the physical is so greatly deprived of this vibrant love and peace, but we should never forget the physical is a school. Remember, you can't have mountains without valleys and you can't have light without darkness. Also, you must remember all souls are a fragment from the body of God. These fragments have been planted in that darkness so those who are ready can float from that horrible darkness and finally make their home in divine love.

"Unfortunately, if the wonders of the astral were openly experienced without effort in the physical, it would be no school at all. However, the measure of mercy from the Divine is far greater than most believe. If a child isn't permitted to get dirty, then it stands to reason that the child has been denied experience. Spirit has granted us the privilege to enter the physical so that we may experience that which we desire."

"But if I could have remembered," she protested, "I could have done so much more to help people. Not only would my life have been better, knowing that I am always protected, ending my constant fears, but I could have shared this knowledge and assisted others."

The teacher smiled. "What makes you think you didn't help others?"

"I just lived a quiet life," she countered. "There was nothing spectacular about it. In fact, I seldom even associated with many other people. I just seemed to live in my own little circle. Nothing great. Nothing noteworthy."

The teacher continued to smile as he motioned toward a distant group of people. "Do you have any idea who these individuals are?" he asked.

She smiled at the approaching figures and after a few seconds, she shook her head, signaling she had no idea who they were.

"I want to thank you," one man said. "I learned from the astral records that due to a brief encounter with you, my entire life was changed!"

She was shocked at such a statement. She wondered why this being would say such a thing. With the complete return of her astral memory, she could recall not only the astral memories, but had complete memory of her physical life. And in all of these memories, she couldn't remember this person, let alone remember changing his life.

Then, to her further shock, another approached with a similar report and thanks. Then there was another. Then another. And another. And still others approached offering love and appreciation.

Not seeming to be unappreciative at such praise, but seriously believing some great error had been made, she opened her heart to them. "I thank you for your love and I offer all of my Godly love to you, but I am afraid you may be thanking the wrong person."

They continued to smile with loving affection, each knowing she was, indeed, the right person.

The teacher, laughing at the strange look on her face, asked, "Didn't you always have a deep love for God or Spirit? Didn't you try to be an example for what you believed?"

She shrugged. "Yes, but I never did anything of any notice."

"Do you remember being taught that by letting the White Light of Spirit flow through, you were opening yourself as a channel for God? By opening the flow, you were being a co-worker with God?"

"Well, yes," she confessed, "but I never thought the teachers really meant it."

"Oh, they meant it!" he said, as he waved his hand in the direction of those who had come to offer their gratitude. "And these are not the only ones whose lives you've changed! In addition to those close to you, your husband, children, grandchildren, parents, aunts, uncles, brothers, sisters, your neighbors, and the dozens of others you've touched with your blessing – there are literally hundreds, possibly thousands, of others who Spirit was able to touch – by passing through you!

"Just as you need a corresponding body for whatever plane you're on, one that vibrates at that particular level, Spirit needs to use a physical body when bringing miracles into the physical plane. If a person isn't able to open up to receive a miracle, by letting Spirit flow through himself, it must come through one who has opened himself to Spiritual flow.

"By exposing yourself to spiritual exercises, you became a pure, flowing channel. When you took an interest in meditation, you formed a bond between Spirit and yourself. By being a channel, you became a beacon, permitting Spirit to touch all around or near you!"

With no further comment, the teacher smiled and returned her shrug, exposing his palms upward, as if to say this was why she was being so graciously thanked.

"How glorious! How wonderful!" she exclaimed. "If only I could have shared in the joy of knowing while such a great thing was happening!"

Turning her loving gaze once again skyward, she had only three words to sing into the blue and yellow sky.

"I never realized...!"

THE COURT OF YAMA

One of the most misunderstood things is the Court of Yama. Also called the Court of Standing, or The Judgment, it is nothing like many may believe. First, it is not a court. There is no judging and there certainly isn't any punishment dealt out. Actually, Yama is a very good thing. It is where we are granted blessings and miracles.

There is no court, no judge, no jury, and no prosecutor. It is a time where all the good one has done is used to determine their level of spirituality.

One might wonder about the bad they have done. The answer is that nothing we regret or are even ashamed of, has any place in this evaluation.

The concept of Yama is much like that of the Monad or Higher Self. We find that only the good we have done is collected and saved. What we think of as negative or waste is passed off, constantly cleansing our essence, much like our body using what is beneficiary and discarding that which is useless.

Karma is the fire that burns away the undesirable. Since Karma took care of the negative in the physical, it no longer has a place at this level.

Through Karmic reaction, every deed we do, whether good or bad, will be either stored or burned up. This is done through the Law of Reaction. For every action, there must be an equal and opposite reaction. So, we pay pretty much for our acts as we progress along in this school.

Since we are constantly paying for negative action, Spirit has canceled the debt – and it is no longer a concern of Yama.

The three important things to remember about this evaluation are 1) There is no court where you are put on trial; 2) There is nothing embarrassing or shameful to fear; and 3) This evaluation is only to determine the degree of reward to be offered.

Furthermore, all of us have already gone through this process before. We should look forward to having such an evaluation, since it is also considered a blessing.

THE SILENT ONES & THE TENTH DOOR

The spiritual experience is a very beautiful and dramatic event. At the same time, though, it is a difficult thing to translate into words. It is much more than a bleeding or crying Icon. I can only guess at what those things mean, but one thing I can say for definite is that miracles surround each of us daily, but for the most part, we are seldom aware of them. But there is a reason for this.

The last thing Divinity wants is to startle us by bringing strange and unusual things into the path of our awareness.

I was shocked when a man told me he hoped he would never have to meet the Silent Ones. That displayed the fact he didn't really understand higher spiritual entities.

They are not galloping ghosts that come and go in a haunting manner. They are actually so close to the understanding of God, that to be in the presence of one would be the same thing as being on Holy Ground.

However, they will never appear in any ways previously written if it would startle, shock, or otherwise upset you. The spiritual experience is a blessed event, but will never occur if the individual is not ready. You are greatly loved by Spirit and nothing will ever come into your awareness that does not bring love, peace and contentment.

When I speak of the Silent Ones, I am not speaking of any Brotherhood or society. They belong solely to the realm of blessings of spirit. They represent the highest achievement mankind can reach. They reside in the Heart of God and are considered to be the Voice of God. They so seldom enter the physical that most religious writings don't even mention them.

Their vibration is so extremely high it is doubtful they could even enter your space without you being immediately aware of them. Your low vibration would seem to receive some kind of super-charge, speeding up the atoms within your aura. A side effect of this is usually feeling dizzy and becoming confused.

One student who experienced such a visit claimed it felt like he had fallen into some sort of vacuum. He could breathe normally, but felt like he had just experienced a popping in his head.

You have been told you are a Channel for spirit. Spirit is (and has been) flowing through you your whole life. By being a channel for spirit, we must permit spirit to flow through our third eye, also called the tenth door.

The beauty of offering this tenth door freely to spirit (or to the Silent Ones who would be able to direct the flow of spirit), is that no demands are made upon you what-so-ever. You are not expected to make lectures, or even go out of your way to do good things for others (although you will probably do this anyway). All you ever have to do is offer your blessing to spirit and accept the blessing spirit returns to you.

When you hear some well-known individual on television tell you he will perform a miracle for you – or heal your money problems – and then asks for money in return, you should question the true spiritual worth. The blessings of spirit can never be bought or sold.

The riches you reap will probably not come from those who spirit has touched through you, but from spirit itself.

It is true, all of us come from the Essence of God, but it is only those who choose to be coworkers with God that are blessed above all others. Even though it may be difficult to believe, or to fully absorb into our consciousness, we must never forget that we can be a coworker or a channel for spirit simply by desiring it.

We don't pay for true miracles of spirit. You aren't sold a blessing. You receive it due to what is in your heart.

Those who are truly "the chosen ones" are those who are the channels for spirit.

THE MOUNTAIN OF LIGHT

I have spent some time at a place I will refer to as my home, since it has always been the place I return to when departing the physical, but I must admit I am unable to determine how distant it may be from other locations. This is because distance and movement are quite different in the astral from the physical. Whenever I have needed to be taken somewhere, the results was almost instantaneous.

Although I remember a great deal about the Capital City, having spent a great deal of time there, I would be at a loss to verify if the mountain was in the city, close to the city, or a distance away. I'm sure anyone else with pre-birth memory would agree with that observation.

Sometimes I have been taken to Aga after I returned to my *home* and sometimes before. On the last occasion, I was taken to Aga and the mountain of light after I had returned to my astral home and was quite ready to move on to a higher state. This time, the journey was to furnish me with information I needed to understand.

A surprising attribute of the mountain is that in addition to being an energy regeneration station, receiving and redistributing spiritual energy so that the astral and physical are able to survive, it is a place where massive amounts of knowledge can be gained by absorption!

You only need to stand before this fantastic thing to gain spiritual insight! Many questions of the cosmic can be quickly cleared up.

Because of my previous desire to carry astral knowledge back to the physical, Yama had decreed I would be allowed to do so. This did not come as joyous news to me though, since I now no longer had a desire to return. Besides my counterpart, Eve, had returned to the astral and was also ready to progress into the more spiritual planes.

Instantly, vast knowledge filled me. I could see every aspect of the life laid before me. I would be able to accomplish many tasks I had desired. However, due to my present reluctance, I wouldn't be required to stay for more than 19 years (unless I chose to). I would be allowed to bring a little memory, have both physical and spiritual guides, and although Eve could not go with me, she would be permitted to assist me spiritually.

That helped ease the situation a little, but I really had no choice in the matter. It wasn't a matter of my accepting the assignment or not. The fact was that the assignment had accepted me!

* An exercise to receive vibrations from the mountain of light would be the contemplation of Aum. It sounds very much like OM and in fact, that's how most do perform it.

271

Actually, this is a very common contemplation, used by millions upon millions world wide.

Sitting with feet flat on the floor, or laying on your back with ankles uncrossed, or sitting in a Lotus Position, chant the sound of AUM.

Even though it sounds very much like OM, you should picture the letters AUM in your mind. Most receive some illumination by thinking OM, but to become properly attuned, the first letter should sound more like AHH than OOO.

With this slight difference, you may be very surprised by the results.

THE GOVERNOR OF THE CREATIVE FORCE

I have mentioned The Creator in the section called "The Great Wall of Darkness", but I need to speak more of this great Being while describing the wonderful city of Aga. Although His true home is in the fourth plane, one can stand in His lower vibrating presence while in Aga.

Previously I have attempted to confirm there definitely is a Creator, but there is so much more that needs to be clarified about this most magnificent and wonderful Being. He is not the angry and jealous beast many would have you believe. Terrible acts of nature should never be referred to as "acts of God". In truth, we are probably more responsible for what we reap than any avenging god would be.

Leaving the mountain of light, I was led by my guide to a place beyond description. To my consciousness it seemed to be made of glass, water, jewels and gold, a thousand miles high and a thousand miles wide! There was actually no way of measuring such magnificence!

Upon entering the site, the grandeur was so great I could not look upon it. I had to look down.

To be completely truthful, I have a hard time understanding that reaction from a physical consciousness. I have tried to evaluate why I acted that way, and the only explanation I can give is it's due to being so suddenly elevated to a position or place you are not yet ready.

You see, in the spiritual worlds, the more perfect you become, the more easily you see your own faults. I had become intimidated by being able to see my own faults!

Adding to that, I realized I was approaching what the entire world would call the Throne of God! Believe me, only the uninformed will say they want to stand before God.

Would you really care to stand naked on a grand stage with an audience of hundreds of thousands? Or even more like hundreds of Millions? Then, add to that, you finally discover you are covered with endless imperfections. Gross imperfections, each of which seems to be crying out for attention!

Well, remember God would be a larger audience than you could ever imagine and this massiveness would be able to see every imperfect thing about you that existed!

I was highly intimidated and of course, I was greatly upset. I hadn't been sent here to see my faults; I had been sent to learn an important lesson.

Instantly, this Great Being seemed to remove a "veil" that was between us.

"Look upon the face," came a silent command from deep within me.

At first I was unable. I was filled with deep, deep shame.
Over and over again the command vibrated within me. Then, slowly, I began to look upwards, but it wasn't because I was trying. It was more like a mother placing her hand under a child's chin and slowly raising his face.

What I saw brought joy to my heart!

It was the warmest, kindest eyes I had ever seen. His smile brought peace to my troubled self and His aura was the pure essence of love!

I saw all of this plus much, much more. But there was something extra special he showed me. Once the Veil was removed, I understood that everyone and everything below the true God Worlds was imperfect. That was to be expected – and He immediately washed away all feelings of shame.

I instantly loved and adored this wonderful and kind being and I still do!

Although He is not the ultimate, this great Being is the Supreme Overlord to all worlds vibrating below the fifth plane (the soul plane).

This is the Governor to all planets everywhere; the Master Teacher to all seekers; the Creator of all physical creation; the Head Principal for the entire schooling system; and the Maintainer of spiritual energy to all life forms we know!

The one thing of primary interest at this time was for me to understand that through my previous desire to teach, I could take part in a new spiritual evolution now unfolding in the physical. This would be done through my teaching about life existing beyond the Earth life. It also became apparent this would not happen unless I agreed freely and of my own accord to return to one last physical life.

Not desiring a long physical stay and it being agreed upon, I returned to a place I call the Garden of Birth. This was always the last stage before re-entering the physical.

In the physical though, due to my own decisions and actions, I have altered the "original blueprint of my life". Instead of an early departure, I have stayed here more than three times my "primary life plan", but it has served many purposes.

This experience also helps to answer the question: is there a life plan laid out for us or not? I understand there is a general direction in which we are led, but we can make the most of it or the least of it as we go along. Also, it shows that nothing is written in stone.

THE GARDEN OF BIRTH

The "garden" is a very beautiful place. While it is inferior to the fourth plane, it is still a hundred times more lovely than anything we know in the physical.

It is both and active and an inactive place. By this, I mean it's sort of like being in a hospital. For the patient there is rest and relaxation, but behind the scenes many workers are carrying out a variety of important functions.

There were primarily two working closely with me. They were an "Interlinking Teacher" and a "Birth Assistant".

The interlinking teacher visually displayed the many possibilities I "could or might" experience in the next incarnation.

The birth assistant dealt more with immediate childhood; things that wouldn't change all that much.

At this time I met two females also making the journey. They were to be my sisters in this new life.

In most cases, brothers and sisters have been related in previous lives, but not necessarily always.

In our case, we were already well orientated together, and they were elated to learn they would have an older brother to look out for them.

One last piece of instruction dealt with the possibility that my life might be extended. If that were the case, there would be certain individuals needed to assist me.

Finally, when the time came for me to go, I again no longer wanted to leave. Strangely enough, a teacher approached and said I would be able to stay a little longer. There would be a slight delay because of a channel closing. I had no idea what that meant, but took delight in the results.

I would be in my twenties before I finally understood what happened.

I was to be born at an earlier date, but my mother received a shock from an electric stove and had a miscarriage.

275

I returned to the beauty of the gardens until she once again became pregnant and was ready to deliver.

This also answers another important question. Is a child killed when aborted? There answer is, of course, a soul cannot be killed. The fetus is only a vehicle. The child scheduled for that particular body will simply be born at another time – much of the time to the same mother when she is ready.

Even if that mother doesn't become a channel, the soul simply enters into another incarnation similar to the one he or she would have experienced with that mother.

CHAPTER 13:

THE MYSTERY OF CREATION AND ITS SOULS

GENESIS

Our understanding of creation is extremely limited – and mostly wrong.

There is a strong insinuation there was nothing, only a vast void, prior to the creation of our Earth. However, science shows such an observation is not only egotistical, but incorrect. Our planet was created just as billions upon billions of other planets have been created throughout eons of time. More than likely, we were created from the blast of a supernova billions upon billions of years ago.

As a child I was taught creation was based on the lesson, "God said let there be light and there was light. Let there be an expanse and God called the expanse sky. Let the water gather and let dry ground appear. Let the land produce vegetation and trees that bear fruit, and it was so. Let there be lights in the sky and it was so. And God made two great lights – the greater to govern the day and the lesser to govern the night."

However, even at this early stage of an explanation for creation, we have come to a roadblock. Here, God is taking the time to create each little element of existence, but then with a casual wave of the hand, creates billions of other planets, empty of all the particular details needed for their makeup. Left unexplained, He just merely refers to them simply as "lights". Then they are supposedly isolated, all being placed on one side of the universe – wherever it happens to be dark. At that time, since man couldn't see stars during the day, it was taken for granted they only existed at night.

Also, we are aware there are an untold number of suns (referred to as greater lights), but in this account He creates only one.

Returning our attention back to Genesis, we find, "God said let the water teem with living creatures and let the birds fly across the expanse." Here again, we have to wonder how all the endless number of species came into existence. Not to mention the different kinds of birds, we have to wonder at all the varieties of water life. He didn't say, "Let there be lobsters, let there be swordfish, let there be sharks, let there be jellyfish," And so on. No, with one mere sentence he created all life in the ocean and sky.

Next, it is suggested he said, "Let the land produce living creatures. And it was so." Here we might stop and ask ourselves a very interesting question. Why didn't He just say, "Let there be life in the ocean, sky and land"?

As far as that goes, why didn't He just say, "Let there be a universe of planets and life"? If creation can come so quickly, with just a simple statement, why not just say one sentence and be done with it? Why take seven days?

Even more surprising is the explanation about the creation of man. It seems God took some dirt and made man, then He had to take a rib from this man to make a woman. Why didn't He just say, "Let there be man and woman"?

Well, the sad fact is that these ancient scriptures were not written by God. They were written by men who had a very limited knowledge about creation.

This in no way should limit us from using our determination to seek more profound and credible answers to the mystery of creation.

Several decades ago, a group of scientists engaged in a highly controlled test. They took a very large container and carefully measured an exact amount of dirt which they placed inside it. Next, they took a young sapling about two feet tall and planted it in the soil.

After many years had passed, they removed the tree they had grown. They carefully removed it and its roots, brushing them very carefully, to make sure every gram of dirt was recovered. They then weighed the dirt and made a most remarkable discovery.

The change in weight of the soil was less than two ounces, however, a twelve hundred pound tree had developed!

Where did all of this substance and weight come from? Could it have come from that two ounces of soil?

While you are pondering this question, let's also take into consideration all of the other miracles of creation going on around you.

We have learned we get an entirely new body every seven years. That means everything in your body. It includes the skull, bones, arms, legs, internal organs, everything.

That doesn't mean every time you reach a seven year period, God comes with a bucket of dirt to give you a new body.

Actually, your process of creation is non-ending. Old cells are constantly being replaced by new ones. This, you are doing without any conscious effort.

This automatic function is taking place at the rate of one million, five hundred thousand cells per minute!

The answer to this great enigma is your "psychic anatomy". This is the energy field completely encasing us and linking us to the higher spiritual planes.

The scientific explanation is, "The psychic anatomy is a collection of different kinds of energy formed into vortexes. These little energies revolve as wave forms. They gyrate in a centrifugal motion constantly repeating the same operation until they are replaced by the next wave of high vibrations coming from an undetermined source." That undetermined source is, of course, the spiritual energy passing to us from the higher vibrating planes.

It was the psychic anatomy of the tree that produced itself, drawing the energy and substance from a higher dimensional world.

It is the same process with yourself. The various organs and structure of your body were developed in combination with your polarity and the higher vibrating energy that gives us life.

By developing an understanding of our various energy fields, we not only solve the mystery of creation, but get a better understanding of what is meant by "being made in the image of God".

God was not a man standing alongside a mud bank making another man out of mud, but is a tremendous Divine Existence really beyond our ability to understand even in this day and age.

Although our world seems solid to us, it is well-known there is no such thing as solid substance. No matter how solid a thing may seem, it is composed of tiny energy constituents called atoms. Each atom is a complete solar system. All of these endless systems are directly controlled by the psychic anatomy which is fueled from the incoming vibrations.

As the atoms are reacted upon, they are able to transform the unseen energies of the psychic body into physical manifestation. That means the energy matter of the higher dimensions is being transformed into physical substance. This, in turn, expands, creating new cells to each family group of atoms.

Dandruff or dead flakes of skin are physical proof of this energy coming from worlds beyond ours.

Einstein was actually the first to open the door to understanding creation with his theory of relativity. The first part of his formula explains all things are not separate from one another.

He discovered mass was created from energy. According to him, they are not two separate things. When energy is exerted into our world, mass is created. Energy is mass. All mass is energy. All things are composed of atoms and atoms are pure energy.

This was proven in the development of the atomic bomb.

In regards to our living cells, when this higher vibrating energy renews our bodies, it draws on previous living tissue. It literally absorbs the life force from it (much like the soul being absorbed from a dead body into a higher consciousness), and pushes the dead tissue mass aside. That is what dandruff really is. It is mass that has been pushed aside to make room for new creation.

When life is withdrawn from mass, that mass will break down to a point in which it returns to energy.

We can better understand this by observing the cycle of life. Nothing simply dies and then no longer exists. Everything will break down and end up returning to the soil, helping to rejuvenate our world.

A STUDY OF ENERGY AND BLACK HOLES

In a scientific study carried out by my study group in 1990, we discovered a fairly new phenomenon called "Energy Balls".

At that time, we presented actual pictures of these strange balls that although invisible to the physical eye, could be captured on film. Some of these pictures were quite astounding in that one could see black balls floating effortlessly in a sea of people. Not only that, but these balls had a variety of sizes. Some were the size of baseballs, or smaller, while the more elevated ones above the crowd were as large as watermelons.

In Europe, a scientist developed a camera and film that could photograph flashing light at 1/1,000 of a second. There was another strange occurrence caught on this film. In addition to the black energy balls, there were lights in the sky not previously seen.

An important factor was that the more lights seen, the more balls were present.

At that time, NASA finally presented pictures of flashing and streaking lights that could be witnessed only on high-speed film. These shots presented on television suggested they were some form of UFOs.

Perhaps there is more truth to this then one might realize. First, any intelligence that could reach across such vast gaps of space would have to be of superior knowledge and ability. This would also explain why more people don't see UFOs. It wouldn't be a matter of "cloaking" themselves, but simply "adjusting their vibration".

In our study of vibrations, we have learned all planes operate on different rates of vibration. We have also learned the higher the frequency, the greater our freedom to perform incredible feats.

Since the flashing sky lights and the floating black holes always accompany one another, we would have to assume these black balls or black holes are a byproduct from a dimension adjustment.

These black balls would seem to be akin to the black holes found in space. Black holes serve the same purpose as many of our garbage-eating predators serve. They suck in discharging energy from the physical to match the astral energy entering our worlds to rebuild and recharge. Just as in a glass of water, some must be poured out if we are to make room for more. If the same water were to be left in the glass, it would eventually stagnate. It is only by creating "a refreshing flow" that the water can stay fresh and healthy.

This is the purpose of the gigantic black holes found in space. This is also the purpose of these smaller rapidly vibrating black holes captured on film.

It is quite evident that when anything enters our atmosphere at a tremendous speed, it would cause invisible atomic holes. This would be matched by higher vibrating energy manifesting as atomic particles needed to fill these newly created black holes.

Carrying this a step further, we can finally understand how our world could be visited not only by distant travelers, but by astral (and higher) visitors as well.

In the past I have suggested you watch for flashing colored lights during meditation. These were described as being a blessing passed from a higher vibrating entity to you.

Another interesting aspect would be so-called ghost hunters. During these encounters, the investigators have usually been met by rapidly shooting lights, instead of phantoms they may had been expecting.

It is also a well-known fact that when such encounters occur, the investigators have experienced "cold spots" where energy was drained from them or from their equipment. This suggests they had a personal encounter with a true black hole, but on a much smaller scale than a cosmic one.

Whether these lights were caused by astral entities or not, the fact still remains that the researchers had a brief encounter with what will eventually be a source of energy for future technology. This could very well be the first step in ending the world's energy problem for all time!

DEATH: THE GREAT ILLUSION

There are endless laws of creation active around us. Regardless if we are aware of them or not, they all re-enforce the fact there is no such thing as death. While there are numerous laws that relate directly to the continuality of life, we will engage in a study of only ten. These ten will be:

#1 - Newton's third law
#2 - The Law of balance
#3 - The Law of motion
#4 - The Law of energy
#5 - The Great law of Hermes
#6 - The Law of interlinking planes
#7 - The Path of spiritual flow
#8 - The Law of Vibration
#9 - The Law of centrifugal force
#10 - The Law of change

1) First is Newton's third law. For every action, there must be an equal and opposite reaction.

Death is stagnant. It cannot produce an opposite reaction and it certainly can't produce life. Life, on the other hand, is a positive and dynamic movement. So, that means its counterpoint has to be a dynamic movement. This law alone makes it clear there has to be life on the other side of the line. This life had to come from some other source and life cannot come from death.

2) Second, in the Law of balance we can see that water seeks its own level. All things must be in balance and the value of any quantity must be equaled by its counterpart. For water to reach any level, it must have an equal force operating on it.

When we fill any size container with water and submerge a hollow tube into it, the water inside will rise to exactly the level of surrounding water. It won't be less and it won't be more.

We can think of our life being as that water and our universe being that tubing. Without some form of counterpoint, life would reach no level at all. It simply would not exist.

3) In the Law of motion we have learned there is no such thing as perpetual motion. All forces must be reinforced, flowing from a higher power source to its lower extension.

In this law we clearly see that life cannot stand on its own. Life would have to be perpetual to keep flowing on. Instead though, each cycle loses its force, no longer having creative ability. So, instead of death, there must be some form of active energy in that mysterious space next to us.

Our substance comes from the energy released to us from the astral, which in turn has received it from a higher source.

4) The Law of energy proves every source of energy has only a limited range of projection. It must constantly be reenergized at or before the conclusion of its range to continue.

This law is similar to the law of no perpetual motion. The difference is that one emphasized the fact all motion must come from a source beyond our range of awareness, while this one shows the mysterious benefactor must continue to supply that energy source for all time.

5) The Great Law as taught by all spiritual teachers is : "As

Above, So Below".

We can learn a great deal about the universe by studying life under a microscope. There is always a plus element.

Scientists admit they haven't been able to dissect (or even see) the spiritual energy that gives life to all things. All things from microscopic to the universe are maintained from a source outside of our physical creation.

6) The Law of interlinking planes teaches that each plane

descends and receives its existence from a previous parent plane and that no plane can stand by itself.

There are an unlimited number of planes, but for the purpose of our study, we usually refer to twelve planes.

In the scope of these twelve, the physical plane is geographically located at the conclusion, the very bottom of all creation.

With this understanding, if any of these planes were to be removed, the planes below would cease to exist.

If the physical was not maintained by the eternal life force, with it being cut off with the removal of a plane, no life at all could exist anywhere in the physical plane.

7) Understanding the Path of spiritual flow, we learn the more you seek spirit in the physical, the more it will recede.

Spirit becomes similar to the evasive rainbow. The more you chase it, the more it disguises itself and seems to be apparent somewhere else. The reason for this is spirit comes from another world and can never be explained by physical means.

8) In the Law of vibration, we understand all molecular

structures must vibrate, being fueled from a primal source, in order to manifest to the physical consciousness.

This gives an indication that "the primal source" is a reflection from the higher worlds – simply called "spirit" by us.

Without the reflection of light, we would not be able to see. Without the reflection of sound vibrations, we are not able to hear. Without the reflection of spirit, no life could exist!

Just as a newborn must have a living mother, life can only come from life. Life cannot come from a void.

9) The Law of centrifugal force states all forces will pull

violently to return to their center. While this mostly describes gravity (which explains why when we fall off a building, we fall down, toward the center of the Earth, rather than into outer space), it also helps us understand "Life Flow".

If there was only life and death, life would cave in upon itself. With nowhere to "connect up" with an energy system, life would become stagnant. This would cause the destruction of all life forms.

10) And last, let's look at the Law of change. Nothing can progress without an outside factor acting upon it. That means we never could have entered into our present technology without assistance.

To give an amazing (and amusing) example of this, we will take a look at something called a procession caterpillar. This caterpillar is noted for its style of advancing along the forest floor. Each caterpillar moves with its head pressed against the rear end of the caterpillar directly in front.

As they advance, they feed upon oak leaves. Recently, a scientist studying this behavior, placed the caterpillars in a wide circle around a flower pot filled with oak leaves. Each caterpillar had its head pressed to the rear of the one ahead.

They proceeded to go around and around the pot until they died of starvation. They perished even though the solution to their problem was right at hand.

Although a dramatic example, it shows that without outside forces working with us, there is very little change in evolution, concepts, or even awareness.

Using a "child prodigy" as an example, how else could a four year old play masterpieces on the piano? Or how could a five year old fluently speak six different languages? Or how could a seven year old complete complex mathematical equations – unless this talent had been previously developed in another life?

Not only do these scientific laws provide proof of life beyond our realm, but they become a part of your general understanding once you return to the astral. It is not the intention of the astral to be in conflict with any religion or particular beliefs. In fact, if what a religion is teaching is based on a reasonable platform of truth, these laws will provide proof for their particular teachings.

BEING A TRANSFERENCE ASSISTANT

In the early stages of spiritual seeking, most believe the "cosmic experience" should be like hitting a homerun ball out of the park. The seeker believes he should be able to escape from – and hover above – this body. He also thinks he should be able to communicate with great spiritual Beings, know all things in an instant, and basically, have control and dominion over all things physical and spiritual. Then, when he fails to do this, he becomes sure there is something wrong with himself.

However, the cosmic experience and the physical awareness of it are six thousand miles apart.

Actually, all of us have had and are having cosmic experiences on a daily basis. Since we are co-workers with God, we are already being used, although most aren't aware.

Just because you may not leave your body and go "shooting" across the universe, it is no indication you are lacking in ability.

The two most fertile fields of activity for the co-worker are : opening our personal aura (which in turn affects others) and working in our dreams.

In the first, there is really little awareness of work you have done. This is because you may have greatly affected someone you merely walked past. But since this was an act of spirit, you won't be aware while in the physical.

In the second, you are given more of an opportunity to put forth your own efforts. This is a good reason to keep a journal of your dreams.

For many, chances are when you had an enjoyable dream, there is a strong possibility you may have been on assignment.

Even dreams that seem insignificant or difficult to remember are important to your spiritual development. Your dreams are a give and take proposition. If you are not giving assistance in a particular dream, most assuredly, you will be receiving it.

Many years ago, I started dreaming about loved ones that I was giving comfort to. Upon awakening though, I was surprised to find I didn't know these people.

In the early stages, I was involved mostly with children. It was always a wonderful experience because of deep spiritual love between us. Night after night, what had been a sad occasion always turned into a beautiful and joyous one as I escorted them to a beautiful garden.

As time wore on, there were more and more of "my children," and I loved each with all my heart! At first, I thought they may be a carry-over from previous life memories, but I soon began to doubt my own sanity. I wondered how one man could have had so many children.

Then the dreams expanded. I was spending more and more time with loved ones, but they were no longer just children. They now came in every conceivable age. They ranged from the very young to the very old – and I still had a deep spiritual love for each.

The people became a part of me, heart and soul. I actually loved each so much that upon awakening, I was torn between emotions. It was sad I was no longer with them, but I would also be content knowing they were happy.

What I was engaged in was, of course, being a transference assistant. I was escorting those leaving this world and returning them to their home in the astral. The love I felt was the "God Flow" between us!

These people were loved by others in the physical and even though I had never known them, I was able to share in that love.

So, instead of a "finality" some might have been expecting, they were, instead, met by someone able to share in their love. This aided them in bringing forth a new blossoming of consciousness, without lingering on the sadness of having left loved ones behind.

Speaking from experience, always remember there is no such thing as death, a death angel, or a grim reaper. There is only change, and that change is always carried out in an atmosphere of love and protection!

YOUR MAGICAL, SPIRITUAL ESSENCE

There are many cultures we consider primitive because of their beliefs. Many primitive people don't want their picture taken because once they understand the concept of a picture, they fear the magic box might trap their soul.

Strangely enough, we find that one who can read the aura, can also tell if someone is still alive simply by looking at a picture of them. According to these readers, a piece of our essence is implanted in every picture ever taken of us.

If the person is still alive, the reader will see a slight white light surrounding the picture. If they are no longer in the physical world, the white light will be gone!

This goes for any picture ever taken of that individual. Even baby pictures stuck away in a family album for sixty or seventy years will still impart that amazing light.

Then, at that moment of physical death, the white light will vanish from every photograph ever taken!

If you have ever doubted the claim that you are a little god, this singular piece of astounding information proves you and God are one-in-the-same.

How can God be everywhere, all of the time? How can *you* be everywhere all of the time? How can all of this "magical" essence suddenly be captured from everywhere in the world all in one second of time, if you truly weren't a little god?

That is not to say your essence is diminished in any way because a piece has been transferred from a picture. You are like a candle flame. No matter how many times you share your "flame", the original flame remains the same.

As amazing as all of this is, it is exactly the same thing for our possessions. It's common knowledge an aura reader can hold an individual's item and tell a great deal about that person. It's the same essence as found in a picture.

Even police have been known to use these readers to help solve crimes or locate lost individuals by "reading" their personal items.

Now knowing beyond a shadow of a doubt we are all little gods, we can finally awaken to who and what we really are.

One might wonder about the difference between a "little god" and a "co-worker with God". All of mankind is composed of being little gods, but most don't know it, don't want to know it, and would even deny it if told.

Meanwhile, the "co-workers with God" not only know it, but are learning to use it for the benefit of others.

When soul, the invisible person, locks out spirit, what communication can it have? The highest spiritual consciousness never intrudes on us, we must always invite it in.

USING PURE SHOTTAMA ENERGY

Shottama is the name given to the primal source of all power. Everything in existence comes from this force.

Some astral readers claim that previous to 20,000 B.C. shottama energy was utilized as an economical form of fuel for transportation. They claim this was especially true for distant planets. According to them, this is the main source used when any are able to reach out to other planets.

Nikola Tesla was not only an outstanding scientist, but one of the forerunners who believed this was a major ingredient in the science of Atlantis.

We might ask ourselves, if we had such fantastic abilities thousands of years ago, what happened? Moreover, we might even wonder why it hasn't been restored, since many scientists, Tesla included, understood how to manifest and use it.

Actually, Tesla did reestablish a formidable power transformer that could convert spiritual energy into physical manifestation, using a series of corresponding towers capable of downloading energy directly into households! It was much like receiving free electricity!

Instantly, we can see this caused tremendous upset among energy and fuel sellers, but the backers of Tesla still went ahead. This was because they also had large dollar signs in their eyes.

However, when the backers finally realized anyone could tap into this energy tower absolutely free, they demanded the tower be destroyed.

Tesla viciously protested, but to no avail. The tower went down and so did all hope of solving future energy problems. Even if Tesla had been able to raise the needed funds, it was too late. The previous backers owned the copyright to the technology, and weren't about to give anything away free.

MANIFESTING IT FOR OURSELVES

Although we may not be able to manifest this energy to light, heat or cool our homes, to run our cars, or use it for other energy related services, we can use it to improve our personal lives.

When instructors teach about shottama, they misconstrue a true understanding of it. These teachers have taught it was a very difficult force to control and would take many years to properly handle.

It seemed this way to them because they weren't using it properly. You have heard martial arts masters speak of it, but they called it the Touch of Death. They claimed one could shoot energy into an opponent and stop his heart. Some could even give demonstrations by pointing at a vase and releasing a shot of energy from his finger tips that smashed the vase.

Of course it would take many decades to master such feats as this! But that is not how the truly spiritually wise will use it.

The whole clue to gaining an immediate response lies in the word "control". We don't want to control the force, we simply want to go with the flow and let it provide for us!